SPORTS

John R. Gerdy

THE ALL-AMERICAN ADDICTION

University Press of Mississippi
Jackson

www.upress.state.ms.us

Copyright © 2002 by
University Press of Mississippi
All rights reserved
Manufactured in the
United States of America

10 09 08 07 06 05 04 03 02   4 3 2 1

Library of Congress Cataloging-in-Publication Data
Gerdy, John R.
Sports: the all-American addiction / John R. Gerdy.
p.   c.m.
Includes bibliographical references and index.
ISBN 1-57806-452-X (cloth: alk. paper)
1. Sports—United States.   2. Sports and state—
United States.   3. Sports—Social aspects—United
States.   I. Title: All-American addiction.   II. Title.
GV583 .G47 2002
306.4'83'0973—dc21   2001046783

British Library Cataloging-in-Publication
Data available

To my father, who taught
me that to be a great athlete you had to work hard;

To my mother, who taught
me that it is far more
important to be a good
person than a great athlete;

And to my children,
Wallace and James, with
the hope that they will
learn the same lessons.

CONTENTS

ACKNOWLEDGMENTS

This book represents not only the sum of forty years of experience in athletics, but also in a significant way, the input and influence throughout the years of many family members, friends, teammates, teachers, and coaches. A few, in particular, deserve mention: My brothers, Greg and Tom, and my sister, Jeannie, whose advice, support, and perspective have always been, and will continue to be, greatly appreciated; others along the way have made a lasting impression, including Ernie Bence, Ed Salomon, Carm DiSimoni, Bo Brickels, Ron Grinker, Cynthia Patterson, Jim Bruning, and of course, Willie Marble.

I am grateful to all those who took the time to discuss ideas or to review drafts, especially Mark Soltz, Mark Sumwalt, Lane Estes, Maureen Devlin, Cynthia Patterson, Kevin Lennon, Neil Isaacs, Ed Salomon, and, in particular, Bob McCabe. Their thoughtful comments and continued interest in my work is greatly appreciated.

Jim Lichtenberg deserves a special measure of gratitude for the active personal interest he took in this project and for his encouragement at a time when it was most needed. And to Jim Murray, who sent me Jim's way, thank you.

I am eternally grateful to Craig Gill, who believed in the book and convinced his editorial board to publish it, and to my copy editor, Debbie Self, and the staff at the University Press of Mississippi for their professionalism, advice, and support.

Finally, to my wife, Follin, for her continued love, patience, and support—thank you.

Portions of this book were taken from previous works of the author: *The Successful College Athletic Program: The New Standard* (Phoenix, Ariz.: American Council on Education/Oryx Press, 1997) and *Sports in School: The Future of an Institution* (New York: Teachers College Press, 2000).

INTRODUCTION

> A man is accepted into a church for what he believes and he is turned out for what he knows.
>
> —Mark Twain

I love sports.

I have been involved in organized athletics my entire life in virtually every capacity imaginable—as a player, a youth league coach, as a fan, and as a youth and college administrator. I believe very strongly that participation in athletics can teach valuable life lessons in ethics, discipline, and teamwork. There is no question in my mind that athletics can contribute in vibrant and meaningful ways to the missions of our nation's educational institutions. Sports also offer a way to connect with others. I know these things to be true; from playing sandlot games as a youngster, to providing me with a clear identity during those insecure adolescent high school years, to getting the opportunity to attend college on scholarship, to earning a living playing professionally, to seeing its effect on children from the viewpoint of a youth sports program director, I have witnessed the positive impact of sports.

I believe very strongly in the power and potential of athletics to mold people and change lives. It did mine. It is this belief in athletics' potential as an educational tool that drove me to choose athletic administration as a career. In short, I have invested heavily in organized athletics because, other than my family, participation in them has influenced my life experience—the person I am and the values I hold dear—more than anything else. That is why I care so passionately about the role, purpose, and influence of organized sport in our culture. I should, for I am a product of the system.

For those reasons, this was a very difficult book to write. What began as an objective, academic look at the role of sport in our culture, soon became highly personal, demanding far more introspection and soul searching than research of fact. When research leads you to question the truth and legitimacy of some of the most basic beliefs, values, and principles upon which you have based your life's work, it is extremely unnerving.

Before proceeding, it is important to distinguish between two major forms of sport in our society; "organized" versus "free play" or "exercise." Sport as "free play" or "exercise" consists of athletic activities that are performed by participants on their own terms, at their own pace, and for their own reasons. Examples of such activities include jogging for fitness, any type of "pick-up" sport, and most recreational activities such as intramural sports at the college level. A group of neighborhood children meeting after school for a game of stickball is the classic example of sport as "free play." The children perform all game-related functions, from choosing teams to mediating a foul ball dispute, without adult supervision. It is the children's game, and any benefit derived accrues directly to the participants. "Organized" sport is an athletic activity that has been institutionalized, such as Little League, high school, college, and professional sports. Such activities have designated coaches and commissioners, official uniforms, league standings, and trophies. There is an emphasis on structure, rules, and procedures, all imposed by adults. Most significant, there is an emphasis placed upon winning. This type of organized sport activity will be the focus of the pages to follow.

My initial research into the evolution of organized sport in America yielded fairly straightforward information and accounts. I found that institutionalized sport that even remotely resembled organized sport of today, with its layers of regulatory bodies, vast promotions networks, and mountains of records and statistics, simply did not exist in America before the late 1800s. American higher education, for example, was in existence for more than 200 years before the first intercollegiate athletic contest (a boat race between Harvard and Yale in 1852) and over 230 years before Rutgers and Princeton squared off in the first intercollegiate football contest. To that point, the formal incorporation of athletics into higher education was never seriously considered. To the leaders of the colonial colleges, education was based upon rigorous study of the classics and devotion to God, which left no time for games.

America's early concept of interscholastic athletics was modeled after programs in the British public school system. Britain's Industrial Revolution of the 1800s produced an expanding middle class. This new middle class became the main clientele of the public schools. With the influx of this "new" type of student (prior to this time the British "public" schools were exclusively for the upper class), headmasters felt the need to organize, supervise, and institutionalize existing games that were previously only loosely structured, run by the students, and often banned by school authorities. School leaders began to embrace the notion that rigorous physical activity, especially team sports like cricket and rugby, made a significant contribution to the development of morality, toughness, and patriotism. It was widely believed that such values were not only transferable to life off the fields of play but were also necessary to govern, maintain, and defend the far-flung British Empire. For much the same reason, rigorous sport was incorporated into the curricula of the exclusive private schools of New England during the mid to late 1800s.

I discovered that the public's acceptance of the value of organized sport was also linked to the fact that America was a nation of immigrants. As such, many of America's traditions had to be invented as little existed in the way of cultural tradition—an important element of defining exactly what it was to be considered "American." Sports were thought to teach typical American characteristics. Thus, sports served a valuable cultural function as a socialization agent for a vast nation of immigrants.

Further, sport was viewed as an effective way in which to train men to defend our country, allegedly teaching character in the form of toughness, discipline, and an unquestioning respect for authority, all virtues valued by the military. It is no coincidence that many terms that have been applied to sports are terms of war. A contest is a battle or war. Offenses and defenses converge at the point of attack. Quarterbacks throw "the bomb."

Finally, the obvious health benefits of athletic participation further eased the formal incorporation of organized sport programs into not only our educational system but into America's collective consciousness, as well, as the notion that a sound body contributed to the development of a sound mind was becoming widely accepted.

But my understanding of the evolution of sport in America took a significant turn upon reading a book by Andrew W. Miracle and C. Roger Rees entitled *Lessons of the Locker Room: The Myth of School Sports.* According to Miracle and Rees, the driving force behind the shaping of American education policy has been economics. Our nation's educational system has been, and will continue to be, influenced and molded by business leaders because they have a strong vested interest in assuring that our schools instill in students—all future potential employees—the skills necessary to be productive workers. America's emergence as an industrial power in the early 1900s required workers trained to be punctual and disciplined, to unquestioningly obey authority, and to work hard—all values that make for good factory workers. Consequently, business leaders took a very active interest in influencing educational reform, particularly at the secondary school level.

The fact that our country's dramatic increase in investment in sport paralleled our country's rise as a world industrial power is no coincidence. The great industrialists needed workers for their factories; workers who were loyal, who responded to authority, and who could work as part of a team—traits that organized sports allegedly instilled in participants. Consequently, business leaders such as J. P. Morgan, J. D. Rockefeller, and Andrew Carnegie pushed to create and helped to finance, for example, the Public School Athletic League (PSAL) in New York. While the aforementioned benefits were influential in its rise to widespread acceptance, it was sports' potential impact on economic development that may have been most responsible for its formal incorporation into our nation's educational system and into the fabric of American culture.

Therein were sown the seeds of the eventual writing of this book, for it created in the back of my mind a question that has refused to go away. This book is an attempt to resolve, at least in my own mind, that question. Specifically, whether the lessons learned and the values promoted through athletics today remain positive and relevant as they relate to helping our nation meet the rapidly changing business, economic, intellectual, and social demands of the twenty-first century. In other words, if athletics were incorporated into the fabric of our nation's educational system because it was believed that participation was valuable in preparing and socializing a work force to meet the human capital needs of an American industrial economy, how do those alleged benefits hold up today? We now live in an information-based, global economy, where the skills necessary to succeed are vastly different from those required over one hundred years ago when athletics was gaining favor as an important educational and cultural resource. In short, the world has changed dramatically in the last

century while the rationale for our significant educational and societal investment in athletics remains the same.

If Miracle and Rees planted the seeds for this book, Bill Curry
watered them.

Shortly after reading *Lessons of the Locker Room*, I participated in
a conference sponsored by the University of Rhode Island's Institute for International Sport. Curry, an integral part of the Vince
Lombardi Green Bay Packer teams that won the 1965 NFL Championship and the first Super Bowl in 1966 and later head football
coach at Georgia Tech, the University of Alabama, and the University of Kentucky, was also a participant. I had gotten to know
and come to greatly respect Bill during my tenure as associate
commissioner for Compliance and Academic Affairs at the Southeastern Conference.

I once heard Bill address his coaching staff about the importance
of abiding by NCAA rules. He left no doubt that his program would
do things the right way. He was powerful and unequivocal. He
encouraged me often and never hesitated to support me, both in
private and in public, in my efforts to highlight the importance of
institutional and academic integrity. For that I am eternally grateful because, at the time, to say that I was not the most popular person in the Southeastern Conference was an understatement.

It was the early 1990s, in the midst of the most comprehensive
and sustained athletics reform movement in the history of American
higher education. Never before had there been so many elements
and interest groups—college presidents, faculty, politicians, an
increasingly aggressive media, and an outraged public—converging
around the idea that major college athletics was out of control and
that sweeping reform was not only necessary, but also critical for the
future health and credibility of higher education. It was a unique
moment in the history of American higher education and an interesting time to be involved in college athletics, particularly in the areas
of rules compliance, academic affairs, and student-athlete welfare.

Athletics reform is about change. More specifically, it is about integrity. The modern-day compliance movement was borne out of a concern that major college athletic programs were out of control. Cheating was rampant, the term *academic standards* as it applied to athletes was considered an oxymoron, and student-athletes in the sports of football and basketball, mostly black, were viewed as pieces of meat, virtually isolated within the athletic culture with their sole purpose being to win games.

As a compliance person, you were viewed as a change agent. More significantly, you were perceived as a threat to a way of life. Coaches and administrators had "done it their way" forever and did not take kindly to anyone who challenged their integrity or the integrity of programs they had built and maintained for decades. And there was no area in the country where resistance to athletic reform was greater than in the Deep South; more specifically, in the athletic departments of the Southeastern Conference.

Most coaches and administrators were not particularly happy to hear from me about their changing responsibilities in the areas of compliance, academics, and student-athlete welfare. To start, the subject matter placed me at odds with those whose behavior was expected to change. I was an agent of change in a culture that was highly resistant to it. Of course, being a Yankee from New Jersey didn't help much. Nor did being an ex-NCAA guy; or a Ph.D., or the fact that I "was a basketball, not a football, guy." So, there I was, a Yankee with a Ph.D. who worked at the NCAA and who hadn't played football, challenging the way things had always been done in the Southeastern Conference.

I got a good taste of the resistance I was facing when, shortly after I had accepted the job, I was asked to outline my plans for implementing a comprehensive conference-wide compliance program at a meeting of the league's athletic directors. A few weeks prior to the meeting, Harvey Schiller, the commissioner who had hired me with the purpose of developing such a program, had resigned to become executive director of the United States Olympic Committee. Naturally, I was concerned about presenting my plan for addressing such contentious matters without the support and presence of the league commissioner. I was flying solo in front of the athletic directors of the Southeastern Conference and their assistants, where football is religion and those who coach and administer it are regional icons. I faced a table full, with a few exceptions, of good ole southern boys whose priorities were clear—God, motherhood, apple pie, and football—although not necessarily in that order.

Being the naive, idealistic, Yankee, ex-NCAA, Ph.D., basketball guy that I am, I proceeded to give them my best rap about the importance of compliance, academics, institutional integrity, and student-athlete welfare and how, with their help, we were going to turn the Southeastern Conference into a model of institutional control for athletics. In short, I spilled my guts. When finished, I had left it all on the meeting room floor.

Silence.

Then, a long-time athletic director leaned out over the table, cleared his throat, slowly turned to me, and said, "Son, I don't know where you are from, but you best remember that you in the SEC now."

While at the time, I wondered what I had gotten myself into, I came to find that, for every "good ole boy" in college athletics resistant to change no matter the price, there are many more who want to do the right thing. Ultimately, they believe that it is possible to run an ethical program that has as its first priority, providing student-athletes the opportunity to earn a well-balanced athletic, academic, and personal experience. Bill Curry was one of them. It would be difficult to find a finer man in college football than Bill Curry. He is thoughtful, totally committed to education, and a joy to talk with because he is intelligent and well read. He always challenges you to think.

At the time of the URI conference, I was becoming increasingly uneasy about the direction organized sport in America was taking, particularly college athletics. While athletics' relationship to higher education has always been strained, it seemed to me that the gulf between athletic values and priorities and those of higher education was growing. Due to increased commercialism, athletic programs seemingly had become more closely aligned with the values of an entertainment, rather than educational, culture. This was disturbing because we have justified our tremendous investment in organized athletics based upon a set of assumptions and outcomes—that participation in athletics supplements the educational process of participants and contributes in a positive way to the goals and mission of higher education—that, seemingly, it was no longer fulfilling. After expressing these concerns, Bill replied, "John, that's nothing new. If you want an example of the disconnect between sports' ideal and reality, do some research on the Olympics in ancient Greece."

Here's what I found out.

From 776 B.C. to A.D. 393, citizens from all over the Greek world traveled to Olympia to witness the Olympic Games. Held every four years, the games attracted spectators from as far away as Spain and Africa. Even in times of war, an Olympic truce would usually allow participants safe travel to and from the games.

But it was more than the games themselves that attracted the masses. The Olympics represented something larger than mere contests of physical proficiency. Sports festivals were created as religious rituals to honor the gods. It was believed that the gods were entertained by the spectacle of man competing against man. There was also wide cultural significance attached to the games as shown in the gathering of diverse segments of the populace, permitting exchanges in philosophy, art, politics, and economics. There were feasts, processions, revelry, song, and dance. Rituals were performed, including one in which athletes swore a sacred oath not to use unfair means in the games. The prize for victory was not money, but rather a crown of wild olives. It was the Olympics' connection to a higher purpose that moved thousands of people to make the pilgrimage to Olympiad to take part in the festivities.

But in 393 B.C., the games were discontinued. While scholars do not always agree upon the specifics of the "rise and fall" of ancient Greek athletics, most agree that the discontinuation of the games was simply the final act in a society's disinvestment in an institution that had long lost its connection to the higher purposes upon which it had been based. Most accounts indicate that after a period of glory and tremendous public interest and investment, the importance of athletics as a cultural institution displayed a pattern of decline and degeneration. Athletics became a victim of its own success, with the pattern of its decline being as follows. As its public appeal grew, the number of athletic events and festivals grew as did the number and size of honors and awards for victors. Increased competition led not only to increased cheating and corruption but also forced athletes to become more specialized, devoting an increasing amount of time to preparing for a particular sport or event to achieve success. Soon experts had to be hired to supervise that training, further promoting the rise of "professional" athletes. The development of a class of elite professional athletes relegated the masses, without the ability or unable to afford the time or money to attain excellence, to the sidelines as spectators, changing Greece from a nation of participants to a nation of spectators.

Sound familiar? Or, to quote that great twentieth-century philosopher Yogi Berra, "It sounds like deja vu all over again."

As Bill Curry suggested, we have been here before. Or rather, the ancient Greeks were where we in America seem to be now. But more interesting to me was the idea that it is possible for a society's interest and investment in organized sport, no matter how influential and powerful a cultural force, to change, and change quite dramatically. If cultural consensus evolves to a point where its perceived impact becomes more negative than positive, societies can disinvest in sports. Apparently, it has occurred before.

So there I was, with serious questions about whether organized athletics' contribution to our nation's educational goals and purposes was as relevant and timely as it once was. This, coupled with the thought that, perhaps, as apparently occurred in ancient Greece, the excesses of sport had become so grotesque that organized athletics had lost any meaningful connection to the "higher societal purposes" it was meant to serve. It was quite a painful revelation for someone who has lived his entire life believing that, warts and all, organized athletics' societal impact was far more positive than negative.

I soon became obsessed with testing my hypothesis regarding sports' impact on our society. I began a very unscientific survey that consisted of asking all kinds of people—now in the hundreds—cab drivers, "soccer moms," friends, family members, people I would meet in the course of my travels—about their impressions of organized sports in America. Specifically, I asked them (and continue to ask people whenever the opportunity arises) to respond to the following statement. "Organized sport has evolved to a point where its overall effect on our culture has become more negative than positive."

I have yet to have anyone disagree with that statement. Not one person has fought me on the point that organized sport in America has "gotten out of control." Even the coaches and athletic administrators I have asked seemed sadly resigned to the fact that we have lost perspective about the role and purpose of sport in America. While certainly not a rigorous survey, the fact that not one person has vigorously disputed the assertion convinced me that I was not alone in my beliefs. As a result, I had no choice but to write this book. In short, I have long felt that the culture of organized sports has changed so dramatically that it is hardly recognizable anymore. Yet, like a drug addict, we continue to inject it into our minds, families, and schools, despite our full awareness of its damaging impact. And my research has done nothing but confirm my suspicion.

Despite these findings and revelations, I continue to love sports. And I continue to believe that, if kept in the proper perspective, they can be a tremendously powerful and positive cultural force. Of that, I am convinced for I have both witnessed and experienced it.

The first step in overcoming any addiction is to come to grips with the fact that you have a problem, that you are addicted. And, with organized sports in America, we have a problem. Sport in America is out of control.

But the purpose of this book is not simply to criticize the current state of organized sport in America. If criticism is to be valid and responsible, it should be accompanied by suggestions for improvement. To that end, I have offered what I believe are thoughtful, practical, and most important, achievable solutions and initiatives to address the problems identified.

That being said, of this I want to be perfectly clear. Despite the way it may sound at times, I am not anti-athletics. Rather, I believe that we have lost perspective regarding the role and purpose of organized sport in our culture and that our cultural consensus regarding the value we place on the development of the mind versus the body, the intellectual versus the physical, education versus athletics, must be restored to a more healthy balance. Do not mistake what may at times be considered unduly harsh criticism in the pages to follow to be the rantings of a bitter has-been ex-jock. They are not. I have no ax to grind. I have absolutely no regrets about my career as a player or administrator. I was blessed with opportunities that many people only dream about. I traveled the world, got an excellent college education, made many friends, and met many fine people along the way. I owe the game a lot. In short, I wouldn't change a thing. I am at peace with my athletic career. At the same time, I have some grave concerns about the current state of organized athletics in America. It is precisely because I care so passionately about athletics that I feel compelled to speak out.

For those of you who have the same concerns, this book is for you. For those who don't, I hope that the pages that follow will challenge you to examine more closely many long-held assumptions regarding the cultural impact of sports. Perhaps reading it will represent, as it did for me with writing it, that highly personal admission that, yes, we do have a problem with organized sports in America. Because only until we admit that we have a problem will we ever be able to begin to address it.

SPORTS

THE ESSENCE
OF THE GAME

The summer after I had decided to stop chasing the dream of a career in the NBA, a college teammate was getting married in Charlotte, North Carolina. The church was not more than a mile from the arena in which we had played most of our college games. I was in the wedding.

I had completed a very successful Division I career at Davidson College just two years earlier, having scored more points than anyone else in the school's history. After being picked in the third round of the NBA draft by the New Jersey Nets, I spent a season playing professionally with the Maine Lumberjacks in the Continental Basketball Association (CBA).

During that long, cold winter in Bangor, Maine, I had decided to give the NBA one more shot the following fall and, if that did not work out, retire from competitive basketball to find a "real" job. I came to this decision after observing far too many twenty-six-, twenty-seven-, and even thirty-year-old CBA players who refused to accept the fact that their chance to make the NBA was long past.

By mid-season I was determined not to follow in their footsteps; thirty years old and still chasing that NBA dream with nothing to show for a twenty-year career but a few faded newspaper clippings. Old newspaper clippings are of little use in getting a job. So, after being released by the Golden State Warriors the following fall, I returned to Charlotte to work as a director of youth sports programs at a YMCA.

One of my wedding responsibilities was to escort family members of the bride and groom from the back of the church to the front before the ceremony. A friend of mine later told me of a conversation he overheard while I was performing these duties. A woman seated in front of my friend pointed at me and asked her companion, "Who is that tall guy walking down the aisle?" The man replied, "Oh, him? That used to be John Gerdy."

Apparently, when I stopped playing competitively, I not only wasn't a basketball player, I wasn't even John Gerdy!

Despite having a great deal of athletic success, I prided myself on being more than simply a dumb jock. My mother had always emphasized to me that while athletic accomplishments were great, what was most important was being a well-rounded and good person. I earned good grades in school, had many outside interests, particularly music and social work, and consciously tried to avoid talking about or calling attention to my basketball career. But that I might be something other than a basketball player, possibly an intelligent or funny person with interests other than basketball, or that I might be someone who he should consider hiring in his business never crossed this person's mind. To him, I was simply a gladiator.

What I failed to appreciate at the time was that my athletic career had, at that very moment, come full circle. From an athletic perspective, I was where I began—not as John Gerdy—but as someone else.

My earliest athletic memory was of kicking a football in the side lot adjacent to our house in Little Falls, New Jersey. I spent thousands of hours kicking that football, often alone, but never lonely as I would visualize game scenarios, imagining myself to be a member of the New York Giants. A fullback named Tucker Fredrickson was my favorite. The Giants had great plans for Tucker, a first-round draft pick out of Auburn. Although he had a few good years, he never met the high expectations of a first-round pick, due to a series of knee injuries. Those were the days when a knee injury often meant the end of your career. But there I was, not thinking about knee injuries, but rather of all the touchdowns I was scoring, not as John Gerdy, but as Tucker Fredrickson.

One of the beauties of sports is the way you can lose yourself for hours with the aid of nothing but a ball and your imagination. One's ability to imagine and construct vivid mental images and concepts is a valuable developmental characteristic, which sport can nurture. Whether playing with others or by yourself, the number and types of games in which you can participate, all with varying sets of rules, each set unique to the particular number and abilities of the players involved, is endless. For example, the rules were different when we played baseball in the school playground as opposed to the park. They had to be because the playing areas were so different. In the park, any decent shot to left field wound up in a busy street. Consequently, left field was out of play. In fact, if you hit two straight balls there, you were out. In the playground, right field butted up against the backside of School No. One, only twenty yards beyond first base. It was our own version of Fenway Park's Green Monster. But unlike Fenway, where a ball hit off the wall results in a hit, in our game, a fly ball off the wall could be caught for an out.

From touch football in the street in front of our house to basketball behind the police station in the center of town, the rules varied. The rules could also be changed depending upon who was playing. Older kids might be required to bat opposite of what they were most comfortable with, or shoot with their "off" hand. But whatever the scenario, we negotiated and policed the rules ourselves. It required imagination, creativity, flexibility, mediation skills, and the ability to communicate with others. Most important, it was fun.

I began participation in organized baseball and football by age seven and in basketball by age twelve. But, despite the excitement of team uniforms and the prospects of winning a team trophy, my fondest memories as a youth are of those pick-up games. There were no adults managing those games and telling us what supposedly was the "right" way to play them. Those games were truly ours. Whether stickball, pick-up basketball, or street football, because they were ours, they were much more fun than any of the games played as part of an adult-organized team. They were more fun because there was no one between us and the game itself. We were just a bunch of kids with a ball playing a game for no other reason than the sheer joy of it. While I dreamed of playing in Madison Square Garden as a New York Knick, I played because it was fun. That is why we all play. When it is no longer fun, we stop, or should stop, playing.

Sports' most fundamental purpose centers on the alleged benefits that accrue to the athletes. Whether a footrace at a county fair in 1800, the Super Bowl in 2000, or the gathering of a group of out-of-shape executives seeking exercise and camaraderie during a lunch-time pick-up basketball game, the most basic purpose of athletics has centered upon the needs—whether they be competitive, physical, or communal—of the participants. Long before athletics were formally incorporated into the framework of our high schools and colleges, people engaged in "free play" or loosely structured, energetic "games" for the sheer joy of participating in a strenuous, competitive, and fun physical activity. To the athlete, the game has always been about being actively involved in what was happening on the field or court. It is the pure enjoyment and challenge of testing your abilities against another that is the essence of sport. Sports' entertainment function, like spectators, is a byproduct of the game, evolving from the competition itself. If anyone was interested enough to watch the action, so much the better. Whether spectators watch, however, is beside the point. The origin of sport in our culture centered on the value or benefits that accrued to the participants.

The most obvious benefit of participation in sport is physical. Virtually every piece of medical research indicates that moderate exercise contributes significantly to a longer, more healthy life. If there is anything that can be said with certainty about sport, it is that regular exercise promotes good health. In short, the ancient Greek ideal that a sound body contributes to a sound mind is, in fact, sound.

But what lured me to sports and what continues to hold me is the essence of the game. What I knew instinctively at the age of eight and know now, after almost forty years of experience in athletics, is that ultimately, what matters in sport is the essence and purpose of the game itself; to have fun, to develop the mind and body, and to connect with others through competition. When sport is done correctly, there is nothing more exciting, rewarding, or powerful. The purity of the game—the beauty of a team meshing together to where the sum equals far more than the parts or of an individual playing to his or her full potential; of looking a teammate in the eye and connecting on a level that needs no explanation, whether it be a back door cut and pass perfectly executed in basketball or a perfectly timed sideline pass in football; the realization that your talent and effort has merged as one with others—remains. That is the essence of the game. And it is why, even to this day, I continue to lace up my sneakers to play lunch time pick-up basketball. This, despite the fact that I will pay a dear price in the form of sore muscles, painful knees, and aching back, for doing so. It is the possibilities inherent in challenging yourself and in connecting with others through competition that keeps me coming back. The lure, to this day, remains irresistible.

It was for those possibilities that I started playing and why I continue to play. It is fun, and it is great exercise. Unfortunately, the forty years of involvement in athletics—between being a kid with dreams and becoming an ex-jock with lots of aches and pains—was much more complicated. Whether it was the uniforms, the coaches, the fans in the stands, the television coverage, the media hype, the governance organizations with their endless meetings of administrators, or the corporate sponsors, it is everything that has happened in the forty years between when I was kicking that football around the yard and now, creakily making my way up and down the court at the YMCA, that has been so complicated, confusing, and ultimately, disappointing.

BUYING IN

It is hard to imagine how a coach, chasing his son around the batting cage with a bat, screaming about not being disciplined at the plate, could possibly be a good thing. But there we were, watching silently, none of us all that surprised or terribly upset at what we were seeing. We had witnessed enough incidents where coaches screamed and yelled at their players. Although the bat was a bit of a new twist for us, it was, in our minds, certainly within the standard deviation of coaches' behavior. We were playing competitive sports, and in competitive sports, coaches yelled, screamed, and threatened. We were ten.

Athletics participation, it is said, teaches important lessons in discipline, perseverance, and hard work. Through involvement in athletics, participants learn such values as sportsmanship, integrity, and ethics. Being a member of a team teaches concepts in cooperation and enhances one's self-image. Community leaders have long asserted that organized athletics instill in participants important "American values," such as honesty, teamwork, and loyalty, all citizenry characteristics that are essential to maintaining a civilized democracy as well as contributing to successful careers in business. Inherent in these claims is the assertion that it is the *process* of participation, rather than the end result, that is most important. Variations on these themes have been articulated so incessantly that they have become indelibly imprinted on the collective psyche of the American public; such a part of our cultural consensus, that we rarely question them. But whenever I hear or read about sports' character-building virtues, my mind invariably returns to the sight of my sobbing and terrified ten-year-old teammate scrambling to keep the batting cage between him and his enraged father.

The unfortunate experience of my youth league teammate aside, our society's heavy investment in sport has depended greatly on the public's acceptance of the idea that participation in organized sports is, before all else, an activity that builds the mind, body, and character of participants. Despite its entertainment value and potential as a revenue-generating enterprise, it has been organized athletics' "higher purposes" that have justified its place as an important American institution, this notion having been drilled into the consciousness of our public psyche by coaches, sports writers, parents, and athletes. The promotion of these assertions has been so thorough that as a society we have accepted them as being the gospel truth.

And for many years, I too, sang that same gospel song.

Learning the Gospel

Like most children, I began playing sports because it was fun. From another standpoint, however, my athletic experience was, and would always be, unique. My father was the head football coach at the high school in our town. While not as important as in say, a small town in Alabama, Texas, or western Pennsylvania, Passaic Valley Hornet football was, nonetheless, very important to our suburban New Jersey community. I also had two older brothers, both of whom played college athletics, and a younger sister who was a cheerleader. In short, sport was the most important thing in our household. In such a family, expectations regarding athletics were high.

There were, of course, times when those expectations were overblown. As a sixth-grader, I was the quarterback on the town's traveling eighth-grade-and-under football team. Though one of the younger team members, I was the logical choice for the position. I was big for my age, could throw very well, and understood the game beyond my years. Some would say that I had been bred for the role. But where the expectations got out of line was when I was also cast as a middle linebacker on defense. Other than the fact that I was the high school coach's son, I had no business being a middle linebacker. I didn't like defense and was certainly not the type of hard-nosed hitter required for the position. I liked Joe Namath too much to be a middle linebacker. John Lonsky, who lived to take the heads off would-be ball carriers, was the obvious choice for the position. My career as a middle linebacker lasted one game before the coaches finally accepted that, regardless of the fact that my father was the high school football coach, I was no middle linebacker.

Despite the pressure accompanying heightened expectations, for a kid who loved sports, there were far more advantages in being the son of a coach. For example, I virtually grew up in a locker room. While others my age were swimming or riding bikes, I was on the practice field as my father put his teams through pre-season drills and in the locker room before, and on the sidelines during, games. I had heard more pre-game and half-time fire-and-brimstone speeches by the time I was ten than most kids hear in a lifetime. Back at our house after the game, I would sit on the landing of the stairs leading to the second floor, while the entire coaching staff gathered for their weekly post-game party. From that perch, I would watch and listen for hours as these coaches rehashed the game, diagrammed plays, argued about players and play calls, told stories, laughed, ate, and drank.

On Sunday mornings, I would awaken to the sound that is unmistakable to any family member of a coach—the whirring of a film projector. Wiping the sleep from my eyes, I would descend the stairs to the living room, where my father, control clicker in hand, living room curtains drawn, the smell of stale beer lingering from the post-game party, was breaking down the previous day's game film. Forward, reverse, forward, reverse, forward, reverse, click, click, click, often taking up to five minutes to run through one play, commenting, cursing, and teaching the game to his three sons. It was all there for me, and I could have as much of it as I wanted. I ate it up, every bit of it.

With a coach as a father and two brothers who were both good athletes, expectations regarding my athletic ability were always high. My short-lived career as a middle linebacker notwithstanding, I was expected to play sports; it was expected that I be good at them; and it was expected that I conform to the values, beliefs, and behaviors of the athletic culture. As is common when a youngster is totally immersed in any culture, the individual comes to unquestioningly accept, and eventually unfailingly espouse, the commonly accepted values and beliefs of that culture. In this case, it was the blind acceptance of the notion that organized athletics, regardless of the environment within which they are conducted, are a positive influence upon not only those who participate, but the community as a whole.

The Values of the Game

When asked to explain the virtues of organized sport, it is its educational and character-building benefits that are most often cited by coaches and parents. Organized sport has been viewed as a way to prepare participants for life, emphasizing sacrifice, teamwork, and the notion that it is not whether you win the game but how you play it that matters most. American business, educational, military, political, and athletic leaders have long embraced the notion of sports' capacity to teach important lessons in discipline, perseverance, and hard work. Through involvement in athletics, participants learn such values as sportsmanship, integrity, and ethics. Being a member of a team teaches concepts in cooperation and loyalty and enhances one's self-image.

General Douglas MacArthur articulated this public sentiment as follows:

> Sports is a vital character builder. It molds the youth of our country for their roles as custodians of the republic. It teaches them to be strong enough to know they are weak and brave enough to face themselves when they are afraid. It teaches them to be proud and unbending in honest defeat, but humble and gentle in victory. . . . It gives them a predominance of courage over timidity, of appetite for adventure over loss of ease. (Chu 1989, 65)

These justifications help explain our heavy investment in sports of all types and at all levels. These alleged benefits are particularly important in the case of sports that are conducted within our educational institutions. While their potential to generate visibility and revenue played a part in high school and colleges deciding to sponsor athletic programs, if such programs could not be tied directly to the educational development of the students, they would be very difficult to explain, not only to faculty, but also to the public. This principle held true in the case of organized youth sports.

Paralleling the development of the "sports as educational" theme was the emergence of the "coach as teacher" ideal. Explaining the role of the coach in such terms served to legitimize athletics' place in the educational institution. Indeed, the first coaches were educators, as many of them were faculty members. The only difference between the English teacher and the football coach, it was said, was that one of them taught in a classroom while the other taught on a field.

Our society's tremendous investment in sport has depended greatly upon public acceptance of the idea that participation was, before all else, an educational activity that built the character of the participants. And, an activity that promoted good health and developed strong character warranted significant public investment.

And, in my case, great personal investment.

Sitting at the top of those stairs, it was easy to believe in all of sports' character-building benefits. The men in that room were all high school teachers, educators who cared deeply about the young people in their program. While they loved the game of football, what drove them was the unyielding belief that through athletics they could help young people grow and mature. They believed unequivocally that the lessons they were teaching on the field applied to life. The athletic culture within which I grew up was an educationally centered culture where priorities and purposes were clear. Athletics was an educational tool; its purpose was to supplement, not override, the primacy of education.

Beyond Character

More than any other American institution, perhaps, organized sports represents the democratic ideal of equal opportunity. Because the rules of play apply uniformly to all participants on the fields and courts, the individual is judged on performance and performance alone. The prospect of participating in an activity where all participants were judged based, not upon color or creed, but equally, by performance alone, contributed to the notion that athletics was an effective vehicle though which to achieve the American dream. For many, particularly those from minority groups or disadvantaged backgrounds, athletics was seen as a vehicle through which to improve their standing in life and, in some cases, even become wealthy. The notion that sports can provide a potential escape to a better life is very powerful. Such a benefit cannot be underestimated in a nation of immigrants. For virtually every immigrant or minority group in our country, sport has been a great equalizer, often the first American institution that offered true equality of opportunity, an important step in achieving the American dream. Sport advocates are at no loss for examples of athletes who attribute their economic and social advancement to having participated in organized athletics.

I, too, believed in the notion of sport as a vehicle for upward mobility. While neither a first-generation immigrant nor from a "disadvantaged" background, basketball was my ticket out of what I viewed as a stifling small town. While I would have attended college with or without a basketball scholarship, earning one allowed me to attend on my own terms. I would be less beholden to my parents than if they had to foot the bill for college. It was an issue of independence, of paying my own way. While Little Falls, New Jersey, was certainly no ghetto, in my adolescent way, I wanted desperately to get out.

Organized sport has also been viewed as something that can bring widely diverse communities together for a common cause. This ability to bridge ethnic, racial, economic, generational, or gender differences can best be demonstrated by considering sports as a topic of conversation. Discussing the local team is a safe way to interact with a friend or a stranger, certainly safer than politics or an upcoming local tax referendum. In the case of small towns, the fortunes of the local high school team is often the primary subject of conversation in the community. A community, region, or nation's support of a team often cuts across racial, cultural, and religious lines, a benefit of no small importance in a nation of immigrants.

Again, this aspect of sports' value was plainly evident to me as I regularly competed with and against athletes of other races. One of my most-enduring memories of summer was of piling into a car to travel to the various outdoor courts in northern New Jersey to play pick-up basketball, often against groups of black and Hispanic players. From an early age, I recognized sports' power, not only as a vehicle to bring together people of various cultures, but also as a way to minimize cultural differences. At the time, the thought of minimizing cultural differences never crossed my mind. My only concern was winning games. The fact that my opponents or team-mates were of another race or religion was irrelevant. The only issue of importance to me was whether they could play the game. Things such as race and income level have little relevance once you step out on the field or the court to compete.

Sport also has a history of shattering racial stereotypes and, thus, has been hailed as an important vehicle for positive social change. Jackie Robinson's breaking of the color line in baseball in 1947, for example, was an inspiration to millions and a catalyst for advance-ment of equality in other fields. Jesse Owens's winning of four gold medals in the 1936 Berlin Olympics was widely hailed as a swift kick in the groin to Hitler's concept of the great Aryan race. Sport has the capacity to give life to social issues. AIDS is one thing, but when Magic Johnson contracts it, it is something quite different. The act of saluting the American flag took on an entirely different context when Abdul Rauof of the Denver Nuggets refused to do so. An estimated one-third of our country is illiterate, but the issue received little attention until the former NFL star Dexter Manley admitted to being one of that group. Thus, from the standpoint of providing an example for positive social change, sport, it is argued, has served the greater societal good.

One of the most effective ways to perpetuate the values and norms of a culture is to recognize and glorify those qualities in in-dividuals. To that end, heroes and role models are used to high-light values deemed culturally important. The characteristics that breed success in athletics—discipline, hard work, commitment to team, being a "winner," and so on—are all traits that are viewed in our culture as being highly desirable, if not defining of our culture itself. Such characteristics are in plain view in an athletic contest. Those who win games are successful. Because they are successful, they must possess those desired qualities in great abundance. We use successful athletes as an example of what we should admire and strive to be. As thousands of coaches have said, a winner in sports is a winner in life. Thus, sports offers an important societal benefit by providing ready-made and easily identifiable heroes and role models.

Finally, organized athletics in America is a multi-billion-dollar business. A professional team, for example, not only provides jobs for coaches, athletes, and administrators, but also provides thousands of other jobs in concessions, the sports apparel industry, the media, and a number of other sports-related industries. From tickets to trading cards, apparel to advertising, the sports industry, it is argued, is a high-powered economic engine and an important tool for municipal revitalization efforts. If this were not so, why would municipalities vie to attract professional sports franchises to their city or region, offering team owners tax and revenue packages worth millions of dollars? In the case of higher education, athletics was incorporated as a university enterprise largely because it was thought that a successful athletic program would help attract the resources, both in terms of money as well as political favor, necessary to support the institution. In short, organized sports are good for our economy and what is good for our economy is good for America.

Whether it be at a high school gym, a college arena, or a professional stadium, millions upon millions of fans are investing their hard-earned money on sports entertainment. With thousands of televised sporting events to choose from, with all-sports channels offering programming twenty-four hours a day, there is no shortage of sports entertainment. Apparently, we will watch anything, at least anything that can be made into a contest that produces a winner and a loser. From the X-Games to an MTV celebrity basketball game, if it can be made into an athletic contest that projects well on television, we will tune in. If nothing else, sport is certainly powerful entertainment.

Getting the Chicken before the Egg?

The purpose of this short review of the benefits of organized sport is to show that in our culture, sport represents something far larger and more important than the games themselves. Without a connection to various "higher purposes," whether they be educational, health related, or as a vehicle for social change, it would be difficult to justify the tremendous amount of time, emotion, effort, and money we spend on organized sports.

By all indications, our investment, at least for the foreseeable future, appears to be growing. For example, the growth of women's sports is only now beginning to gain steam. According to American Sports Data, Inc., 41 million females (six years and older) participated on a "frequent" basis in some sport, fitness, or outdoor activity—a 30 percent increase from 1987. During this time period, female sports participation in team and individual sports has risen 26 percent. Even more impressive is the 33 percent participation increase since 1987 in female fitness activities. Females now account for 53 percent of the "core" fitness participant segment. Female participation in school team sports, like basketball, softball, soccer, and volleyball, keeps rising as well (Sporting Goods Manufacturing Association 1997, 5).

More people are investing more time in watching more sporting events. Attendance at sporting events has risen decade after decade even while the number of televised sporting events has skyrocketed. Our emotional investment in sport seems to have increased as well. Our financial investment has never been higher. Athletes are making more money than ever could have been imagined twenty years ago. College coaches are earning six-figure contracts simply for allowing their student-athletes to wear a particular brand of sneaker.

Cities are offering ever-larger incentive packages to attract professional sports franchises to their communities. Bigger stadiums are
being built. College athletic budgets are increasing. Ticket prices
are skyrocketing. The influence of organized sport in our culture
continues to grow, largely because of our belief that sport is connected to various "higher causes." The advantages of organized
sports participation on the athletes and our society generally have
become so ingrained in our collective American psyche, that they
have become American "truths"—unquestioned and virtually unas-
sailable. To question the validity of these supposed benefits is tan-
tamount to questioning America, motherhood, and apple pie.

Sport's influence in our culture has never been bigger. The
resources we lavish upon athletes and the programs that support
them have never been greater. Sport has never been more popular.

But is it better? Are the alleged benefits of organized athletics
real, or have they been perpetuated to support what has become a
large consumer of our nation's resources? Is sports' connection to
the various "higher purposes" previously mentioned real?

It is important to ask such questions because if organized sport
does, in fact, build character, generate economic growth, bring
communities together, contribute in positive ways to educational
institutions, improve the health of our populace, and contribute in
a dynamic way to our educational institutions, perhaps we should
invest more heavily in it. Perhaps we should pump even more
money into our high school and college athletic programs. We
should start more children in youth sports at even younger ages.
We should invest even larger amounts of public tax dollars in professional franchises and encourage year-round participation in
organized, highly competitive sports leagues. If these claimed links
to higher purposes are real, perhaps we should be watching even
more sports on television.

But what if organized sport in America is not doing all of these
things? What if we determined that, on balance, when all of the

positives and negatives are tallied, organized sport has become more of a negative, than a positive, influence in our society? What if we determine that organized sports' only redeeming value is in the entertainment it provides, that it has no lasting or significant positive link to any of its alleged higher causes? Is sports' entertainment value alone enough to justify our heavy personal and societal investment? To make this determination, we must approach the issue with a clear, open, and honest perspective. Specifically, we must determine exactly what sport represents, the images it projects, the values it promotes, and the behavior it encourages.

Evaluating sports' impact on our society is a difficult challenge. It is difficult because sport undoubtedly has the potential to do all of the things it claims to do. Sport can build character and teach lifelong lessons in discipline, teamwork, and sportsmanship. Sport can bind a community, and it can promote social change. Sport can teach humility and compassion for a competitor. And sport can have a positive impact on our health.

But the question remains, is it doing these things? And, if not, what do we do as individuals and society? These are the questions that will be explored in the pages to follow.

3

THE ALL-AMERICAN ADDICTION

I know the addiction well. I have spent countless hours at games, watching them on television, or reading about them in newspapers and magazines. I have to willfully resist snapping on the television to check out that night's big game, or to catch a quick sports news update from ESPN. I am drawn to it like a moth to flame.

Sport's lure is powerful; often irresistible. On far too many occasions, I have found myself sitting on the sofa, beer in hand, wasting away the afternoon or evening mindlessly flipping from one sporting event to another. I awake from my sports-induced coma, awash in feelings of guilt that I was not doing something more productive. Periodically, I muster the nerve to fight back. I vow to turn off the television set . . . at the next timeout. Often, when the moment of truth arrives, I cannot raise my arm to do so. Taking comfort in the fact that the game will be decided by the next timeout, I settle in for more. But rarely is the contest decided by the next commercial break. So, I would continue to sit, sometimes all day.

I am not alone. There are lots of us out there. Millions. Perhaps you have been there, too.

We have become addicted to sport; it is our society's opiate. We plan our days, weekends, and even vacations around it. If it is on the television anywhere near us, at home, the local bar, or a restaurant, we invariably turn to watch. We can't even get away from it in the car as we tune to the incessant wail of sports talk radio. And we'll do whatever we need to do to get it; twenty-four hours a day, seven days a week, from Key West to Seattle, Maine to New Mexico.

While a little escapism is not harmful, addiction is. Although not as destructive as an addiction to drugs, educationally, intellectually, and personally, a sports addiction can be very harmful as it lures us into physical inactivity and a mindless stupor.

Like a drug addiction, being a sports fan offers little of long-term substance or meaning. It allows us to escape our problems and ignore the issues we face, and it undermines our attempts to solve them. We invest our effort and emotion in sports stars and teams rather than improving our own lives by reading, writing, learning a new skill or how to play a musical instrument, or simply engaging in some meaningful conversation with a friend or family member. It is not enough to watch one game. We must watch the next and the next. Like a drug addiction, we need to repeat the act again and again and again just to feel normal. And, as with drugs, addiction to sports adversely affects those around us: friends, spouses, and children. "The love of sports can become so consuming that it corrodes all but the strongest unions between husband and wife. When a fan pours all of his emotion into baseball, basketball, or football, there is very little left for his wife, children, career, and community. That is a recipe for marital disaster" (Putnam 1999, 169).

For example, how many thousands of times does conversation come to a standstill the moment a game is turned on? Rather than interacting with a friend or family member, our eyes and attention turn instead to the tube, where we slowly slip into a collective ESPN-induced stupor. Rather than getting involved, sport makes it easy for us to choose to sit idly and watch, television remote in hand. Sport is what we talk about when we want to avoid thinking or talking about anything meaningful or important. Like crack addicts sitting around their pipe in a dream state waiting for their next "hit," we sit in front of our televisions, unresponsive to the world around us, eyes glazed over and minds numbed, totally absorbed in a sports fantasy "trip," waiting for the next big play.

Yet, we don't mind our addiction. In fact, we embrace it. Sport is pure, it is wholesome, it embodies the "American way," showcasing champions and providing us with winners to worship and emulate. We don't mind our addiction to sport because it is the All-American addiction. And because it is the All-American addiction, we don't believe we suffer any consequences from it. But we do. To understand those consequences, we must determine what it is we have become addicted to. In other words, what is sport today? What has it evolved into? What values, images, and behaviors are associated with it? Exactly what is it that we have been mainlining into our minds each and every day? These questions are the focus of the remainder of this chapter.

What Have We Become?

I had never been subject to a "hard frisk." Not one of those cursory checks for a hidden flask on the way into a Rolling Stones or Bruce Springsteen concert, but rather, a thorough pat-down; shoes to chest. The kind of search where you realize "these guys mean business!" Yet, there I was, submitting to one at the door of what was billed as a "sporting event." A security guard explained, "These fans are crazy. They'll throw anything."

I chuckled at the thought of anyone getting worked up over an ECW (Extreme Championship Wrestling) Professional Wrestling match. Professional wrestling is not a *real* sport. It is staged entertainment. Everyone knows it is fake. The winners are pre-determined and the idea is to get in as much "wrasslin', dancin', trash talkin', and entertainin' " in the amount of time allotted until the next scheduled television commercial. How can that be considered *real* sport? If I wanted to witness *real* sport I would have gone to an NBA game. Secure in my knowledge that what I was about to witness had nothing to do with sports, I settled into my seat for a night of low-grade entertainment.

But as the evening wore on, it began to dawn on me that what I was watching sure looked like the *real* sporting events I had seen recently. During "player" introductions, there were flashing, glittering, and whirling lights, pounding music, and lots of smoke. Athletes preened, pointed, chest bumped, and "high fived." About every other match, a scantily clad women accompanied the wrestler to ringside under the guise of being a "manager" or "ring mate."

Somewhere around the third match, it clicked. It wasn't that the ECW looked like a "real" sporting event, but rather, that the last NBA game I watched, not only looked, but felt, strikingly like a professional wrestling event. I couldn't distinguish between the opening introductions of the Chicago Bulls or the grand entrance of former University of Kentucky basketball coach Rick Pitino minutes before tip-off at Rupp Arena and the tag team of Rob Van Dam and the Great Sabu. There was every bit as much preening, pointing, chest bumpin', and high fivin' and every bit as much pomp, pageantry, glitter, and glam. And it looked to me that there wasn't much difference between the ECW's "head cheerleader," the lovely Lady Francine, and the Laker Girls or UNLV's cheerleaders. All were simply women portrayed as sex objects in a sideshow as the men dueled it out in the main event.

The ECW fans in Dayton, Ohio, were every bit as vocal and serious about the fate of the Sandman and the Dudley Boys as those in New York are over that of Allan Houston. After a wrestler leaped off the top turnbuckle, descending fifteen feet onto an opponent who just happened to be sprawled out on a table at ringside, splintering the table and cutting himself, the fans, sweaty and red-faced, burst into a wild-eyed, lung-busting, fist-waving chant of "E-C-W, E-C-W." They could have easily been chanting, "Let's go, Knicks!" The same sweaty red faces and wild-eyed looks I had seen on numerous occasions at Giants Stadium or the Southeastern Conference basketball tournament and the same fists waving and lungs busting. I was not going to be the one to tell those ECW fans that their "sport" wasn't real.

The day where hard frisks become a normal part of entering a real sporting event may not be far off. Some athletes might say they are long overdue as it is not uncommon for fans to throw coins, batteries, and other assorted objects at umpires and opposing players. One of the reasons the Chicago Bulls were disappointed in not being able to wrap up their 1998 championship in Chicago was the fact that they would have to return to play in front of the notoriously rabid Utah Jazz fans. It wasn't the noise that distracted the Bulls, but rather the coins that were apparently thrown at them.

There was a time when the thought of comparing professional wrestling and the NFL, NBA, or major college sporting events was unthinkable. The lines of distinction were simply too clear. Wrestling was staged. Rivalries were created and then hyped. What transpired outside of the ring was every bit a part of the show as what went on in it. It was entertainment, pure and simple. *Real* sports were something entirely different. They were serious. It was the game that mattered. But there is very little difference between today's professional, and increasingly, college sporting events and an ECW or WWF event. In fact, the NBA has gotten so far away from being about sport, that the league does not feel the game is interesting enough to entertain fans without help of an organist or taped snippets of deafening "rev up the fan" music blaring incessantly in the background . . . during play! Even the ECW respects their "sport" enough to turn the music off during the match.

To describe an NBA or NFL game or the Final Four as a "sporting event" is no longer accurate. These events are entertainment extravaganzas, subject to all the promotional and marketing gimmicks of a three ring circus. Even the issue of games being predetermined can be called into question. Concerns regarding game fixing at the college level are increasing. And there is always "league interest" in certain teams advancing into the next round of the playoffs. Do you think NBA and NBC executives breathed a sigh of relief when Michael Jordan and the Chicago Bulls finally put away the Indiana Pacers to move on to the 1998 Finals? Indiana versus Utah? What kind of television ratings would that generate?

Today, sport is packaged, merchandised, and marketed as entertainment. It is more about money, television ratings, advertising rates, and corporate sky boxes than it is about sport. Think it's simply a coincidence that ESPN is the abbreviation for the Entertainment Sports Programming Network? As Dick Vitale might say, "It's showbiz, Baby!"

Our "Sportainment" Culture

In his book entitled *Spoiled Sport*, John Underwood writes about sport's better days. While he does not claim that sport of yesteryear was "cleaner" (there has always been enough cheating, bad sportsmanship, arrogant and immature athletes, unscrupulous agents, and greedy owners to go around), he does, however, maintain that sport was "purer" because it had far less commercial value to be manipulated for economic gain. Thus, Underwood contends, it was simpler and more appealing. Because of its growing public appeal, it is increasingly being manipulated by "marketplace ethics" in the quest for greater economic return for investors, owners, and television networks—from the flow of the game being interrupted for television timeouts, to the blaring music played during the game, to labor strife and lockouts, to the smoke, fireworks, and glittering lights of longer and longer player introductions. In Underwood's words, "It has been transformed into economic snake oil. From something wonderful, it has been made grotesque by commerce. It has been distorted and polluted by money, and the never-ending quest for more. It has been appropriated by a growing army of owner-entrepreneurs who made a remarkable discovery after the 1950's: that sport was not sport at all but a tool for extracting incredible riches from the sports-hungry populace" (Underwood 1984, 5).

Sport has become a commodity, to be bought, sold, and used to generate profit. And, as is natural with any commodity, it eventually becomes "corporatized." In the movie *Rollerball*, James Cahn plays Jonathan, the world's best rollerball player, a sport that is remindful of the roller derby days of Joanie Weston and the San Francisco Bay Area Bombers. But this game has a far more deadly twist. Competitors fight for possession of a cantaloupe-sized solid-steel ball. Points are scored when the ball is deposited in a small goal. Heavily plated motorcycles circle the track alongside players on skates, who are outfitted in weaponry that include leather arm and hand gear adorned with blunt metal spikes and plating. Competitors are routinely dragged off the playing surface with what are depicted as life-threatening or life-ending injuries. Meanwhile, play does not stop.

Interestingly, Jonathan does not play for a city, state, or country but rather a company, a multinational corporation, competing against other worldwide corporate giants. While it is easy to dismiss *Rollerball* as merely an entertaining, futuristic, sci-fi musing, the fact is, we may not be that far from the "corporate sport" depicted in this movie. Just who is it that members of the Los Angeles Dodgers play for anyway? The people of L.A. or the Fox Corporation that owns the team? Does Tom Glavine pitch for the city of Atlanta or the Time-Warner Corporation? And what corporate conglomerate owns the New York Knicks and the Rangers these days? Increasingly, it is more likely that "your city's" team is not "your city's" at all, but rather, a corporation's—representing simply one commodity in its vast multinational asset portfolio. And with B Sky B, Rupert Murdoch's British Satellite TV company, purchasing Manchester United, Britain's richest soccer club for $1 billion, the days of the family-owned professional franchise are numbered.

Rollerball's "championship" game, a game where there were no rules and no time limit, where the "contest" ended when all competitors but one was left alive, presented a telling glimpse of our sports future. With the blood sport Extreme Fighting gaining popularity; a "sport" where the contestants are locked in a cage and the only rule is "no eye gouging," *Rollerball's* "end game" does not seem so far-fetched.

The result of the "corporatization" of sport, is that, as in any business, all decisions are influenced by the bottom line. According to Underwood,

> The padrones of sport are milking it dry. They have inflated ticket prices to the point where a trip to the ballpark for the average family is now an adventure in high finance. They move their clubs and players from city to city like gypsies, or threaten to if demands for a new stadium or a better lease or a few million dollars' worth of improvements are not met. They cater to the whims of television by playing games at all hours and twisting the seasons around and stretching them out so that they overlap and smother each other in the endless grubbing for money. (Underwood 1984, 10)

The line between sport and entertainment has become hopelessly blurred. In fact, they have become one. Increasingly, in this sports/entertainment hybrid, it is the television network executives who are calling the shots, packaging, promoting, and now, even creating, sports entertainment events. The Goodwill Games, for example, were created and run by the Turner Network, now owned by Time-Warner. To attract more Generation X viewers for corporate sponsors, ESPN invented the X-Games. These "games" were created, not necessarily as sporting events, but rather as television entertainment programming—soap operas with sweat. Briefly, we even had the

Extreme Football League (XFL), a joint venture between Vince Mc-
Mahon, owner of the World Wrestling Federation, and NBC Sports,
where players were encouraged to smash quarterbacks and to date the
cheerleaders. Sport purists have raised the obvious questions about
the effect of such preprogrammed "sportainment" on the integrity and
purity of athletic competition. They are wasting their breath. There
are no issues of integrity, purity, and sanctity of such "competition"
because they aren't sporting events at all. They are entertainment spectacles. This evolution, however, has come at a cost.

> Sports have become valuable entertainment goods, and new mass
> media, particularly radio and television, have at once sold and shaped
> those goods. The financial opportunities opened up by the marketing
> of sports have enticed the most talented people onto our playing fields,
> have encouraged new ways to develop that talent, and have given us
> ever-improving, often astonishing displays of physical excellence. . . .
> Even as our athletes soar to unheard-of heights, we are in danger of
> losing sight of all values beyond winning. In the worst case, we become
> complicit in a system that makes money its god; we find ourselves
> watching televised spectacles that bury athletic competition with com-
> mentator's babble, with advertisers' useless products, with a cult of fame
> and glamour; and we ignore the destruction of our most physically gifted
> young people's bodies through drugs pushed by a systemic compulsion
> to win at all costs. (Gorn and Goldstein 1993, 248–49)

But we have moved beyond simply winning at any cost. Today,
the driving force behind sports is profit. And in sports, profits
result not necessarily from winning, but from being entertaining.
But in transforming our athletes into entertainers, we have trivialized sport. Those things that we have long valued in sport—
its ability to promote good health, develop character, encourage
sportsmanship, and bring people together—are simply no longer
important. It is the athlete's or team's ability to drive television
ratings and profit margins that is of paramount importance in our
sportainment culture. It is a sad day when Latrell Sprewell's entertainment value actually increases as a result of choking his coach.

From an entertainment value standpoint, Sprewell is worth more money because more people are going to tune in to see if he flips out again. In our sportainment society, athletes' deeds and examples in areas such as sportsmanship and character are relegated to the back seat because it is their entertainment value and potential to generate profits that drive their value to the team, the league, and the television networks. Sadly, the game itself has become secondary to its entertainment value, as are the players and fans who support it.

The Culture of Sport

Day after day the sports pages present us with examples of the negative effects of the commercially driven, win-at-any-cost mentality that drives our sports culture. Cheating is rampant. For example, thousands of athletes use steroids to enhance their performance, despite the likelihood of their use causing sterility, damaging the heart and liver, and causing psychological and emotional instability. This, while athletics is hailed as being a way to "keep kids off drugs" as popularized by the bumper-sticker slogan "Do Sports, Not Drugs." Perhaps a more accurate slogan would be "Wanna Play the Game? Ya Gotta Do Drugs."

The culture of sport also undermines academic institutions and intellectual values. In the locker rooms and on the sidelines, signing a pro contract and buying a fancy sports car is valued far more than earning a college degree. To many coaches and athletes, getting to the "Big Show," rather than earning a college degree, is what college is all about. Coaches scream at seven-year-olds for committing an error in a T-ball game. Parents attack Little League umpires or fatally beat each other at youth hockey games. Things have gotten so bad in this regard, that more than two dozen state legislatures have approved or are debating bills that stiffen penalties for attacks on referees. School districts are forced to play games behind locked doors for fear of spectator violence. This is what we have become, all in the name of sport. This is our All-American addiction.

There was a time, not long ago, when these excesses could simply be blamed upon the win-at-all-cost mentality that pervaded the sports culture. But that is no longer the case. The driving ethos in sport today is that it must be entertaining enough for television. We can't simply play sports for fun and exercise; we must elevate any competition to epic proportions. Heated rivalries are recast as holy wars. The meeting of two undefeated teams is billed as the "Game of the Century" or at least this week's Game of the Century. Even at the youth sport level, it is not enough to simply play within your town. Traveling all-star teams must be formed to see which town reigns supreme. The warped purpose and value of youth sports programs is reflected in the almost unbelievable comments attributed to Jeff Laravie, coach of the third-grade select team for the Centerville (Ohio) Basketball Club. "We don't want to lose a ballgame because we played kids equally. It's sort of like a business: I'm trying to put the best product on the floor" (Vinella 1998, 1).

Something is wildly out of proportion when drawing 2 million fans into a professional baseball stadium during a season is no longer enough to ensure financial success or when the Minnesota Timberwolves pay twenty-one-year-old Kevin Garnett $125 million over six years, $35 million more than owner Glen Taylor paid for the entire Minnesota franchise in 1995. Of course, Garnett's contract is small potatoes compared to the one signed in 2000 by shortstop Alex Rodriguez with the Texas Rangers—$252 million over ten years. That total exceeds by $2 million the price Tom Hicks paid for the Rangers in 1997. Or when a high school senior signs a multimillion-dollar contract to be a spokesperson for a sneaker company before he attends his senior prom let alone scores a single NBA basket. It is a gross distortion of our cultural values when ten- and eleven-year-olds are not only taken out of school to train ten hours a day but placed in a position of risking serious long-term damage to their health because they are pressured to maintain a petite body frame. These are mere children, thrust onto a world stage when they should be home playing on the playground with other ten-year-olds. This is what organized sport in America has become. This is our All-America addiction.

An ESPN Mentality

Television has affected virtually every aspect of our games, distorting not only when but also how they are played. "Because television networks make money by, in effect, renting audiences to advertisers, they have considerably less interest in the internal structures, particular histories and traditions, or distinctive rhythms of a given sport—except insofar as they affect the number of viewers" (Gorn and Goldstein 1993, 237). The most obvious example of this negative influence is how television timeouts lengthen games and disrupt their natural rhythm. Starting times for World Series games require that children on the East Coast stay up past midnight to see the last out and college basketball games are scheduled to meet the programming needs of television executives rather than the academic needs of the "student-athletes" who play them.

We have been tricked into believing that the only worthwhile sport is "big-time sport." And, to be considered big-time sport, it must be on television. "The real impact of television lies in its pervasiveness: that there are so few sporting experiences that have not at least been exposed to—and therefore in an important sense measured by—the professional ethos of televised sports" (Gorn and Goldstein 1993, 241). We have been duped into believing that unless you are worthy of an ESPN highlight, you are not worthy as an athlete. It is no longer enough to play simply for the camaraderie, the intrinsic values gained, or the sheer joy of participation.

The impact of this ESPN mentality on the individual athlete is tremendous as it is the driving force behind how an athlete determines his or her "success." Most athletes are conditioned to believe that the only successful athletic career is one which ends in the Olympics, NBA, NFL, or other major professional leagues. I witnessed the tragic results of this throughout my athletic career, particularly while playing professionally in the Continental Basketball Association. Despite having athletic careers that provided the chance to get a college education, travel the world, and open countless doors of opportunity, many of us considered ourselves failures because we didn't play in the NBA. Many never recover from having been a "failure" at the ripe old age of twenty-two.

The Lure of the "Big Time"

Our obsession with wanting to be a part of "big-time sport" is so pervasive that we will do most anything to be connected to it, no matter how distantly. Sports apparel advertisements implore us to "look like the pros." Sports equipment manufacturers tell us that their products will help us to "play like the pros." We wear our T-shirts, hats, and parkas adorned with our favorite team logos like a badge of honor. Family, friends, coaches, teachers, and other assorted "wannabes" and hangers-on "invest" in the careers of potential future star athletes, providing favors and clamoring for their attention and affection like a toddler reaching out for his mother. And when the athlete "fails," it is often these wannabes who somehow feel betrayed. The athlete feels that he has let these people down, regardless of whether he ever wanted them along for the ride. It is a burden that many athletes find stifling. And it is a sad commentary on our lives when we invest so much time, energy, and emotion chasing another's elusive dream of athletic stardom.

The lure of the "big time," with its big money and high visibility, can be overpowering, often causing even the most-experienced, level-headed athletes, coaches, and parents to lose perspective regarding an athlete's career. All of us are susceptible to its potency, easily causing us to lose sight of athletics' purpose and our own core beliefs and values.

I experienced sports' capacity to warp perspective in a very personal way. I was a child prodigy in the sport of basketball. Most of my early success had to do with the fact that I was very big for my age, had two older brothers, both of whom were very good athletes, and a father who was a football coach. I literally grew up in locker rooms and on athletic fields and courts. I was always competing against bigger, older, and stronger players. Thus, at an early age, I developed not only the necessary ball-handling and shooting skills of a guard but the competitive instincts of an athlete. Those skills and the many competitive experiences against much older players served me well when playing against kids my own age. I started on my high school varsity team as a freshman and still hold the New Jersey state scoring record for a freshman competing on the varsity level. Upon high school graduation, I ranked third in career scoring in New Jersey history and was recently named one of Passaic County's top twenty-five athletes of the century.

My father was a physics teacher and a very successful high school head football coach. He recently retired from coaching after forty-eight years on the sidelines. Obviously, to be in the game for that long, he believes strongly that participation in athletics teaches positive character traits and values. As an educator, he believes that the value of athletics lies in the process of participation rather than the end result. Although he was disappointed that I did not want to play high school football (I was obsessed with basketball), he slowly got over it as I achieved success on the court. I was a great source of pride in his life as I received a scholarship to Davidson College where my success continued. Upon graduation, I was thirteenth on the NCAA all-time Division I career scoring list. I was voted 1979 Southern

Conference Athlete of the Year and Davidson retired my jersey. An NBA career was a distinct possibility.

As I climbed the competitive ladder, my father became increasingly invested in my career. Such interest and investment is quite natural for a parent. After all, he is my father, and he only wanted what was best for his son. He is an intelligent man, a good father, and has been involved in athletics his entire life. But the lure of the big time is powerful. Even with all of his experience, my playing in the NBA became too important to him. He wanted me to succeed so badly, the definition of "success" being to play in the NBA, that he began to lose sight of the fact that it was my career and not his. In short, it became more important to him than it did to me. This, coupled with my desire to "do it my way," resulted in much conflict and took much of the joy out of what should have been a fun and exciting experience for both of us.

My father meant well. He had witnessed how hard I had worked at the game and how important it was to me that I "make it." He simply wanted me to achieve my dream and, for that, I love him. Now, as a parent myself, I can understand and appreciate his perspective at the time. But, although such behavior is understandable, an athlete's career can never become more important to a parent, brother, sister, friend, or coach than it is to the athlete himself. This scenario is not uncommon, having been played out over and over again in thousands of households throughout our sports-obsessed culture. While I did not play in the NBA, I had a very successful career. I had lots of fun, played professionally in the Continental Basketball Association, traveled the world, earned a free college education, and made many lifelong friends along the way. I have no regrets and nothing to be ashamed of. Nor should anyone else.

The big-time sport mentality's effect is so pervasive it can overtake an entire city, region, or state. Municipal leaders actually believe that the only way they can ever be considered a big-time city is if they house one of the major sports league's teams. Time and time again, precious tax dollars are appropriated to subsidize extraordinarily wealthy team owners and their millionaire players. Despite the fact that fans may have to drive over pot-holed roads to get to them, new stadiums and arenas are built on land donated by the city, complete with luxury suites, prime office space, and state-of-the-art practice facilities, all financed by taxpayers. And as thanks, we get the privilege of getting to buy a Coke in a souvenir plastic cup for seven dollars.

And we have become so mesmerized by the bright lights, high salaries, and glitter and glamour of big-time sports that we have come to believe that it is only the gifted who are deserving of the best in coaching, training, and participation opportunities, leaving the vast majority of our population with athletic opportunities that are less than adequate or with no opportunities at all. From the pee-wee league to the college campus, our sports programs cater to the "athletic elite." Gifted athletes receive an ever-increasingly disproportionate share of athletic budgets and resources while the majority sits and watches. Meanwhile, our nation becomes more obese. If we truly believe in the value of athletic participation, rather than being blinded by the bright lights of "big-time sport," quality participation opportunities should be available to all. But that is not the sport to which we have become addicted.

This is where we are. This is what sport in America has become. It is no longer about the participants or about playing for the sheer joy of competing. It is not about health, education, social mobility, or racial equality. It is about entertainment, money, ego, image, and getting on television. It is not even about getting our fifteen minutes of fame, but rather latching on to someone else's fifteen minutes by wearing logo-laden sportswear and cheering loudly. In sum, we have lost perspective.

Apologists are likely to dismiss these criticisms, claiming that sport is merely a reflection of the values and behaviors of our society. Perhaps they are correct. Perhaps the evolution of sport in America is simply reflective of our societal values—capitalistic, media driven, and consumption based. Certainly there is an element of truth to such a claim. It is, however, too simplistic an argument, a cop-out to explain the unacceptable behavior of athletes and the warped values that drive sports teams and institutions. While there may have been a time when the values and behaviors associated with organized athletics merely reflected those of society, that is no longer the case. Organized sport in America has become too pervasive an influence to be considered merely a reflection of cultural values. You cannot have it both ways. You cannot claim that athletics develops character, builds community, and promotes positive values but, when the dark side of organized athletics rears its ugly head, claim that sports is merely a reflection of society. The relationship between the values of sport and the values of our culture is symbiotic. While cultural values certainly influence what we see and hear about on the fields of play, the inverse is also true. What occurs on the fields of play influences cultural values and norms.

Rodman Is Reality

The culture of organized sport in America has changed so dramatically that we can hardly recognize it as sport anymore. Nicholas Dawidoff, author of *The Catcher Was a Spy: The Mysterious Life of Moe Berg*, aptly described the shifting culture of American sports in a *New York Times* op-ed piece regarding Major League baseball's decision to open its 2000 season in Japan with two games between the New York Mets and the Chicago Cubs. "When the corporate instincts that have given us chain stores, fast-food restaurants, and theme parks invade our pastimes, they bleed them of the dash of strangeness that attracted us in the first place. If you market your culture too much, marketing becomes your culture" (Dawidoff 2000, A-31).

This dramatic change has presented us with a troubling dilemma. Although we may continue to watch and support sport, perhaps more out of habit than anything else, we don't particularly like what it represents, what it has become, and how it makes us act. The problem is that we don't know what to do about it. So, like a drug addict we continue to inject it into our minds and bodies. It is as if we have ordered filet mignon from the menu only to be served sirloin steak. Do you simply eat the sirloin because you are hungry and it is not worth the time and effort to return it? After all, it is still red meat. Or, do we return it and demand what we have paid for?

Of course, organized sport in America is not all bad. There are plenty of coaches and athletic programs committed to instilling positive values in participants. There are thousands of athletes who benefit greatly from athletic participation. And there is a degree of value in sports' entertainment function. But while it is not all bad, it is clearly not what it is supposed to be. The fact is, an honest, rational argument can be made that organized sports' overall influence within our culture has become more negative than positive, that the moral basis upon which it was built has crumbled to dust and, as a result, has left it devoid of meaning. Merely the fact that such an argument can be made should certainly give us reason to pause.

As with any industry, profession, or group of people, there will always be a small percentage of irritants or bad apples. Generally, it is a distinct minority, say, for the sake of argument, 3, 4, or 5 percent. The specific number is beside the point. What is important is that it is a small number of people, practices, or incidents, not enough to offset the vast majority of positive aspects or people in the whole. When the numbers are small, a few bad apples can be tolerated. Today, however, it seems as if everywhere we turn, we witness, read about, or experience some aspect of organized sport's excesses.

Whether crass commercialism, unsportsmanlike conduct, rampant cheating, or the petulant off-the-court behavior of twenty-year-old multimillionaires, the excesses are no longer a distinct and small minority. Whether the excesses of organized sports have become 20, 30, or 50 percent of the whole, whatever it is, it has become too much.

The most fitting example of what organized sport in America has evolved into is Dennis Rodman. What rankles sports "purists" about Rodman is that he has simply taken what sports has become—an exercise in self-promotion and crass commercialism— to the extreme. It is no coincidence that he skipped a practice session during the 1998 NBA Finals to appear with Hulk Hogan in a nationally televised professional wrestling event. Rodman did not create our "sportainment" culture, he simply recognized it for what it is and created a persona and self-marketing strategy to take full advantage of that reality. In fact, Rodman may be the smartest and most honest of all athletes. In terms of the way in which success is measured in sports today—money and publicity generated through media coverage and television ratings—Rodman is one of the most successful athletes of our time, representing, most graphically, the values of our mega-commercialized sports industry.

As much as it may disturb us to admit it, Dennis Rodman is the poster boy of our All-American addiction. Like a heroin addict, we have looked in the mirror and come to realize that we do not like what we see. But the fact is, we have gotten what we have asked for from our All-American addiction—and he is Dennis Rodman.

SPORT AND A
CIVIL SOCIETY

With only a few minutes left in a close game, I stepped to the foul line for a free throw. We were playing North Carolina State in Reynolds Coliseum, their home court in Raleigh. As the official handed me the ball, I noticed the

fans behind the basket, veins popping out of their necks, eyes red with rage and bulging from their sockets, screaming at the top of their lungs for me to miss. I was certain that their heads would explode. They not only didn't like me, they absolutely hated me. I thought, "At least they haven't spit on me . . . yet." It wouldn't have been the first time I had been spit upon. That had happened on a number of occasions after beating a rival school on their home court while in high school. Running back on defense after hitting the shot, I remember thinking how sad it was that a simple game could evoke so much hatred.

Most discussions of civil society focus on those things that bind a community. Honesty, trust, equality of opportunity, and civic responsibility are all values that contribute to the making of a democratic and civil society. A civil society is built, not upon the pursuit of self-satisfaction or personal advantage but, on the principles of justice, intellectual excellence, civic purpose, and care for others. If a society is to thrive, there must exist among its citizenry, a basic set of cultural understandings, behavioral norms, ethical standards, and humanistic values. There is much evidence that a robust civil society is related to a better quality of life. Data from hundreds of studies indicate that civicly engaged communities have more success in education, health, government, economics, and programs addressing crime, drug abuse, and urban poverty (Putnam 1995).

Sport, it is said, promotes the essential qualities of a civil society. The term *sportsmanship*, for example, implies a commitment to honesty and fair play. Teamwork demands that the goals of the individual not overshadow the greater purpose of the team. Sport not only teaches the value of winning, but also lessons in empathy, understanding, compassion, and humility, all learned when one falls on the short end of the final score. With countless examples of what can be accomplished when issues of race, class, and religion are cast aside in the quest of a common goal, athletics promotes the democratic ideal of equal opportunity.

In the minds of most Americans, sport's enduring value rests in its potential to influence, shape, and promote in participants ideals such as honesty, integrity, respect, compassion, and sacrifice, all standards upon which a democratic, civil society rest. In fact, in an effort to highlight the relationship between what transpires on the playing fields and that which occurs off of them, some sports organizations, most notably, the National Federation of State High School Associations, have begun to refer to sportsmanship as "citizenship."

But in today's mega-commercialized sport, complete with its media-hyped, overpriced superstar coaches and athletes, corporate luxury sky boxes, and twenty-four-hour-a-day television coverage, is it possible that sports' link to these "higher causes"—to the ideals of a democratic and civil society—no longer exist? Has sports' capacity to promote the lessons and values of a humane and civil society been lost in the age of ultimate fighting and Super Bowl commercials that sell for more than $50,000 a second? The purpose of this chapter is to examine organized sports' impact on the cultural principles and attitudes that contribute to the establishment and maintenance of a civil society.

Sportsmanship for a Civil Society?

It is the promise of a fair contest that forms the foundation upon which all athletic competition is based: competitors all playing by the same rules, each with an equal chance to win the game—no quotas, no prejudices, and no lies—only the opportunity to compete on equal footing. Without the element of trust— that a standard set of rules will govern participation—our "games" would cease to exist, replaced by chaos. This ethical dimension, referred to as "sportsmanship," is organized athletics' most powerful link to the fundamental principles of a civil society— honesty, integrity, and trust.

In athletics, sportsmanship and fairness is supposedly a sacred standard. At the first practice of the season, coaches announce that everyone will get a "fair shot" to make the team. Coaches repeatedly assert that the color of an athlete's skin, religious beliefs, or political persuasion mean nothing; on-the-field performance is the only criterion upon which playing time will be awarded. Inherent in that claim is the underlying assumption that athletes will be competing on a level playing field. This assumption carries over to games: coaches and athletes will play by the rules, and referees and officials will enforce them fairly. The essence of sport, then, is built upon the principles of honesty, fairness, integrity, trust, and ethical behavior.

Given these assumptions, it is argued that involvement in sports naturally enhances an individual's moral and ethical development.

The largely unquestioned acceptance of this claim has fueled the belief that sports' impact on our culture is positive, which in turn, has made the sponsorship of athletic programs seem not only logical, but essential in molding positive values in young people.

The process of instilling these specific values, as well as others such as toughness and perseverance, is commonly referred to as building "character." But how do we know those lessons and values are being instilled in participants? Research to support this assertion has been, until recently, sketchy. There is, however, a growing body of research suggesting that the moral and ethical reasoning skills of intercollegiate athletes might actually be less developed than nonathletes.

Over the past few years, Jennifer Beller and Sharon Stoll, both of the University of Idaho's Center for Ethics, have evaluated thousands of high school and college student-athletes and their nonathlete peers on their cognitive moral reasoning development. They have found that "revenue-producing athletes, whether at NAIA, Division III, Division II or Division I, are significantly lower in moral development than their peer group, and individual and non-revenue-producing athletes." Further, they found that "revenue-producing athletes are not morally, developmentally dysfunctional when they come to athletics, rather the competitive process appears to cause a masking of moral reasoning processes" (Stoll 1996).

The classic example of the "masking" of the moral reasoning process is illustrated by Stephen Carter in his 1996 book titled *Integrity.* During a televised football game, a player who had failed to catch a ball thrown his way hit the ground, rolled over, and then jumped up, celebrating as if he had made the catch. Though apparently screened from the play, the referee awarded the catch. After review of the replay, it was obvious that the player had dropped the ball. The broadcaster commented, "What a heads up play!" meaning, in Carter's words, "Wow! What a great liar this kid is. Well done!"

Carter continues:

> By jumping up and celebrating, he was trying to convey a false impression. He was trying to convince the officials that he had caught the ball . . . So, in any understanding of the word, he lied. . . Now, suppose the player had instead gone to the referee and said, "I'm sorry, sir, but I did not make that catch. Your call is wrong." Probably his coach and teammates and most of his team's fans would have been furious: he would not have been a good team player. The good team player lies to the referee, and does so in a manner that is at once blatant (because millions of viewers see it) and virtually impossible for the referee to detect. Having pulled off this trickery, the player is congratulated: he is told that he has made a heads-up play. Thus, the ethic of the game turns out to be an ethic that rewards cheating. (Carter 1996, 5)

David L. Shields and Brenda J. Bredemeir, from the University of California, Berkeley, reviewed the body of research available regarding sport and character development in their book *Character Development and Physical Activity*. The following excerpt calls into question the blind acceptance of such claims.

> Let us state our conclusion first. The research does not support either position in the debate over sport building character. If any conclusion is justified, it is that the question that is posed is too simplistic. The term *character* is vague, even if modified with the adjective *good*. More important, sport experience is far from uniform. There is certainly nothing intrinsically character-building about batting a ball, jumping over hurdles, or rolling heavy spheres toward pins. The component physical behaviors of sport are not in themselves moral or immoral. When we talk about building character through sport, we are referring to the potential influence of the social interactions that are fostered by the sport experience. The nature of those interactions varies from sport to sport, from team to team, from one geographical region to another, from one level of competition to another, and so on. . . . The word *character* is often used synonymously with personality. Not surprisingly, then, a number of early researchers were interested in whether sport influenced the personality characteristics of participants. Most studies conducted on this question have followed one or more of three strategies (Stevenson, 1975): a comparison of athletes with non-participants, a comparison of elite athletes with less-advanced sport

participants or the general population, or a comparison of athletes participating in different sports. In all three cases, results are inconclusive. (Shields and Bredemeir 1995, 178

Sport, in and of itself, has no intrinsic moral effect. Rather, it is the environment within which the athletic activity occurs or is observed that influences our ideas, perceptions and, ultimately, our behavior. Far too often, however, that environment has not encouraged positive sportsmanship-related behavior. For example, how were the principles of good sportsmanship illustrated when Indiana University basketball coach Bobby Knight hurled a metal chair across the court, Mike Tyson bit Evander Holyfield's ear, and former Ohio State football coach Woody Hayes punched an opposing player? Coaches at all levels, youth league included, incessantly berate officials, justifying such behavior as simply "working" the game to gain a competitive edge. The number of coaches' ejections at the high school level is at an all-time high. Some high school leagues have discontinued the practice of shaking hands with opponents following games, fearing that fighting will erupt. There have been instances of youth and recreational leagues being discontinued due to rampant cheating. Universities have discontinued sports for various periods of time (San Francisco and Tulane in basketball and Southern Methodist in football) as a result of coaches' and administrators' blatant disregard of NCAA rules.

According to Fred Engh, president of the National Alliance for Youth Sports, reports from the twenty-two hundred chapters of that organization show that about 15 percent of youth games involve some sort of verbal or physical abuse from parents or coaches as compared with 5 percent just five years ago (*New York Times*, May 6, 2001, 30).

The decline in sportsmanship, fair play, and honesty extends beyond the fields of play. Perhaps the most glaring example of this decline are the revelations that it was commonplace for International

Olympic Committee members to sell their votes for the election of host cities. IOC members were regularly recipients of lavish gifts. In the case of Salt Lake City's bid for the 2002 Winter Games, members and their relatives received more than $1 million in cash, scholarships, and other inducements from Salt Lake bid officials. This corruption is particularly grievous given the Olympics' promotion of the ideals of amateurism and fellowship of diverse cultures.

The erosion in the belief that athletic participation teaches positive sportsmanship behaviors is so extensive that most people have come to consider the term *sports ethics* an oxymoron. The general attitude regarding the place of ethics in sports has evolved to where far too many parents, coaches, and athletes themselves believe that ethical behavior no longer has a place in athletics—that is, of course, if you want to win. Even at the youth sport level, many coaches believe they are not responsible for teaching ethical behavior, but rather that their only responsibility is to win games. In thinking back over my career, I am hard pressed to recall any coach who routinely emphasized good sportsmanship to any great extent. Other than to grudgingly shake hands after a contest, the only consistent reminder about anything to do with the rules was to push them as close to the limit as possible to gain a competitive edge. In fact, on one occasion in college, I was yelled at by a coach for shaking hands and chatting with an opponent whom I knew from high school.

Despite claims that athletics teaches the ethical values of fair play and honesty, the reality of our win-at-all-costs sports mentality strongly suggests otherwise. This attitude manifests itself in many forms. What message is sent, for example, when a college coach cheats when recruiting a high school prospect? Or when the coach instructs an athlete to "do whatever he has to do on the field to get the job done" or that "it is not cheating if you do not get caught?" The message is simple—forget about ethics and honesty—just win! Being a "good sport" is no longer a valued characteristic because it is believed that in being one, a competitor "loses the edge" that can be the difference between winning and losing. And the seemingly endless string of NCAA allegations, investigations, and sanctions relating to recruiting and academic fraud suggests that our youth need to look elsewhere for a lesson in ethics and honesty. Sportsmanship, it appears, has gone the way of the peach basket and leather football helmet.

Our expectations regarding sportsmanship have become so low as to be virtually nonexistent. We no longer expect or even hope that athletes will display it. We have accepted the fact that sportsmanship is no longer a part of sport. George Vecsey, a columnist for the *New York Times*, accurately captured our attitude toward sportsmanship in a February 21, 1999, column titled "Don't Worry: Sportsmanship Won't Be Catching." Vescey recounts how a professional soccer team in England, Arsenal of London, won a match on a disputed goal. Arsenal, however, did not accept a 2-1 victory because the winning goal was tainted by an apparently innocent breach of ethics and, instead, offered their opponent, Sheffield United, a rematch. Vescey expressed his wonder that the "incident happened in professional sports, where sportsmanship seems to come along once a millennium." He continued,

> In our own bloated and tedious sport of American football, let us harken back to last December, when the Jets received a gift victory because officials mistakenly ruled that Vinny Testaverde had crossed the goal line. I never expected kindly Bill Parcells to say, "Hey, we don't want to make the playoffs because of some mistake by the refs." . . . I never expected the Yankees to volunteer that a young man had unintentionally turned a fly ball into a game saving home run in the 1996 playoffs and gracefully refuse the gift . . . Au contraire. Athletes are conditioned to fool the officials, to stumble backward and draw the foul, to elicit sympathy. . . Gamesmanship lives . . . I reassure everybody that this is not the start of some fearful epidemic of sportsmanship. (Vescey 1999, sec. 8, 9)

Despite all the examples of the lost principle of sportsmanship (and there are countless more), we continue to justify our investment in organized athletics upon its ability to teach it. How can we continue to do so when, according to a 1999–2000 study by the University of Rhode Island's Institute for International Sport, 26 percent of NCAA Division I basketball players agreed to some extent that their teammates would expect them to cheat if it meant the difference in winning a game? Given these numbers, it is no stretch to say that sportsmanship is no longer a part of organized sport. Despite our refusal to admit it, it has become a common belief that to be successful at the elite level, you cannot afford to be ethical and honest because being so places your ability to win at risk.

There is no denying that winning is important. But if we have come to believe that success cannot be achieved honestly, that the price for winning is a compromising of ethical principles, the very notion of sport having any larger societal value must be seriously questioned. If the most basic principle upon which sport is built— that contests are fair and honest and that athletic participation teaches sportsmanship—is flawed, isn't then, the credibility of the entire institution of sport?

The Humble and Respectful Athlete?

While athletes are trained to compete fiercely, they are allegedly taught to respect teammates and opponents. These lessons in compassion, sympathy, empathy, and respect influence the way we treat and relate to one another as human beings. It is difficult, however, to find behavior that is respectful of opponents when watching athletics today. The dancing and gyrating that follows a big basket or a touchdown, the standing over a fallen opponent or the mugging for television cameras after a big play, and the general "in your face" mentality of sport hardly promotes humility, empathy, compassion, and respect for an opponent.

For example, in Sturgeon Bay, Wisconsin, a father punched an umpire for not calling a balk on an eleven-year-old pitcher. In Wagoner, Oklahoma, a thirty-six-year-old T-ball coach was convicted of choking a fifteen-year-old umpire during a game. In Riverdale, Georgia, a coach shot a father in the arm after the father had complained that his son was not pitching enough. An attorney in Princeton, New Jersey, has developed a practice based upon defending youth league umpires and officials who are assaulted by coaches or parents. Things are so bad that the National Association of Sports Officials now provides assault insurance to umpires and referees at all levels of play. The insurance covers legal fees, medical expenses, and lost revenue from missed games.

Speaking of officials and umpires, what lessons were taught regarding respect for authority—another character trait allegedly taught through athletic participation and a cornerstone of a civil society—when Latrell Sprewell, then of the Golden State Warriors, choked his coach? Or when Roberto Alomar, then of the Baltimore Orioles, spit in the face of an umpire simply because he disagreed with a judgment call? Or, when Nick Van Exel, then of the Los Angeles Lakers, bumped an official, or Dennis Rodman head butted one? Or worse, what does it say about the values of sport in America when Major League baseball's response was to suspend Alomar for the first five games of the following season rather than the upcoming playoffs? Or when John D. Freerick, who arbitrated Sprewell's appeal of his termination by the Golden State Warriors and his one-year suspension by the NBA, reduced the suspension by one-half year and determined that the team could not terminate Sprewell's contract because his attack on coach P. J. Carlisimo was not an act of "moral turpitude"? Or when the New York Knicks subsequently signed Sprewell to a multi-year, multi-million-dollar contract? The message is clear; sportsmanship, ethics, compassion, and respect for your opponent no longer matters. If you have athletic ability you can do just about anything you please.

The general decline in respect and compassion for opponents is perhaps best exemplified by the attitude of Pat Riley, considered one the NBA's great coaches. Apparently, Riley fines players for helping an opponent off the floor. His reasoning is that you compete much more effectively if you consider competition the equivalent of war and view your opponent as a mortal enemy. Such an approach is absurd and pompous. A game is meaningless when compared to the destruction and lives lost in a war. To think that helping a fellow competitor off the floor will somehow weaken an athlete's resolve to win the game is ridiculous. The Chicago Bulls of the 1990s regularly helped opponents off the floor. Such displays of civility and respect certainly did not hurt their ability to win championships.

And such attitudes are not limited to male athletes. As women's sports have grown in popularity, the females are mirroring the attitudes and behavior of the men. Clarissa Davis Wrightsil punched Cindy Brown in the head during the 1997 American Basketball League's All-Star Game. Nancy Lieberman-Cline was fined $500 by the WNBA for clutching Jamila Wideman by the throat during a game. Kim Braatz-Voisard of the Colorado Silver Bullets baseball team sparked a bench-clearing brawl when she charged the mound after being hit by a pitch during a game against the all-male Americus Travelers. Advertisements for the 1998 NCAA women's basketball tournament had a decidedly "in your face" tone. And for an extreme example of unsportsmanlike conduct, the viscious attack by members of figure skater Tonya Harding's "camp" on Nancy Kerrigan. Women athletes have also adopted the men's habit of dancing, gyrating, finger-pointing, and preening over a fallen foe after a big play. These are but a few examples of the folly of thinking that women's athletics are any less prone than men's to the decay in standards of sportsmanship.

It is bad enough when athletes display unsportsmanlike conduct, but far worse when leagues and television executives turn a blind eye toward it. While league spokespersons publicly discourage and occasionally discipline perpetrators of poor sportsmanship, privately, they realize that controversy creates interest in the product, sells tickets, and increases viewership, which is why sports leagues and television exist. How else can you explain the weak penalties—usually a game suspension and a small fine for an athlete earning millions—levied when pro athletes fight?

There has been more than one athlete who has cashed in on being unsportsmanlike; John McEnroe in tennis, Brian Cox in football, Dennis Rodman in basketball, Albert Belle in baseball, and Mike Tyson in boxing have all benefited, in terms of public visibility and interest, from their "bad boy" image. These athletes' sportsmanship transgressions have not only been tolerated, but glorified through continued coverage by the media. And it is not only the media who embrace such "bad boys." The Detroit Pistons, the NBA, and NBC aggressively promoted the "bad boy" image of the Piston's teams of the late 1980s and early 1990s. And it sold.

Coaches are quick to overlook an athlete's poor sportsmanship and moral indiscretions if they believe the athlete can help them win a championship. And, despite what some fans may say about wanting to feel good about the athletes that "represent" their cities, they would cheer for Timothy McVeigh if he were scoring touchdowns for their team. The fact is, in our win-at-all-cost society, when it comes to the final score, sportsmanship is for losers.

Teamwork in a Civil Society

One of the most fundamental of all democratic principles, and an essential element of a civil society, is that the individual has an obligation to the larger community. While individual rights are cherished in a democracy, they are tempered by the belief that citizens have a responsibility to ensure that individualism does not trample upon the greater societal good. This notion of individual rights, balanced by personal responsibility, is a fundamental tenant of a civil society.

In athletics, this relationship is described as teamwork. Coaches preach it constantly, and championship teams claim to have it. According to sports advocates, it is a fundamental lesson of athletic participation and one that can be readily applied to life beyond the fields of play. For example, corporate leaders look for it in their employees, and it is an essential element in successful family relationships.

But does organized sport promote teamwork? Amidst all the commercialism, high salaries, self-promotion, entertainment, and profit-driven priorities and behavior that we have come to accept as being a part of organized athletics, could it be that the concept of teamwork in sport has become distorted? The five players on the court for an NBA team are just as likely to resemble five corporations, with separate products, marketing strategies, and bottom lines, than five athletes working together for a common goal. The concept of "paying your dues" appears lost on athletes and young coaches. Everyone wants the big money, and they want it now! High school players don't even have the time to stop off at college for a few years before collecting their million-dollar pro signing bonus; that is, of course, if a college can't put together an attractive enough "package" for them to stop by for a year.

Coaches speak of how sport builds loyalty between teammates, coaches, and players or between a player and a city or college. Today, professional players jump from one team to another so often that the stadium vendor's cry of "you can't tell the players without a scorecard" has never rung more true. With owners' commitments to keep a franchise in a city lasting only until another city offers a more lucrative set of tax incentives or builds a better stadium, you now need a scorecard to tell what city a franchise will be playing in from year to year. A college coach's concept of loyalty is shaped more by the size of their financial "packages," complete with a sneaker deal, television show, summer camp arrangements, and loaner cars than any commitment to student-athletes, a university, or education. And the marketing of sports has taken a decidedly individualistic tone. It is no longer the Los Angeles Lakers versus the Miami Heat, but rather Shaquille O'Neal versus Alonzo Mourning.

Teams must play well together to win a championship. So, in this sense, sports can teach us about working together, sacrificing for the good of the group, and loyalty toward teammates. But that is where the lessons stop. Once off of the fields and courts, sports is a free-for-all, governed by a bottom line of "getting mine and getting it now." Athletes and coaches see the millions of dollars being generated and simply want what they feel is rightfully theirs. But how do you explain to your child that athletes, coaches, and even sports franchises will leave a team or a city at the mere scent of a better deal elsewhere?

Further, sport does very little to promote personal responsibility for one's own actions. Rather than accepting responsibility for a loss, players and coaches point fingers of blame toward referees or teammates. This, despite the fact that players and coaches make poor decisions and fail to execute their assignments throughout the entire game. Athletes and coaches have become so pampered and coddled that they simply cannot admit that their failure may actually be a result of their own actions.

We have become so confused about what it is that sport is supposed to represent, so blinded by media accounts and perceptions about what sport is supposed to be about, that we could not even give Dennis Rodman, one of sports great team players, his due. Rodman understood, perhaps better than anyone, that the only place where teamwork and sacrificing for the good of the team matters, is on the court at game time. What more could you ask from a teammate in basketball? He was a tenacious defender and rebounder, an excellent passer, an energetic presence; he dove for loose balls (who does *that* anymore?); and he didn't care if he ever shot. He did all of the dirty work, all of the things that win championships. Once he stepped onto the court, Rodman was the ultimate team player, and he has five championship rings to prove it.

Off the court, however, he was looked upon with disdain as being too individualistic, a distraction, and not a team player. But Rodman understood that everything connected with the game is about entertainment and self-promotion. He knew that teamwork, loyalty, and sacrificing for the group have nothing to do with anything that occurs off the fields of play. Other than the actual playing of the game itself, sports has very little to do with teamwork and loyalty. Thus, our continued attempts to draw parallels about "sport values" relating to loyalty, teamwork, and personal responsibility to anything other than what occurs during play is misguided.

Building a Sense of Community

A civil society is held together not only by common values, but also by institutions that bring various elements of a community together. College athletics offers a good example of sport's unifying function. As university enrollments have increased and diversified, athletic teams have promoted institutional unity and school spirit. The entire university family, from faculty, students, and local fans, to alumni living in faraway places, can usually rally around the university's athletic teams. This potential to unite an increasingly disparate university community was one of the justifications for its formal incorporation into higher education. Possibly the best example of sports unifying potential is the United States hockey team's win over Russia and subsequent Olympic Gold Medal victory in 1980. This victory brought our country together in a way that very few other events have.

There are, however, risks in relying on sports to bring a community together. For example, universities that use athletics to solve the problems of a fragmented community run the risk of making athletics, and not educational and academic excellence, the primary purpose of the institution. Although a football or basketball program can unite a university community in a way that an English department cannot, the primary purpose of the institution remains, as it always has been, educational. In short, a winning football team does not make a quality educational institution.

Further, placing such a heavy emphasis on sports' unifying function promotes a community mindset that college athletics is more about the fans and campus community than it is about the participation of student-athletes. A successful team in terms of win-loss record, although pleasing to fans, alumni, and the media, may cover up fundamental problems within an athletic program such as low graduation rates, illegal activities, or abusive coaches. While a few wins may unite the campus community in the short term, it may result in long-term disintegration of community trust if the athletic department is not meeting its fundamental educational responsibilities to its student-athletes or contradicts broader institutional goals.

These same concerns apply to high school sports, as explained by Andrew Miracle and Roger Rees in *Lessons of the Locker Room*:

> It is victory in sport that creates community spirit, and that victory may be at the expense of the community down the road. For example, incidents in high school sports may initiate or perpetuate local rivalries which unite "us" against "them." Moreover, since high school sport has an intergenerational element (i.e., grandfathers and sons may have played for the same school team), it helps to create the impression of cultural continuity rather than cultural change. However, community ethnic or racial tensions caused by the attempts of minority groups to take a more active role in community politics may find their way into high school sports. While a winning team may temporarily allay or cover up these tensions, it is no substitute for community reform.

Communities are always in a state of change and sometimes high
school sport is symbolic of the status quo, especially in the eyes of the
"disenfranchised." (Miracle and Rees 1994, 155–56)

In the case of a city or a region, a sports team can serve as a
powerful community symbol. By virtue of having an NFL, an NBA,
an NHL, or a Major League baseball franchise, the city, at least in
the minds of its residents, is considered a "major-league city." However, placing too much emphasis on this designation may serve to
overshadow more-important community concerns such as poor
schools, crumbling infrastructure, inadequate housing, and declining public services. Further, what is assumed will unite a community may, in fact, do the opposite. Professional sports teams
routinely threaten to relocate to another city if significant financial incentives are not provided to the franchise. Such incentives
might include the building of a new stadium or significant tax
breaks. While some claim that losing a professional sports franchise
will lend a significant blow to community pride, others claim that
providing such incentives amounts to nothing more than corporate welfare. Others could care less about sports. With school systems underfinanced, poverty rising, and public services being
eliminated, using tax dollars to support extremely wealthy owners
and their millionaire players is thought by many to be the worst
example of misplaced community priorities.

Another example of sports' potential to divide is the major
league team that is viewed by the minority community as being
racist or antisemitic. Consider the repeated stereotypical and
racist comments of the Cincinnati Reds owner Marge Schott
regarding African Americans and Jews; the Atlanta Braves relief
pitcher John Rocker about minorities, gays, and immigrants; the
New York Knicks guard Charlie Ward's comments about Jews; or
the continued use of Native-American names and symbols as
team mascots can be particularly divisive. Such examples illustrate

organized sports' capacity to bring very divisive community issues to the surface and can exacerbate divides that prevent the future resolution of issues far more important than whether a pro sports franchise remains in town or wins a championship. And, despite a recent increase in participation opportunities for women as a result of Title IX, the sports establishment has done little to include women. American sports continues to be largely an activity that unites men in a celebration of male accomplishment while women cheer them on or sit on the sidelines.

Us Versus Them

For many fans, however, an evening at the ballpark or arena is nothing more than an opportunity for a night out. For these, the final score is far less important than sharing experiences with fellow fans. Despite the fact that they may have little in common, sport allows people with vastly different backgrounds to talk about "their" team. In today's increasingly diverse, impersonal (Internet), and far-flung society, the common threads that sport fandom provides have value.

Increasingly, however, it seems as if our "fandom" has crossed over a line where it is no longer simply about a pleasant evening out, but rather an affirmation of self, of one's beliefs, attitudes, and identity, that the performance of your favorite team is a direct reflection on your worth as a human being. Many take their connection to a team so seriously that when their team wins, it is an indication that the values and what they and their team "stand for" are validated. We won, so therefore we are right and good. We are the best—number one. Such a strong perceived connection between the performance of a sports team and the validation of a fan's self-worth raises the stakes of games to an absurd level. Such attitudes promote a win-at-all-cost mentality that is certainly unhealthy from a societal perspective, and in many cases, destructive.

In an increasingly diverse culture, it becomes more important that we find things that bring people together. Sports' ability to do this, however, is limited. The very nature of sport serves to divide rather than to bring people together. Inherent in any sporting event is the dichotomy of "winner" and "loser," "us" versus "them," "home team" versus "visitors." The fundamental premise upon which sports is based is to pit competitors against each other in a battle for domination. The result is an event where a group of people are gathered together, not for the purpose of pulling for a common cause, but to root against each other. Not only is the action on the field violent and uncivil, so too is the environment in the stands. Chants of "Kill the umpire!" for example, are almost as much a part of baseball as the cry, "Play ball!"

It is becoming more difficult to categorize a professional sporting event as wholesome family entertainment. Increasingly, children are exposed to loud, obnoxious fans, excessive vulgarity, and numerous displays of public drunkedness at such events. Fighting among spectators is common. New York Jets fans, possibly the most antisocial of all, "routinely fight with each other, hurl batteries onto the playing field, and fling mounds of garbage into the concrete walkways that surround Giants Stadium, where the Jets play their home games. The most notorious incident occurred at a Monday night NFL game in 1988, when several fans ignited fires in the stands. The resulting mayhem led to fifteen arrests, five hospitalizations, fifty-six ejections from the stadium, and forty fistfights" (Putnam 1999, 173). In 1996, fans entered the ring throwing chairs at the controversial conclusion of a boxing match between Riddick Bowe and Andrew Golata at Madison Square Garden in New York. While such scenes of mayhem occur less frequently in the United States, they are quite common in South America and Europe, particularly at soccer matches. This, in contrast to a musical concert, where the purpose of the event is to bring the audience together through music, with the entire audience rooting for the same goal, a great performance.

And it is likely that fan behavior will become even more abhorrent in the future as international competition in sports like soccer and golf generate increased interest. Consider, for example, the deplorable behavior exhibited by Americans at the 1999 Ryder Cup in Brookline, Massachusetts. Fans shouted insults and yelled, "Choke," at European golfers as they were putting. Even the American golfers, in what is considered to be the most gentlemanly of sports, were dancing in the fairways and spraying champagne as their competitors were lining up their final putts. Yes, American fans are turning into sports hooligans, just like those soccer lads in Britain.

It is no stretch to challenge sports' unifying benefits as being overblown. While the winning of a championship may serve to bridge community fissures, sports' impact in this regard is temporary and superficial. What binds one group invariably excludes others, and the very nature of athletic competition serves to divide rather than unite by pitting opponents against each other to create winners and losers, good guys and bad guys. In short, sports' ability to bind a community in meaningful, productive, and long-term ways is limited.

Sports Violence and a Civil Society

A civil society requires that we resolve disputes peacefully. And, true to form, advocates argue that athletics contributes to our ability to do so as sports are a positive outlet for aggression. To the contrary, organized athletics does far more to glorify violence and aggressive behavior than it does to promote civility and conflict resolution. Instant replays and highlight shows repeatedly present recaps of the most violent "big hits," all in excruciatingly slow motion. "While the newspapers heap acclaim upon the most skillful athletes, the players and coaches often recognize the most violent and brutal players as the real heroes. We reward and condone violence and aggression among youth and when as adults these people behave violently and aggressively, we blame it on man's animalistic nature" (Scott 1971, 173).

Rather than promoting peaceful coexistence, the culture of many of our sports promotes confrontation and glorifies violence. Ultimate fighting, for example, pits competitors in a ring with no rules other than a prohibition against eye gouging. How much different are such spectacles than those conducted by the ancient Romans where men and women were often forced to engage in mortal combat with lions and gladiators or were pitted against one another in gory fights to the death? Are we far behind the Romans in our sport "evolution"?

There is growing concern regarding the affect of athletic participation on the ability to peacefully resolve off-the-field conflicts, with particular attention being paid to violence against women. Accounts of athletes physically abusing women seem to appear in our nation's newspapers weekly. Although research has not conclusively proven that athletes commit this type of abuse at any greater rate than the male population at large, there is evidence to suggest that the problem is more severe among them.

One of the few studies of athlete violence against women was published in May 1995 in the *Journal of Sport and Social Issues.* Titled "Male Student-Athletes Reported for Sexual Assault: Survey of Campus Police Departments and Judicial Affairs," the study reviewed 107 cases of sexual assault reported at 30 NCAA Division I institutions from 1991 to 1993. At ten schools, male student-athletes were accused in 19 percent of the assaults, though they comprised only 3.3 percent of the male student body (Crosset, Benedict, and McDonald 1995, 126–40).

Although broad conclusions should not be drawn from such a limited study, it does raise the following questions. Could it be that athletes, conditioned to resolve on-the-field conflicts with violence, have a more difficult time resolving off-the-field conflicts peacefully? Do sports condition and develop such aggressive tendencies, which then carry over into nonathletic situations? In short, what is the affect of such a highly visible institution that increasingly glorifies and promotes violence on efforts to maintain a civil and humane society?

Laws of Its Own

A society can not function effectively without a common understanding of values, principles, and behavioral expectations. Such an understanding helps guide behavior of people toward each other. Similar to an athletic contest where one team plays by one set of rules while the other by another, without a common understanding of behavioral expectations, the result would be chaos.

It is widely believed that sport is one of our country's most-effective vehicles through which to socialize our diverse population by instilling the values and expectations that bind our American culture. Our tremendous investment in sport then, is justified not simply in that it provides entertainment but also upon its ability to build community, socialize citizens, and make our lives and culture richer by promoting those values that are essential in a civil and just society.

Unfortunately, it appears that the values and behavioral standards and expectations within the athletic culture actually run counter to those essential to the functioning of a civil society. Honesty and integrity are quickly forgotten in the quest to win games. Cheating is expected, trust is nonexistent, violence is embraced, disrespect for others is flaunted, and equality of opportunity exists only on the fields of play. The "in-your-face" mentality of athletes hardly suggests that sport is teaching humility, empathy, conflict resolution, and compassion for others. And the emphasis on self-promotion and marketing of the individual athlete suggests that team sports have become more about "me" than "we."

Most disturbing however, is that despite the rhetoric about organized athletics' ability to build character and instill discipline, involvement in athletics very clearly teaches that if you are good enough, common societal standards of behavior simply do not apply to you.

Perhaps the most tragic example of our athletic system's tendency to instill in athletes a sense of entitlement and of being above the standards of a civil society is the 1989 rape case in Glen Ridge, New Jersey, in which a seventeen-year-old girl classified as "educable mentally retarded" was sexually assaulted by a gang of popular high school athletes. This incident was chronicled by Bernard Lefkowitz, a Columbia University journalism professor, in a book entitled *Our Guys: The Glen Ridge Rape Case and the Secret Life of the Perfect Suburb*. What makes this book so compelling is that the author goes beyond a simple account of the event and court proceedings that followed, to analyze the attitudes and behavior present in the small suburban town that contributed to and influenced the event. Specifically, Lefkowitz cites that the town's obsession with the success of its high school football team as contributing to the creation of a "Jock Elite." (According to a 1941 Yale University study, Glen Ridge placed "too much emphasis on producing winning teams at the expense of social values.") Glen Ridge High School football players were coddled and placed on pedestals to such an extent that it warped their sense of social propriety and responsibility. These athletes thought they were above not only the law, but common standards of civility and behavior as well. For example, they were responsible for viciously trashing the home of a classmate at an unsupervised party, despite the repeated and desperate pleas of the hostess. Yet, they went unpunished. No one dared take on the football juggernaut—not parents, coaches, or teachers.

While this example may be extreme, it is hard to argue that our society's obsession with organized athletics has created an attitude among athletes that if they are good enough, the rules don't apply to them. There are simply too many examples of athletes who, despite repeated criminal offenses, violations of team rules, or run-ins with the law, are welcomed back to the fields of play with open arms. As the former New York Yankee pitcher Jim Bouton once said, "They'd find room for Charles Manson if he could hit .300."

Bouton is not far off in his assessment of the priorities of the leaders of organized sport. In their book *Pros and Cons: The Criminals Who Play in the NFL,* Jeff Benedict and Don Yaeger randomly sampled 509 NFL players and found that 109 (21 percent) had been formally charged with a serious crime, including rape, kidnapping, assault and battery, weapons possession, drug dealing, driving while intoxicated, domestic violence, and even homicide. Yes, *one in five!* That means there is more than a 20 percent chance that the NFL athlete a parent holds up as a role model for their children has a criminal record.

Apologists state that behavior and attitudes displayed in organized athletics merely reflect the values and behaviors of society generally. As mentioned earlier, the relationship between our society and sport, as it applies to influencing cultural values and behaviors, is symbiotic. The problem is that in organized athletics only one thing matters—winning. How you win, whether gracefully or arrogantly, or what you do to win, whether it be deliberately injuring an opponent, offering under-the-table cash to a high school all-star to attend college, or injecting your body with a performance-enhancing drug, simply does not matter. In the sports world, the end always justifies the means.

These negatives would not be much of an issue if it weren't for the fact that we have promoted organized athletics as our culture's most-effective vehicle to teach lessons in sportsmanship, ethics, and fair play. It is due to this belief that we, as a culture, have invested so heavily in organized sports. We have held athletics up on a pedestal as some superior, more wholesome, more important, and yes, more "American" an activity than involvement in the choir, the debate team, or the drama club. Athletes are looked upon as being "good kids" and "leaders," while the kid playing electric guitar in a band, who also happens to have long hair and an earring, is looked upon as a "freak," a troublemaker, or worse. Most parents would likely want their child to emulate Shaquille O'Neal the basketball player rather than Shaquille O'Neal the rap artist. Athletics is motherhood and apple pie, pure and All-American. We believe, without question, that if our children are involved in athletics they are being exposed to good, solid, wholesome values.

But are they?

Could it be that organized athletics' effect on our culture, at least as it applies to its contribution to the creation and maintenance of a just and civil society, has become more negative than positive? In the world of sports, cheating is winked at; a lack of civility to competitors is considered a positive attribute; violence is glorified; and the promotion of the individual, often at the expense of the group, is tolerated. In sport, there are no rules of civility. There is no trust. There are no standards of acceptable behavior, or, if there are, they can easily be bent, broken, or amended if the player is good enough. In the athletic culture, there is no order and but one rule: win at any cost. The question is whether that cost has become too high.

DUMB JOCKS IN THE GLOBAL ECONOMY

> **Dumb jocks are not born, they are being systematically created.**
>
> —Harry Edwards

The evolution of sport in America is strikingly similar to that of athletics in ancient Greece. In both cases, as sport grew in popularity, so did the rewards that came with success. Increased prize money and the prospects of becoming a widely recognized celebrity heightened the emphasis placed upon winning, resulting in increased "professionalization" of athletics. The consequences of such developments in ancient Greece were that "athletics was compressed from a broad-based cultural ideal to the practice of a select few, and within this group the old values of well-rounded performance, cultivation of the whole body, and the importance of beauty and grace were lost. The connection between athletics, cultural education, and nobility withered, and the athlete came to be seen as crude, limited, and base" (Hatab 1991, 36).

It is not unreasonable to claim that a similar imbalance between athletics and education exists in America today. For example, when a school district or university is faced with budget cuts, it is far more likely that a program in the arts will be downsized or eliminated while the athletic program remains untouched. Many of our major universities appropriate $20 to $50 million to an intercollegiate athletic program that serves a few hundred students while intramural programs, potentially serving the entire student body, operate on a fraction of that. Academic standards are continuously loosened or, in many cases, dropped altogether, for a youngster who displays athletic talent. With school systems in disrepair, politicians think nothing of appropriating tax dollars to build a stadium for a professional sports team and its billionaire owner and millionaire players. Accounts of cheating, corruption, a widening gap between athletics and the educational process, astronomical salaries, and athletes acting as if their star status exempts them from societal standards and norms of civil and lawful behavior seem to occupy more space in newspapers than accounts of games. These are simply a few examples of a society that seems to have lost its sense of the proper relationship between sport and education, between the development of the mind and of the body.

The purpose of this chapter is to explore the relationship between athletics and education in America. We will explore this relationship from two perspectives, the effect of athletic participation on the educational, intellectual, and personal development of the athlete as well as organized athletics' impact on our country's educational values and institutions.

Preparing Workers for the Twenty-first Century?

That a culture of anti-intellectualism might exist in our organized sports programs should come as no surprise. The reason athletics were incorporated into our public school systems had little to do with education. Community-based youth sports programs, such as the Police Athletic League, were formed for other reasons as well. The driving force behind the development of such programs were the great industrialists of the early 1900s. Rather than having an interest in educating through sport, these business leaders looked upon organized athletics as a means to train, socialize, and control a workforce. Through sport, youth could be taught to conform to the rules of the existing culture. Further, industrial America required workers to be loyal, dependable, in good physical shape, able to work as part of a team and, above all, obedient. Sport, it was believed, instilled these characteristics. In the minds of Andrew Carnegie, J. D. Rockefeller, and the like, there was little room for lofty thinking on the assembly line. Factory owners of that time did not want their line workers to be great thinkers, preferring that they passively conform. "The leaders of American industry felt that their workers needed to be loyal and punctual, but not necessarily good academically" (Miracle and Rees 1994, 178).

The most critical aspect of the discussion regarding our nation's changing sport and educational landscape, and the focus of this chapter, relates to the role of athletic participation in developing the skills necessary to succeed in the workplace of the day. While the above-mentioned character traits may have been desirable in the workforce of the early 1900s, they may not be for a twenty-first-century workforce that requires different skills, attitudes, and behaviors. As our economy becomes less physical and more cerebral, business leaders have expressed increasing concern regarding the inability of our educational system to develop in their future workforce the educational skills needed to keep American companies competitive in today's high-tech, information based, global economy. A common complaint is that too much emphasis, not only in terms of dollars, but more important, in time and effort, is being placed upon maintaining highly competitive athletic programs, often at the expense of educational programs in music, math, art, foreign languages, or the sciences.

Texas businessman H. Ross Perot's involvement in an educational reform effort in that state in the mid-1980s provides an excellent example of athletics' negative effect on educational priorities and outcomes. One element of Texas's reform packet required students involved in extra-curricular activities to earn at least a "C" in all of their courses. This aspect of the reform initiative received the most attention as it would apply to student-athletes. Apparently, many Texans were interested in education reform provided it did not affect the quality of their high school athletic programs. Such an approach to educational reform is hardly a recipe for preparing our workforce to compete successfully in the Information Age.

While punctuality, hard work, discipline, a strong body, and the ability to produce in a team environment are all desirable worker traits, preparing our country's workforce to compete successfully in the information-based, service economy of the new millennium will require much more; specifically, the ability to reason, think creatively, adapt to change, manage large amounts of information, critically assess data, and improved math, verbal, and communication skills. The Information Age will require strong minds developed in the classrooms more than strong bodies developed on the playing fields. What Andrew Carnegie considered to be good worker skills for purposes of advancing America's economic interests in 1900 may not be considered adequate to advance America's economic interests in the year 2000 and beyond by today's business leaders like Perot or Microsoft's Bill Gates.

Creating Dumb Jocks

Nathan McCall, in a book of personal essays entitled *What's Going On*, writes about anti-intellectualism and the sports culture, with particular attention to how it impacts black youth. "So many brothers get sucked into what seems like a basketball cult because they're conditioned to see themselves—and even aspire to be seen—as athletic mules rather than as thinking men. Almost from the jump, they're encouraged—by the media, by whites, and even by the unwitting black athletes they admire most—to buy into images that lead to self-defeat" (McCall 1994, 11).

McCall asserts that those who buy into this obsession, encouraged by glitzy ad campaigns featuring black athletes hawking sneakers and soft drinks while performing superhuman physical feats are missing a larger point, "They think they're on top of the world because they can do a three-sixty or shatter a rim. But they haven't figured out how to transfer their ball-playing skills to the mental sphere. Their confidence and brilliant play mean that with similar time and devotion they could perform equivalent intellectual feats off the court. But they don't seem to get it" (10–11).

John R. Hoberman, a professor at the University of Texas-Austin, gets it. In his book, *Darwin's Athletes*, Hoberman argues that not only does sport draw far too many inner city youth away from the classrooms and towards the playing fields and courts, but that sport continues to serve up imagery and metaphors that reinforce racism. Specifically, America feels comfortable in believing that blacks do so well in sports because they are mentally inadequate and that their well muscled, dark bodies, seen night after night on television battling it out on the fields of play, reinforces stereotypes about black brutishness. Hoberman asserts that while we are busy glorifying black athletes for their physical exploits, we downplay or ignore black accomplishment in other, more meaningful areas. Not only does our sports obsession reinforce racial attitudes and stereotypes of blacks, it has also served to instill in the minds of far too many black youth, the idea that they are good at sports and sports alone.

Despite the belief that sports contributes to the educational process, there is virtually no connection between the two. The pervasive image of the athlete is that of being dumb. Far too many coaches discourage the intellectual development of their athletes while we turn our heads and cheer on. With the athlete doing little to fight this image, the public believes it. Why else, for example, did we marvel at, and so many media representatives go to such lengths to explain, the success of Princeton's men's basketball team? (McCabe, 2000). How could a group of intelligent Ivy Leaguers be a great basketball team? The message is clear: athletics and intellectualism are conflicting ideals. We assume good athletes are dumb.

The image of the dumb jock is pervasive. From advertisements that depict athletes as violent brutes to the jokes that are told around the water cooler at work, to the popular television series "Coach," with its collection of dimwitted coaches and athletes, the message is consistent: while we enjoy watching their feats of physical prowess, when the game is over, we discount, or even ridicule, athletes' lack of intelligence.

As for jokes about dumb jocks and the Mickey Mouse "academic" curriculums in which they enroll, how about this one?

Question: How many basketball players does it take to screw in a lightbulb?

Answer: The whole team. And everyone gets credit for the semester.

Joking aside, the notion of the dumb jock is more than simply a tired stereotype. It is real. I got a sobering taste of the effects of a life immersed in the jock culture while playing professionally with the Maine Lumberjacks in the Continental Basketball Association. Upon receiving our paychecks one day, a few team members went to the bank to cash them. After depositing portions of my check into my savings and checking accounts, I took the remainder in cash. Noticing all of the paperwork, a teammate asked what I was doing. I had to explain that if you deposit your money in the bank, you can get it out at a later date. He stood, entire paycheck worth of cash in hand, amazed.

Ordering a simple meal in a restaurant could provide an interesting glimpse into the limited life jocks often lead. A teammate asked a waitress whether they served pork or beef sausage. He explained that he felt very strongly about not eating pork. The waitress expressed her regrets, informing him that the sausage was made of pork. "That's OK," my teammate responded as he took another look at the menu. "I'll take the bacon, instead."

The factors contributing to the evolution from pee-wee phenom to dumb jock are complex. Despite the negative image of the dumb jock and regardless of the fact that the values and behaviors often promoted through athletics can be self-defeating, the pressure on youngsters to conform to the commonly accepted image of the athlete is very powerful.

Absolute obedience, discipline, and conformity—coaches demand nothing less from their athletes. From the moment youngsters step onto a playing field, coaches begin to drill into them the importance of unyielding dedication and commitment to the sport and to the team. Coaches set absolute standards for attitudes and behavior, all centered upon molding a group of individuals into a team. As a result, a form of "group think" envelops the team, with all the athletes buying into the same set of attitudes, beliefs, and behaviors. Athletes are repeatedly told that only by subordinating individual behavior and goals for the greater good of the group will the team succeed. This attitude is exemplified by the common coaching adage, "There is no 'I' in Team."

Such a controlled, authoritative environment hinders an athlete's ability to think and act for himself. There is a fine line between a healthy dose of discipline and an autocratic, militaristic dictatorship. Blindly obeying any and all commands is not necessarily a blueprint for success in life. A bit of healthy skepticism is important, as is believing that you have the right to ask questions and challenge authority. Coaches, however, train athletes to respond to their demands without so much as a blink of an eye. In the heat of battle, quick and unquestioning response to commands can make the difference between winning and losing. While that may be true on the fields of play, expecting the same blind loyalty when the games are over is problematic.

Collegiate coaches want to control their athletes' academic schedules, where and when they eat, who they socialize with, and when and where they sleep. Coaches claim that they exert such control because they "care about" their athletes. The fact is, most coaches do not trust their athletes to make intelligent, responsible decisions for themselves because they do not believe athletes are capable of doing so (they are dumb!). What coaches care most about is eliminating anything that might be construed as a "distraction" to their athletes' focusing on peak athletic performance. Such "distractions" often include academic responsibilities, extracurricular activities, and opportunities for social and cultural enrichment. The result is athletes who cannot think for themselves.

In an article that appeared in GQ titled "My Body, My Weapon, My Shame," Elwood Reid, an author and former major college football player, explains the type of behavior that is expected of jocks:

> I began to realize that as a potential college-football recruit, I was expected to behave like one. I had to shake hands and look scouts in the eye and thank them for coming to see me. I had to talk sports, tell them who my favorite players were, what team I liked in the Super Bowl. I had to be smart, but not too smart. Grades mattered only because colleges like "no risk" players, guys who can be recruited without the worry that they'll flunk out. I couldn't tell them that I didn't care who won the Super Bowl, that what really mattered to me was books. That when I finished *One Flew over the Cuckoo's Nest* or *Heart of Darkness*, my heart beat faster than it ever had on the football field. I knew that I had to keep this part of me hidden and let the scouts and coaches see the bright-eyed athlete they wanted to see. (Reid 1998, 119)

Limiting Worldview?

That coaches would expect such behavior from their athletes should come as no surprise. Typically, those who end up in coaching or athletic administration are products of the authoritarian athletic culture.

Most coaches are ex-athletes. To advance up the coaching ladder, they have to mirror the behaviors and expectations of veteran coaches. The further up the career ladder a coach or an administrator climbs, the more intense the expectations for conformity. Athletics is a very incestuous culture where conformity is embraced and difference is looked upon very suspiciously; where toughness, obedience, and unquestioned loyalty is rewarded while intellectualism, sensitivity, and free thought is ridiculed. It is naive to think that this attitude exists only at the college and professional levels. From day one, athletes are conditioned to conform to team standards of thought and behavior. Coaches reward those who are strong, not smart; tough, not sensitive, unquestioning in their loyalty, not thoughtful and reflective.

One of the most interesting studies of the effect of athletic participation on student-athletes was conducted by the sociologists Peter and Patricia Adler. The Adlers virtually became a part of a Division I basketball program for a five-year period. Their observations are outlined in their 1991 book titled *Backboards and Blackboards: College Athletics and Role Engulfment*. Based upon extensive interviews and observation, among the conclusions they drew was that after a four- or five-year intercollegiate athletic experience, student-athletes often had a much narrower "worldview" than when they entered the university.

The Adlers found that upon initial enrollment, student-athletes had a broad range of interests and goals in the academic, social, and athletic areas. However, during their time on campus, they were forced to make decisions that pitted their academic or social interests against their athletic interests. Invariably, decisions were made in favor of athletic interests. For example, if a student-athlete wanted to go to a movie with a nonathlete but the coach had planned a social event with a booster of the program, the student-athlete felt pressure to attend the team function. Or, if a coach thought a particular major was too demanding and would thus affect athletic performance, it was "suggested" that the student-athlete enroll in a less-demanding major.

Because of the intense pressure to constantly show one's "commitment to the program," student-athletes were continually forced to make decisions that would further their athletic goals, while pushing their academic or social aspirations into the background. Like the muscle that atrophies from inactivity, the result was a dwindling of student-athletes' social and academic interests in favor of athletic interests. Although much in athletics, such as travel to new and exciting places, has the potential to expand the student-athlete's worldview, the Adlers argued that the overall experience may, in some cases, actually narrow the student-athlete's perspective.

> Despite its structural fit within the trends current in American society, the engulfment of college athletes raises questions and conflicts that cannot be easily answered. On the one hand, these young men are spending formative years sacrificing themselves to entertain and enrich others, lured by the hope of a future that is elusive at best. For other students, this kind of narrowing and intense focus may lead to a prosperous career in such fields as medicine, law, education, or business. For college athletes, however, their specialization, dedication, and abandonment of alternatives leads to their becoming finally proficient at a role that, for most, will end immediately following the conclusion of their college eligibility. For those fortunate enough to achieve a professional career, the end comes only slightly later.
>
> It is ironic that these athletes are thus partly socialized to failure; although some sustained the athletic role temporarily, they were released by the system at the end of four years engulfed in a role destined to become an "ex" (Ebaugh 1988). College athletes entered the university thinking that they would expand their horizons and opportunities in a variety of ways. They ended up narrowing their selves enough that their more grandiose expectations were not met. (Adler and Adler 1991, 230)

Even at my school, Davidson College, a small liberal arts institution with high academic standards that competed at the NCAA Division I level, we felt the tension between academic and personal goals and athletic responsibility. Despite the fact that from an institutional standpoint, priorities relating to athletics and education were clear, some coaches did not hesitate in pitting academic and athletic interests against each other. Whether it was the subtle pressure not to schedule a lab class that would conflict with practice time or suggesting that it would be in your best interest to stop spending so much time with a particular group of students (non-jocks), coaches subtly pressured us to conform to their athletic dreams, goals, and expectations rather than to our academic and personal dreams, goals, and expectations. It didn't take long for us to figure out that far too many coaches are interested only in the bottom line, immediate athletic results of their "players," not the long-term personal and intellectual development of their students.

The fundamental purpose of education, and often a stated purpose of athletics itself, is to provide youngsters opportunities to broaden their life experiences and to make decisions both good and bad and to learn from those decisions. Our schools and colleges are in the business of expanding horizons and teaching young people the love of learning. Is it possible that involvement in highly competitive school and intercollegiate athletics might actually do the opposite? Does participation in elite athletics actually narrow focus and self-identity and restrict decision-making opportunities?

Athletes and the Work Ethic

One of the more interesting twists on the educational and character-building benefits of sport participation relates to work ethic. Discipline and the drive to work hard contribute greatly to success on the fields of play and in life. Of that there is no dispute. But does participation in sport instill these character traits more than any other intense training activity such as learning to play a musical instrument? Does participation in athletics breed these traits at all?

While it takes discipline and hard work to succeed in athletics, the success that results from such hard work on the fields of play may, in the long run, actually distort an individual's work ethic.

From the moment a young person is identified as an outstanding athlete, he or she is pampered by coaches, fans, teachers, fellow students, and even their parents. "You're special. Don't worry about those details. We'll take care of them for you. Concentrate on playing ball." These are the not-so-subtle messages communicated to the athlete. The athlete is coddled and in many ways given a "free pass" through life.

> His athletic accomplishments, while frequently demanding hard work, self-discipline, and self-sacrifice, receive great praise from principals, superintendents, local newspapers, service and booster clubs, politicians, and community leaders. For the attention he brings to his school and community his elders are grateful. His teachers and coaches begin to bend rules to make sure that he is able to excel at what he does best. Fellow students treat him with a mixture of awe and respect, and he finds himself pursued by the most desirable girls in his school. From an early age, the athlete finds that the pleasures of the world are his reward for athletic accomplishment; that he is treated differently from the rest. (Gorn and Goldstein 1993, 243)

This is an example of the age-old argument of whether sports builds character or simply reveals it. It is unquestionable that sports reveals character. How the athlete acts on the field or the court reveals a lot about him or her as a person. But it is also quite clear that involvement in organized sports can contribute greatly to a demise in character, morals, and values. There have been many good, hard-working, and humble athletes who, after achieving success on the fields of play, begin to believe all of their press clippings. Many cannot handle the adulation gracefully; they become "big-headed" and begin to feel that, because of their star status, they are entitled to certain perks, benefits, and privileges.

At first, they may be embarrassed by the attention, but in time, athletes begin to not only enjoy such special treatment, but also to expect it. Whether it be the teacher who gives the leading scorer on the basketball team an "A" despite the fact that he rarely showed up for class or the local restauranteur who lets the quarterback eat for free, such treatment instills in the athlete a warped sense of entitlement. Because he is a "star," the athlete begins to expect that everything will be either given to him or taken care of for him, which hardly instills a positive work ethic.

I got a depressing look at the result of things being "taking care of" for athletes during my season of professional basketball. Upon the completion of preseason training camp, I set out to secure more permanent living accommodations as the team would no longer arrange and pay for our lodging. I will never forget how bewildered a teammate was when faced with even the simple task of finding an apartment. He had no idea of how to go about renting an apartment, connecting a phone, or paying a deposit. This was someone who had spent four years on a college campus! My teammate had become accustomed to, and thus expected, things to be "taken care of" for him, including the arrangement of an apartment.

Another example, as told by a faculty athletic representative of a major college program, involved a matter as simple as retrieving baggage after a plane flight. Asked why he was wearing the same outfit three consecutive days, a student-athlete explained that he had recently returned from a trip home and the airlines had lost his luggage. As it turned out, he did not understand that he was responsible for retrieving his own bags. When he was traveling with the team, it had always been "taken care of" for him.

> It's becoming increasingly difficult to find a professional basketball player who has ever held a real job, even a part-time one. Even stars with good images, such as Detroit Pistons forward Grant Hill, admits he's never worked a real job in his life.
> "No," says Hill, a little sheepishly. "In my free time I played basketball. Summers, weekends, every chance I had. I suppose that's not the best way to develop values, but that's how it is these days." (Wetzel and Yeager 2000, 183)

In many cases, even the most fundamental decisions—their daily schedule, where, when, and what they eat, when they go to bed and wake up in the morning—are made for athletes by coaches intent upon improving their "focus" on athletic performance. The result is that athletes' understanding of the fact that in the "real world" you not only have to work hard but also must accept personal responsibility for your actions, is underdeveloped, or in some cases, never develops.

As cited in the previous chapter in relation to the issue of moral and ethical reasoning, there appears to be some empirical evidence of the potential of involvement in organized sports to have a negative impact on the development of certain positive character traits. While it may be impossible to empirically measure the effect of involvement in athletics on an individual's sense of entitlement, I have seen far too many cases of this occurring not to believe that some effect exists. I, too, at various times during my career, was guilty of feeling entitled due to my status as an athlete. With all of the adulation athletes receive, it is completely understandable how it could happen.

Defending the Status Quo

There are many with a vested interest in promoting the principle that participation in sport is an educational and character-building activity. To justify their place in the educational community, coaches and athletic administrators must demonstrate that what they do has educational value. These individuals are well served to promote this belief because its widespread acceptance secures their power and status not only in the educational community but also in the public's eye. Even at the professional level, it is beneficial to promote sports' role in teaching such lessons as it makes the professional product—whether it be a team, league, or athlete—a more attractive and marketable commodity.

If the public senses that positive traits are being taught and displayed, they will be more inclined to buy a ticket, purchase team apparel items, or watch a game on television.

The educational justification for sport serves those in the athletic establishment in another important way. An unquestioned acceptance of this ideal relieves coaches of accountability for teaching in a responsible manner. Coaches, who are supposed to be teachers, curse their students and impose arbitrary rules about hair length, clothes, and social life, and no one thinks twice about it. A college or high school coach can justify punishing an "undisciplined" student-athlete, running a few "bad apples" off the team and out of a scholarship, or verbally abusing an athlete simply by stating that he or she is "teaching discipline and life lessons." Thus, teaching methods deemed unacceptable for the classroom can be justified on the playing fields in the name of "educating" and building character.

This is not to say that organized, competitive athletics cannot be culturally and educationally enriching. Athletics has enormous potential as a very powerful supplement to the educational process provided we take the time and make the effort to make it so. The problem, however, is that the system is not structured with those purposes in mind.

For example, sports advocates cite the tremendous educational opportunities afforded through the extensive travel that is a part of elite athletic competition. Undoubtedly, travel is educational and can broaden the horizons of athletes. However, as someone who has been on road trips too numerous to count, team travel is not about providing an educational opportunity or a personally enriching experience for the athlete. Team travel is about winning a game. Very rarely are meaningful educational or cultural outings a part of athletic travel. The common road trip itinerary looks something like this: bus to airport, board plane, bus to hotel, unpack, bus to gym or field, practice, back to hotel, dinner, sleep, breakfast, pre-game walk-through at gym or field, back to hotel, to game, to bus, to plane, to bus, to home. To consider such an itinerary culturally enriching is a stretch.

While our investment in athletics has been sold on the assumption that participation contributes to the educational and personal development of the athlete, the culture of athletics actually discourages educational achievement and personal development. Coaches and athletic administrators are not interested in developing Phi Beta Kappas and Nobel Prize winners. Their job is to win games. To win games, they must produce great athletes. To develop great athletes, coaches do whatever possible to get their athletes to "focus" as much of their time, energy, and emotion on athletic development and performance. The pressure for a young athlete to conform to a coach's or a team's athletic expectations and the appropriate "jock mentality" is tremendous. The result is a narrowing of perspective and worldview.

My experience of touring behind the Iron Curtain with a USA basketball team in 1979 provides an example. From the moment we got off the plane in Russia, everywhere we turned it seemed, there were posters, billboards, and statues of Karl Marx, Vladimir Lenin, and Joseph Stalin. You couldn't go anywhere in Moscow and Kiev without seeing some propaganda image with Russia's "Big Three" peering over your shoulder. A few days into the trip, a teammate looked at me, puzzled, and asked, "Who are those dudes, anyway?" While no world history scholar, I was able to explain the fundamentals of communism and their role in Russian history. After all, my generation was weaned on the politics of the Cold War. My teammate, intent throughout my rudimentary discourse, thought for a moment, shook his head, and marveled, "They sure do get a lot of 'pub' [publicity] over here. Who's their agent?"

While sports advocates are quick to point out that my teammates' worldview was expanded simply by traveling to Russia, the fact is, the only reason he learned anything about Russia or its history was because he asked a question. There certainly weren't any educational side trips on our itinerary. We were there to play and win games. Period.

Despite repeated claims regarding organized athletics' value as a vehicle to educate, expand the mind, and broaden horizons, the fact is, the concept of the "dumb jock" is real. Worse, however, is that Harry Edwards is correct. Dumb jocks are not born; they are being systematically created by an athletic culture that has as a very low priority the educational, intellectual, and personal development of the athlete.

Undermining Our Educational Values and Institutions

Because of the tremendous visibility and influence of school athletic programs, their impact on the values of, and public attitudes toward, our schools, colleges, and universities is enormous. Competitive interscholastic and intercollegiate athletics have become so entrenched within the educational system that it is difficult to imagine our schools and universities without them; athletics and education are inseparably linked, feeding off of each other, all for the greater good of the institution.

Unfortunately, athletics' impact on our intellectual values and educational institutions strongly suggests otherwise. Similar to what occurred as sport became wildly popular in ancient Greece, as school and college sport in America grew in popularity, its relationship to education has become skewed. Rather than strengthening our educational values and supplementing the missions of our educational institutions, organized athletics actually undermines them. Despite our unwillingness to acknowledge it, there is a fundamental inconsistency in the relationship between athletics and education. Simply put, the forces that drive athletics and those that guide educational policy are, for the most part, diametrically opposed.

For example, coaches are driven to win games. Coaches rationalize their intense drive by indicating that if they do not win they will be fired. While that may be true to some degree, the fact is, coaches coach because they are highly competitive and have a tremendous desire to win. Athletic administrators, most of whom are ex-athletes or coaches with the same type of competitive drive, must help their coaches win games to fill stadiums to generate revenue to pay for the expense of the program or the team. If the athletic administrator does not meet budget, he or she will soon be out of a job. Such goals are short term—to win next week's game.

The goal of our educational institutions is to prepare individuals to be productive citizens for the rest of their lives and, in doing so, keep our nation a vibrant and strong world power. As is always the case when balancing short- and long-term goals, conflicts arise. These inherent conflicts have nothing to do with "good guys" versus "bad guys"; they are simply the realities of two very different cultures. There is not a coach in the country, at any level, who does not want every one of his or her athletes to be successful in life after their playing days are over. The problem, however, is that for too many coaches it eventually comes back to winning games. Thus, it is easy to understand why coaches and athletic administrators are primarily interested in maximizing athletic performance. In short, the pressure to win to generate the revenue necessary to support athletic programs or teams, coupled with their own hyper-competitive drive, places the long-term academic interests, goals, and priorities of our educational institutions in direct conflict with the highly competitive, short-term, economically driven interests of the athletic establishment.

The National Collegiate Athletic Association exists, in large part, to monitor athletic abuses and, as stated in its constitution, "to maintain athletics as an integral part of the educational program and the athlete an integral part of the student body." While a laudable ideal, many argue that the organization operates more as a trade association and public relations arm for collegiate athletics, and is hardly interested in an educated or informed student-athlete. For example, when Congress initiated the "Right to Know" Act to require universities to make public the graduation rates of its student-athletes, the NCAA lobbied forcefully against it (Zimbalist 1999, 12).

The extent to which organized sport subverts our nation's educational interests is substantial. At the grade school and high school levels, athletes are passed who have not mastered the required work. The prevailing notion is that it is acceptable if Johnny can't read as long as he can play. Coaches plead the case of "a good kid, whose only chance at a better life is through an athletic scholarship and he won't be eligible for that scholarship unless he passes this course." Far too often, the teacher or principal complies, not wanting to be responsible for denying a youngster his "only chance." Unfortunately, everyone knows— classmates, parents, coaches, teachers, and Johnny himself—that Johnny did not deserve to pass. The effect on the academic credibility of the institution is enormous. Such acts, and they are far from isolated, serve to cheapen the value and standing of education in our communities.

This academic fraud is perpetuated when our institutions of higher learning spend significant resources recruiting and later admitting Johnny, despite the fact that he is unqualified to perform college work and unlikely to graduate. Once the "student-athlete" is enrolled, it becomes all too clear that the primary reason for being at college is to produce on the fields of play. All else— education, social life, and personal development—occupies a distant place on the list of priorities for what in reality is an "athlete-student." All this in the name of "educational opportunity." All at the expense of academic integrity.

There is no better example of the way in which such academic fraud undermines the integrity of our educational institutions than the following quote from the Charlotte Hornets forward Elden Camp-bell. When asked if he had earned his degree from Clemson University, he apparently responded, "No, but they gave me one anyway."

For a more personal example, in August 1992, while associate commissioner of the SEC, I sat in on a meeting of the conference athletic directors. My purpose was to review a series of NCAA proposals aimed at increasing academic standards for athletes. As the discussion dragged on, a prominent athletic director warned, "Hey, this is an athletic conference. We've got to be careful that we don't get lost in all of this academic stuff." Two other athletic directors concurred.

Athletics undercuts the integrity of our academic institutions in other ways. The obscenely large salaries that NCAA Division I and I-A universities pay their football and basketball coaches is an example of institutional priorities that are wildly out of balance. It is not uncommon for these coaches to make more money than the university president, and in some cases, many times more. For example, Auburn University's head football coach, Tommy Tuberville, gets paid between $750,000 and $900,000, depending on the team's performance. That is four times the salary of Auburn's president at the time, William Muse. The University of Florida's football coach, Steve Spurrier, reportedly earns up to $2 million a year when broadcast contracts and other benefits are included. What does providing a football coach such a salary imply about university priorities? According to Ted Gup, a lecturer at Georgetown University and a freelance writer, it says a lot. "As one who has taught at universities for 20 years and who has witnessed a generation of students come and go, I can attest to the fact that plenty of harm is done. Our children, our institutions, and our communities are paying dearly for our society's obsession with winning and the dollars that follow. The grossly disproportionate resources and attention given to big-time college sports infect our institutions with corruption, venality, and hypocrisy" (Gup 1998, A-52).

But isn't it the institution itself that decides to hire, fire, and pay coaches such exorbitant salaries? Absolutely. But the larger question is whether the highly competitive, win-at-all cost culture of athletics is simply antithetical to the values and culture of the academic community.

Beyond this warped salary structure rests the issue of the status that is bestowed upon popular coaches; a status that is far out of proportion to their contribution to positive academic outcomes. There is no more tragic example of this imbalance than Indiana University and its basketball coach, Bobby Knight. Despite a videotape showing Knight choking a former student and various accounts of threatening behavior directed toward an athletic department secretary and the athletics director, the university retained the coach. And these episodes were only the most recent in a string of abusive and embarrassing episodes. As Ellen J. Staurowsky, associate professor of sports sociology at Ithaca College, wrote in the June 5, 2000, *NCAA News:*

> For those unpersuaded that the corruption in big-time college sports does not translate into the corruption of the ideals of higher education, pause long on this event because it serves as a clarifying moment. There can be no doubt in this case that athletics accomplishments, including three NCAA championships, 24 NCAA tournament appearances, five Final Four appearances and their attendant attachment to power and money, have trumped the courage of a former student who was grabbed by the throat and choked during a practice three years ago. . . . As in the movie *Wizard of Oz,* not only are we not in Kansas anymore, we are nowhere near higher education in this scene. We are smack-dab in the middle of Darwinian Survival of the Fittest mores and unchecked American capitalism where the lowest class is expendable and the producers maintain their positions, despite otherwise intolerable behavior. And for what? A college basketball program? (4)

Despite the fact that Knight was dismissed after an angry confrontation with a student a few months later, for too long, his transgressions and the university's unwillingness to respond to them in an educationally responsible manner illustrated most clearly that big-time athletics' fundamental purposes and modus operandi have drifted hopelessly outside those of the mainstream university community. Here is an instance where a young person came to an educational institution to study and learn, and he was choked by a "teacher" . . . choked! A university community would have never permitted a history professor or an English professor to choke a student. And that is precisely where the problem lies. The sad reality is that we do not think of major college student-athletes as students at all, but rather hired guns, entertainers, and dumb jocks. As a result, they are denied the same rights as all other students, that being the right to have a quality educational experience and earn a meaningful degree. This situation cuts two disturbing and, ultimately, very revealing ways. Not only is it another case where a popular and powerful coach is not held accountable for acting in an educationally irresponsible manner, but it is also a vivid example of how student-athletes are not thought of as students at all. When a university does not dismiss a coach for choking a student, big-time athletics has clearly gotten out of control.

In short, college athletics has created, American higher education has tacitly endorsed, and our society celebrates, a culture that accepts the notion that it is an educational institution's responsibility to provide the very best in athletic facilities, coaching, and support so elite athletes have every opportunity to develop their athletic abilities to the fullest. While there is nothing inherently wrong with wanting to provide the resources and support to help an individual develop fully as an athlete, the problem is, that goal has become the primary purpose of the student-athlete's stay on campus. As a result, the educational and personal development of the student-athlete has become an afterthought. Sadly, we have come to accept the notion that if during the student-athlete's years on campus he or she *happens* to get an education, it is a bonus. This, as opposed to a culture and system that *expects* a young person to develop fully academically, intellectually, and personally while he or she happens to play sports. It is the athletic development that must be a pleasant byproduct of the educational process, not the other way around. We simply can no longer tolerate a system that demands athletic excellence but accepts educational mediocrity or less, for no matter how small a group of students. The negative impact of such a system on institutional credibility and public perception is simply too great.

Embracing an Entertainment Culture

Despite the claims of many that college sports has never been healthier or more popular, it is becoming increasingly difficult not to notice the negative effects that popularity is having on our academic institutions. According to William C. Dowling, professor of English at Rutgers University, the tremendous growth in commercialization of college athletics has eroded American higher education's intellectual and academic values. The tremendous influence, says Dowling,

> of TV networks, major corporations, athletics gear sponsors like Nike, etc., has gradually eaten its way into the heart of American higher education through Division IA sports, a "society of the spectacle" entirely willing to see academic and intellectual values collapse so long as sales and advertising revenues remain hugely lucrative. . . . The fans who view the Tostitos Fiesta Bowl on television are watching not only a football game but a demonstration that the same culture that generated *The Jerry Springer Show* and cable-TV wrestling has been able to penetrate, and to hollow out from within, the university as an institution. (Dowling 2000, 31–33)

James J. Duderstadt, president emeritus of the University of Michigan, writes provocatively about the growing separation between athletics and the core values of the educational institution in his book, *Intercollegiate Athletics and the American University: A University*

President's Perspective. Duderstadt's contention is that in an effort to increase public popularity, athletic departments have had to embrace the values and principles of an entertainment culture. His concern is that those entertainment values are, in large part, contrary to those of the academic community. While he acknowledges that most of intercollegiate athletics are valuable and appropriate activities for higher education, "big-time college football and basketball stand apart. They have little if any relevance to the academic mission of the university. They are based on a set of values that, while appropriate for show business, are viewed as highly corrupt by the academy and deemed corrosive to our academic mission" (Knight Commission 2000).

Thus, Duderstadt poses the question of

> whether it makes sense for the 21st-century university to conduct commercial activities at the current level of big-time college football and basketball. Is there any logical reason for an academic institution, with the fundamental mission of teaching and scholarship, to mount and sustain a professional and commercial enterprise simply to satisfy the public desire for entertainment, and the commercial goals of the marketplace? Why should the university squander its resources, distract its leadership, and erode its most fundamental values and integrity with these commercial activities, particularly at a time when it will face so many other challenges in responding to the changing educational needs of our society? (Knight Commission 2000)

In short, there is a cost associated with the decision to embrace the values of an entertainment culture, and the cost has become particularly high for educational institutions.

And the Gap Is Widening

While it is no secret that the gap between the athletic and academic cultures on our college campuses exists, what is particularly disturbing is that the chasm between the two cultures is apparently growing. Worse yet, is that such a gap exists not only in major college (NCAA Division I) institutions, but also at schools in NCAA Divisions II and III, which spend less money and place much less emphasis on athletics.

In their ground-breaking book, *The Game of Life: College Sports and Educational Values*, William G. Bowen and James L. Shulman, president and CFO, respectively, of the Mellon Foundation, utilize a vast database gathered by the foundation to analyze a wide range of assumptions and trends relating to athletics on campus. The study involved the examination of the academic records of over ninety thousand students from the entering classes of 1951, 1976, and 1989 at thirty-two institutions: four large public universities, including Michigan and North Carolina; four Ivy League schools; nine other private universities, including Tulane and Stanford; seven co-ed liberal arts colleges, including Swarthmore and Williams; four all-women's colleges, and four historically black colleges. The data have been used in a number of studies the foundation has supported.

The authors used the massive database to make the following observations—supported by dozens of tables and graphs—about the role of sport at academically elite institutions. The findings are particularly striking because the trends most people associate with athletic powerhouses like Michigan show up at even smaller colleges. For example:

- Athletes enjoy a huge advantage in the admission process even more than members of minority groups and children of alumni.
- Athletes tend to underperform academically compared with their peers, but more important, with what their high-school grades and test scores predict.
- Athletes do not show any signs of having acquired leadership skills, based upon their life experiences following

college. While many athletes think of themselves as strong leaders, generally, they don't exhibit leadership.

• Contrary to popular belief, recruitment of athletes has no marked effect on either the socioeconomic composition of colleges or their racial diversity.

• The data flatly contradict one of the strongest myths about college athletics—that winning teams, and especially winning football teams, have a large, positive impact on rates of philanthropic giving to the institution.

• It appears that a distinct "athletic culture" exists in essentially all sports at all levels of play, including the Division III coed liberal arts colleges. This culture tends to separate athletes from other students and exacerbates the problem of academic performance. For example, athletes were highly concentrated in certain fields of study and in certain residences. "In this atmosphere, athletics are naturally emphasized, and the upcoming game might easily get more attention than the term paper. The evidence of disappointing academic performance is found not only in football and basketball, but in lower-profile sports like tennis and swimming, among both men and women" (Shulman and Bowen 2001, A-29).

• Female athletes, whether at women's colleges or coeducational ones, are beginning to follow the same pattern as men, as women's teams adopt the same recruiting practices and levels of intensity.

• What may, however, be the most significant of their findings is that the primary reason for schools placing such a heavy emphasis on athletics—a desire to please alumni— is apparently a myth. When the authors surveyed alumni, they found that "in general, alumni favored decreasing their school's emphasis on inter-collegiate competition, not increasing it. Those who made the biggest donations assigned lower priority to intercollegiate athletics than to nearly every other aspect of college or university life that they were asked to rank" (Shulman and Bowen 2001, A-29).

The fact that these issues and problems seem to apply to schools at all levels of play, is particularly interesting. This revelation certainly broadens the debate about the potential pitfalls of sponsoring competitive intercollegiate athletics from one that was previously limited to major college, full-scholarship programs such as Michigan, to include non-scholarship Division III programs such as Williams. The authors argue that sports' impact on admissions and on academic performance is more significant at small liberal arts colleges and Ivy League institutions because athletes make up a larger percentage of the student population. Athletes generally make up less than 5 percent of the student body at schools like Michigan versus over 30 percent at many liberal arts institutions.

As if the above-mentioned findings were not disturbing enough, the authors discovered that in virtually every category, these negative athletic effects are becoming greater. This is so because the level of intensity of everything connected to the athletic experience, from recruiting to individual commitment to the sport to the level of play, has increased at all levels of sport, from pee-wee leagues to professional leagues. In short, the chasm between athletics values and priorities and those of the academic community is becoming greater.

Shulman and Bowen's study is the most extensive and provocative examination of intercollegiate athletics' effect on the campus culture. Their findings, if not earth shattering, are certainly myth shattering. Which leads to some fundamental questions. While the authors believe that involvement in sports can and should be a fun and healthy way to build community spirit on a campus, they challenge trustees, parents, and society to consider "what role specialized sports talent—as opposed to participation in sports as one part of a well-rounded application—should play in admission. Does it make sense for a liberal arts college or university to assign a large share of its scarce admissions places to students who, on average, fail to take full advantage of academic opportunities? The root question is broader: With intellectual capital ever more important, how great a role should hand-eye coordination play in deciding who is given educational opportunity?" (Shulman and Bowen 2001, A-29).

The Influence Filters Down

Colleges are not our only educational institutions demonstrating warped priorities relating to athletics. H. G. Bissinger, in his book *Friday Night Lights*, explains how athletics undermines educational priories at Permian High School in Odessa, Texas. He noted that the cost of boys medical supplies at Permian was $6,750. The cost for teaching materials for the English department was $5,040, which included supplies, maintenance of the copying machine, and any extra books besides the required texts that a teacher thought it might be important for the students to read. The cost of game film was $6,400. Meanwhile, the English department had just received its first computer, which was to be used by all twenty-five teachers. An English teacher with twenty years of experience, Larue Moore, earned a salary of $32,000 as compared to the football coach, who also served as athletic director, earning $48,000 and the free use of a new Tauras sedan each year. And, during the 1988 season, Permian spent $70,000 for chartered jets for the football team's travel (Bissinger 1990, 146–47).

Such imbalance prompted one teacher to fume, "'This community doesn't want academic excellence. It wants a gladiatorial spectacle on Friday nights.' As she made that comment, a history class meeting a few yards down the hall did not have a teacher.

The instructor was an assistant football coach. He was one of the best teachers in the school, dedicated and lively, but because of the pressures of preparing for a crucial game, he did not have time to go to class. That wasn't to say however, that the class did not receive a lesson. They learned about American history that day by watching *Butch Cassidy and the Sundance Kid*." (Bissinger 1990, 147–48)

Wayne Flynt, Distinguished University Professor at Auburn University, speaks often about misplaced educational priorities. During an April 25, 1990, speech, Flynt discussed the release of a study indicating that four of Birmingham's ten high schools had no students who scored at or above the national average in reading, math, language, and science between 1985 and 1987 and, of the six remaining high schools, 17 percent was the highest number of students scoring at or above the national average. He noted that not only was Birmingham's system well above the average for the state, but that "of nearly 400 high schools in Alabama, about 370 field football teams. But only 286 offered a foreign language course in 1988 and fewer than 100 offered full-fledged computer courses."

Even when opportunities to teach meaningful lessons arise, institutional pressure to win and generate revenue prevent coaches and athletic officials from doing what is educationally responsible. A most glaring example of this occurred in Tuscaloosa, Alabama, during a game between the University of Alabama and UCLA in the 1998 NCAA Division I women's basketball tournament. Alabama won the game 75-74 after the officials blew two calls in the final 0.8 seconds.

While attempting to inbound the ball under their opponent's basket, an Alabama player ran the baseline, which should have been called a violation. The player then threw the ball almost the full length of the court where it was tipped by both an Alabama and a UCLA player at Alabama's foul line. The game should have ended there. It didn't. Apparently the timekeeper, who had been Alabama's timekeeper for twenty-five years, forgot to start the clock. Meanwhile, an Alabama player caught the ball, squared to the basket, and hit the game-winning shot.

Alabama officials declared that they had won the game fairly, that missed calls are a part of the game. Yes, missed calls are a part of the game, but the primary justification for the game even being sponsored by an educational institution is supposedly to teach life's larger lessons. Alabama's coaches and administrators were presented a golden opportunity to do just that; a teachable moment of tremendous magnitude had occurred in front of a national audience. Such an opportunity will likely come only once in a lifetime. And they missed it. If sports was really about teaching, Alabama's coaches and athletic officials would have done the right thing and refused to accept the tainted victory. If college athletics was about sportsmanship and character, Alabama would have insisted that UCLA advance to the next round of the tournament. If college athletics was about education, it would have been *expected* that Alabama coaches and athletic officials do the right thing. But sport is not about those things. It is about winning. It is about the achievement of short-term athletic goals regardless of whether they come at the expense of long-term educational development and priorities.

Coaches as Educators?

Coaches have a tremendous amount of influence over their athletes. Further, the head football or basketball coach is often the most-visible representative of the educational institution. Given such influence and visibility, their impact on educational values and institutions is enormous. Coaches have been cast as educators and teachers and as an integral part of the academic community. But, here again, the chasm between myth and reality is wide and growing. To fully appreciate the influence of coaches on educational values and institutions, it is best to consider the college coach.

At the time athletics was formally incorporated into higher education, coaches were usually faculty members who also happened to coach. Just as athletics was an extracurricular activity for students, so, too, for the English professor. But as public interest in college athletics grew and its potential as a revenue-generating enterprise increased, institutions began to employ full-time professional coaches. This fundamental change in the coaching profile has not, however, stopped those in the athletic community from continuing to insist that coaches are, before all else, educators. The playing field or court, they insist, is a coach's classroom and the lessons taught there in discipline, teamwork, and sportsmanship are just as important as the lessons being taught in the lecture hall or chemistry lab.

But the realities of major college athletics suggest otherwise. Coaches are neither hired nor evaluated upon their commitment to education. In today's high-pressure world of college athletics, coaches, particularly in the sports of football and basketball, are hired and fired based upon their ability to produce winning teams that generate revenue.

Arguably, the college coach's job description has changed more in the last twenty-five years than any other in higher education. Most Division I football and basketball coaches will agree that the actual teaching and coaching of their sport and their involvement in the off-the-field interests of their student-athletes occupies an increasingly smaller percentage of their time. Coaches are now the most recognizable personalities on campus and thus have been asked to be more involved in university-wide fund-raising and public relations efforts. The pressure for coaches not only to win, but also to be accessible to the media has increased dramatically. Finally, many coaches have become full-fledged entrepreneurs with their own television and radio shows, summer camps, shoe contracts, and endorsements.

As a result, coaches are viewed as slick-looking, fast-talking entertainers and entrepreneurs rather than educators—far more concerned about winning games than graduating student-athletes and largely viewed as having little connection to the educational community. Simply put, the "Coach as Educator" ideal has gone the way of the leather football helmet.

The evolution of the recruiting process has also effected significant change in the "Coach as Educator" ideal. Before recruiting became a highly sophisticated and international operation, prospects heard about athletic programs through newspapers, letters, phone calls, and word of mouth. Alumni and "talent scouts" would identify prospects and perform most of the face-to-face off-campus recruiting. In the 1930s, for example, Northwestern University appointed almost fifty "alumni counselors" to scout for football prospects (Lester 1995, 137). In some cases, a prospect might show up on campus without any recruitment. How that has changed! Recruiting is now looked upon as the life blood of a program because coaches understand they will not win many games with mediocre talent. Thus, considerable time and money is spent recruiting prospects not only nationwide, but worldwide.

This increased emphasis on recruiting has resulted in a shift in the desired credentials and background of assistant coaches. Thirty years ago, the most important hiring criteria for an assistant coach were teaching ability and head-coaching experience. College head coaches looked for experienced assistants who were committed educators. Candidates with those credentials were usually found in high schools, which were filled with head coaches with master's degrees and years of classroom experience.

Today, the most important characteristic an assistant coach must possess is the personality and ability to sell the program to seventeen- and eighteen-year-old high school All-Americans. "You recruit 'em and I'll coach 'em," orders the head coach. If an assistant coach cannot deliver top-notch talent on a consistent basis, he or she will not be an assistant coach for long. The result is that the qualities and background of a committed educator are simply no longer a valued component of an assistant coach's credentials.

Further, many highly qualified high school head coaches, particularly veteran coaches with families, are reluctant to become a college assistant coach because of the travel required to be a successful recruiter. And, after experiencing the hands-on coaching and decision-making responsibility required of a head coach, high school coaches do not have much interest in becoming simply a recruiter at the college level. The result is that there are fewer college coaches cast in the traditional "Coach as Educator" mold as an increasing number are entering the college ranks immediately after their playing days are over.

It can also be argued that the motivation for entering the profession has changed. Young people used to enter coaching because they loved the game and were committed to utilizing sports as a vehicle to teach. Coaches certainly did not coach to get rich. My father has been a high school coach for forty-eight years. In 1950, he earned $100 as an assistant baseball coach, $150 as an assistant football coach, and $400 as the head basketball coach. As a head football coach from 1955 to 1973, he never earned more than $2,400. In 2000, he earned $4,200 a year as an assistant football coach.

After serving for seven years as a high school teacher and coach, Bo Brickels, my former coach at Davidson, earned $6,000 as an assistant coach at Rice University in 1967. He was also required to teach a few courses. Most head basketball coaches during that time were earning $12,000 to $15,000 per year. Many taught or had summer jobs to supplement their income, for theirs was not the type of salary that would make one rich and certainly it was not greater than the institution's president.

But college coaching now offers the opportunity to not only become wealthy, but also to become a national celebrity. Head coaches often command salary "packages" worth hundreds of thousands of dollars.

Even key assistant coaches can earn a six-figure income. These packages include endorsement opportunities, shoe contracts, television shows, and income from summer camps. And with games being televised nationally, a coach can quickly become a media star. Could it be that young people are entering the coaching profession for different reasons than thirty years ago? Could it be that the possibility of significant compensation as well as national celebrity status attracts a different individual to college coaching? And, as a result, have we placed student-athletes in the hands of "coaches" who have more interest in getting rich and becoming a celebrity than they do in education?

One of my most disheartening moments at the Southeastern Conference occurred over the issue of the way in which coaches perceive themselves. The conference conducted a diversity training workshop for athletic personnel at each conference school. One of the workshop exercises involved compiling a list of personal descriptors, such as "white," "female," "married," "southerner," or "administrator." The workshop leaders would then call out a few of the descriptors, asking anyone in the audience who identified with that descriptor to stand. The purpose of the exercise was to demonstrate that it is far more difficult to stand in front of a large group if you are the only person the descriptor applied to than it is when you are one of ten or twenty people to which the descriptor applied. My dismay resulted when the workshop leader asked for anyone who identified with the term "educator" to stand. Invariably, only about half of the group would rise. It was very revealing to see that many coaches and administrators remained seated. Either they did not understand the exercise or they simply did not view themselves as educators. To be involved in college athletics as either a coach or administrator and not consider yourself to be first and foremost, an educator, is quite frankly, inexcusable.

Reference must also be made to the fact that many of the points presented regarding the "Coach as Educator" also apply to athletic administrators. Similar to the shift in the desired credentials of coaches, there appears to be a growing trend to hire athletic directors with strong business credentials, in many cases, compiled outside the academic community. An informal survey of Division I-A college presidents conducted by Eastman & Beaudine and reported in the *NCAA News* revealed characteristics that presidents seek in athletic directors:

> Strategic Thinking—the ability to develop, evaluate and implement short- and long-term plans.
>
> Knowledge of and sensitivity to gender equity issues and regulatory procedures.
>
> Ability to manage complex financial issues and budgets.
>
> Capability to direct a large and diverse staff, including coaches.
>
> Marketing expertise.
>
> Strong public speaking, writing and media relations skills.
>
> Creativity and problem-solving abilities.
>
> Effective human resource talents for dealing with parents, students, faculty, booster groups and sponsors. (Eastman and Beaudine 1996, 13)

Incredibly, in these desired credentials there is neither mention of academic background or achievement nor of an appreciation for, or understanding of, the role of athletics within higher education and the ability to function within that environment. While it is important for an athletic director to possess the business acumen to balance a budget, one has to wonder what effect such a trend is having on the educational priorities of athletic programs, and in particular, on the academic and personal welfare of student-athletes.

There has also been a significant shift in the background and preparation of high school coaches. There was a time when it was generally accepted that a high school coach was also a high school teacher. But with the de-emphasis on physical education programs in high school, coupled with the low pay scale for high school coaching, there has been an alarming increase in the number of high school coaches who have no connection to the school other than through the team they coach. Many of these coaches have never taught in the classroom and have little training or certification in coaching techniques or philosophy. For many, their only "training" is their observations of how others perform the role or their memories from their own high school career. Often, these coaches model their behavior after the professional and college coaches on television which, for obvious reasons, may not be the most appropriate behavior for high school coaches. Further, the only school facilities such coaches set their feet in are the locker room and the playing field or court. That being the case, there is simply no opportunity to integrate the coach into the academic community. Many coaches have absolutely no appreciation for, or understanding of, educational and academic expectations, practices, philosophies, and mores. The result is that there is no link between what occurs on the fields of play and the educational institution because the leader of the sports team—the coach—has no connection to the academic institution. As a result, the goals, purposes, and culture of the athletic team often runs counter to those of the school specifically and to education generally.

Charles Barkley Was Correct!

As would be expected, the commentary that accompanied Michael Jordan's second retirement announcement on January 13, 1999, was extensive. Everyone from coaches, fellow players, historians, and financial analysts offered their take on the impact of the retirement of one who, second to Muhammed Ali, has been the most influential athlete of our time. Undoubtably, he was the most marketable, and to some, the most positive role model of such stature. Ervin "Magic" Johnson summed up the feelings of many when he commented, "He's an icon, a one-man show. It's going to be a devastating loss. It's a loss for basketball, but for kids too, in terms of not being able to see a superb role model in action" (*Lancaster Intelligencer-Journal*, January 14, 1999, C-2).

Why is it that when people in other occupations retire we do not refer to the loss of a role model? Why is it that we do not think of a teacher, policeman, doctor, or scientist as a role model? Obviously, there is the issue of visibility. Sports performers are highly visible. But so are movie stars and musicians, yet we do not accord them the same role-model status and responsibilities as we do athletes. Perhaps it is our admiration for their pure physical ability, the ease with which they do things of which we can only dream. Or, maybe it is because the results of their efforts are so real. Immediate and starkly apparent, their actions have an impact on the final score, the difference between winning and losing.

Athletes are America's heroes. Children idolize them, wearing uniforms with their names emblazoned on the back and imitating the way they run and shoot. Adults admire them, placing them before their children as someone who should be emulated. We hold athletes up on pedestals without thinking why. Our unquestioned belief in the athlete as a role model is a major justification for our heavy investment in organized sport.

But what is the effect of our adulation of athletes upon educational and intellectual values and institutions? Are they good role models? What qualifies them to be role models? Or, was Charles Barkley correct when he claimed, "I am not a role model! I am a basketball player!" Barkley's very honest proclamation created quite a stir, particularly among parents and those in the athletic establishment. Barkley, however, was exactly right. Athletes are not in the position to be role models, particularly educational role models. Very little in their backgrounds, at least educationally, qualifies them to be placed upon a pedestal for our children to emulate. These are the same people we consider dumb jocks!

What do we really know about athletes when our only contact with them is what we observe on television and read in the sports pages? Is the fact that athletes can run fast or jump high reason to encourage our children to model their behavior after them when the ability to run fast or jump high will be a skill of very little value in the information-based, global economy and workforce of the twenty-first century?

Sport history is filled with great athletes who engaged in less than admirable behaviors. Babe Ruth was reported to be a compulsive adulterer and heavy drinker. Mike Tyson served three years in prison for rape. The list of athletes accused of domestic violence include Scottie Pippen, Lawrence Phillips, and Jose Canseco, and the legal troubles of various members of the Dallas Cowboys in the 1990s is legendary.

Twice an All-American on the University of San Francisco basketball team that won fifty-five straight games and two NCAA championships, a member of the gold-medal-winning Olympic team in 1956, and center on the fabled Boston Celtic teams that won eleven NBA championships in thirteen years, Bill Russell is one of the most successful athletes of our time. Despite such success, he was often criticized by fans and the media because he refused to sign autographs. One of his reasons for not doing so was that he saw no connection between his basketball ability and the expectation of fans that he be a "role model" for their children.

"During my career, people would come up to me and say, 'Great game, Bill. I want my son here to grow up to be just like you,'" Russell wrote in *Second Wind: The Memoirs of an Opinionated Man*. "I began to wonder. Those people didn't know a thing about me personally; for all they know, I might be a child molester. Yet, here were parents saying they wanted to model their children after me, instead of after themselves. I began to cringe at those comments; instead of flattering me, they made me sad. Over the years, I would learn better than anyone that my basketball skills and my parental ones were very different qualities" (Russell 1979, 102).

There are significant risks in placing athletes on pedestals as role models. Athletes are human beings, with the same failings and weaknesses as you and I. This fact was brought home with vivid clarity during the 1999 Super Bowl. The Atlanta Falcons safety Eugene Robinson was arrested the night before the game on a charge that he solicited a prostitute. What makes this example particularly poignant is, that morning, Robinson was awarded the Bart Starr Award, presented to the player with outstanding moral character by the religious group Athletes in Action. Robinson had been involved in many charities and spoke often of being a born-again Christian. While this one incident should not define what otherwise had been a positive image and career, it shows the folly of holding up an individual as a role model simply because he or she can run fast and jump high.

Todd Crosset contributed a very insightful chapter to *Sports in School: The Future of an Institution* in which he debunked the myth that athletes are effective role models. The focus of his chapter was not to suggest that there are not role models. According to Crosset, there are plenty of strong, positive role models. Most, however, do not appear on television every weekend. Parents, relatives, neighbors, teachers, and any number of persons who come into regular contact with children can be positive role models. Crosset points out that no one can be a positive role model without regular, sustained contact with the person whom he or she is trying to influence. To think that an athlete, whom a child sees only on television or reads about in the newspaper, can have a dramatic influence on the day-to-day values, behaviors, and attitudes of a youngster is ludicrous. "A young person may model a batting stance or jump shot after a sports figure. But to expect or even suggest that admiration for an athlete's ability to run fast or jump high will cause someone to change his or her personal behavior, values, or beliefs in meaningful and long-lasting ways, is misguided. While an athlete's visit to a hospital ward to cheer a child stricken with cancer may brighten that child's outlook, it is highly unlikely that one-time visit will alter the child's personal behavior" (33).

There are many athletes who are wonderful people—good, honest, and hardworking. But these athletes are not admired for their personal characteristics but rather for their athletic accomplishments. Why is it, for example, that the high-scoring forward who happens to be on academic probation is lionized by the media and the public and pushed as a role model by the athletic department while the back-up point guard with the 4.0 GPA is ignored? Why is the star hailed as a willing community servant after participating in a largely staged photo-op at a basketball clinic but that same back-up point guard's weekly trips to volunteer at a local soup kitchen go unnoticed?

That very scenario was played out with my brother, Tom, a full scholarship football player at Virginia Tech in the early 1970s. Tom volunteered twice a week for two semesters at a local day care center in Blacksburg. One day, the star quarterback arrived at the center with an entourage of reporters and photographers in what would be a staged public relations photo opportunity. Predictably, an article, complete with photos, appeared in the next day's paper, hailing the quarterback as a diligent public servant. This, despite the fact that his previous day's one hour visit was the first time he had stepped through the day care center's doors.

Despite what we claim to be the reasons for embracing athletes as good role models—good work ethic, discipline, and so forth— it is their on the field and court performance that we glorify. We exalt their strength, size, speed, meanness, and ability to jump high, not their intellect, compassion, and off-the-field accomplishments. What type of a role model is it who feels a sense of entitlement because he has been catered to since junior high? What kind of a hero is the coach who wins a college championship with illegally recruited athletes? Is an athlete who has physically abused his spouse someone we want to place on a pedestal for young boys to emulate? Is it wise to use as a role model someone whom, when the game is over, we consider to be a dumb jock?

The link in our minds between athlete and dumb jock is so strong that to think that athletes are positive educational role models is ludicrous. The best example of the folly of placing athletes on pedestals as educational role models is the well-intentioned but woefully misguided National Basketball Association's "Stay in School" program. To ask a group of athletes, many of whom were waved through high school, admitted to college not for academic, but athletic, reasons, and more than half of whom dropped out of college before graduating, to participate in a program designed to advocate to children the importance of staying in school is insulting.

> The very qualities a society tends to seek in its hereos—selflessness, social consciousness, and the like—are precisely the opposite of those needed to transform a talented but otherwise unremarkable neighborhood kid into a Michael Jordan or Joe Montana. Becoming a star athlete requires a profound and long-term kind of self-absorption, a single-minded attention to the development of a few rather odd physical skills, and an overarching competitive outlook. These qualities may well make a great athlete, but they don't necessarily make a great person. On top of this, our society reinforces these traits by the system it has created to produce athletes—a system characterized by limited responsibility and enormous privilege. (Dudley 1994, 47)

As Crosset (2000) correctly concludes, "Despite what parents, coaches, athletic administrators, and athletes themselves might think, an athlete's ability to affect behavior is limited almost entirely to specific, on-the-field or court athletic actions and attitudes. In short, the common belief that athletes are role models has been blown wildly out of proportion" (33).

In fact, athletes may be the last people upon which we should want our children to model their behaviors. It bears mentioning again, the 21 percent of the NFL players who were found to be formally charged (arrested or indicted) with a serious crime. That means that when a young child is standing in line to seek an autograph of an NFL player, there is a one in five chance that the person signing that autograph is a criminal. Many athletes whom we place upon a pedestal for our children to worship are hardly the types of people after which the children should model their behavior.

It is important to note that the athletic establishment, from college coaches and athletic directors to professional teams and owners, has a tremendous stake in promoting the athlete as role model/hero. Promoting athletes as positive role models creates public good will which leads to a more favorable opinion of your department or professional team. Glorifying the feats of athletes creates heroes, which creates public interest in your team, which sells tickets and merchandise, which generates profits. Those most interested in creating heroes and role models, regardless of whether they are worthy role models, are advertisers and corporate sponsors. Advertisers and corporate sponsors' main purpose is to create heroes to sell products. That is why Nike spends millions of dollars creating and burnishing the image of "their" sports heroes who, by the way, happen to be wearing Nike shoes while they are performing their feats of heroism. The process of creating and building up heroes and role models in sports today has little to do with role models and everything to do with corporate profits.

Encouraging youngsters to emulate professional athletes amounts to sending them on a mission to find the Holy Grail or the Fountain of Youth. With the odds of being a professional athlete infinitesimally small, encouraging young people to focus their attention upon and model their behavior after athletes will likely distract them from education and other goals and interests—activities every bit as capable of building the same positive character traits as athletics but which offer the added bonus of providing the likely opportunity to convert their efforts and interests into a stable job in the future.

In short, it is not in our society's best interests to ask or expect athletes to be role models, not because they are not worthy or do not possess admirable qualities, but because of the characteristics and abilities we have chosen to exalt in them; specifically, their physical accomplishments. An athlete is someone who plays a sport very well—not a brain surgeon or a responsible parent. Nor is an athlete a counselor for troubled children or a scientist searching for a cure for cancer. The athlete is simply very proficient at a physically demanding activity. As we head into the information-based, global economy of the twenty-first century, where personal and societal success will be dependent upon brain power, creative thought, and the ability to manage large amounts of information, are the qualities associated with becoming a great athlete the qualities we want our children to emulate?

In a more general sense, one has to question the broad messages regarding attitudes and behaviors that are advanced through promotion and presentation of sport. When watching a sporting event in its entirety, from the pre-game show through the advertisements to the post-game show, a very distinct set of images and values emerge. Sport has become more about winning at any cost than about teaching valuable life skills. Players are hardly respectful and sportsmanlike to opponents with their aggressive, "in your face" attitudes and violent behavior. Anyone claiming that sports teaches unselfish play, humility, and modesty hasn't witnessed the excessive gyrating and showboating that accompanies even the most routine of plays. Such displays of individualism simply do not square with the "subjugation of the individual for the goals of the team" ethic. With players and coaches seemingly changing teams yearly, and franchises changing cities at the mere scent of a better stadium deal, the claim that sports teaches concepts in loyalty holds no water.

If we were really honest about our expectations of athletes as role models, we would acknowledge the fact that we only want them to be role models when it is convenient, when we can afford them to be. In other words, when our favorite teams are winning. We have a tendency to overlook their transgressions if they can help us win. For example, after his reprehensible display of bigotry in his comments in a *Sports Illustrated* interview, John Rocker received a standing ovation from the Atlanta Braves fans upon his return. Quite frankly, when push comes to shove we are far less interested in role-model behavior than on-the-field performance. We will put up with most anyone, Albert Belle and Dennis Rodman being examples, if they help our teams win.

There is hardly a kid in America who doesn't or hasn't, at some time, looked upon a professional athlete as a bigger-than-life hero. I had many, most of them from New York professional teams: Joe Namath of the Jets, Tom Seaver of the Mets, and just about any New York Knick from the 1969 championship team. The athlete as hero is part of American sporting legend and lore. Of course, the more involved you become in athletics, the farther up the competitive ladder you climb, it becomes increasingly apparent that athletes are like everyone else, with the same flaws and hang-ups as your next-door neighbor or the mailman. In fact, professional athletes are so much like everyone else, so common, that it is comical how we yearn to build them up into something that they aren't or could never be. The farce of the athlete hero came to a hilarious end for me while I was in training camp as a rookie trying to make the New Jersey Nets. At the time, the Nets' leading scorer and resident star was the late John Williamson, or, "Super" John Williamson to the fans. A stocky guard who had a knack for bulling his way into the lane for medium-range jump shots and strong drives to the hoop, Williamson was an excellent offensive player. He was also a nice guy, very gregarious, and he was always friendly to me, despite the fact that he had no particular reason to be so. I was simply an unknown third-round pick who was unlikely to make the team. I liked John a lot.

The year was 1979 and John had come into camp overweight and out of shape. Nonetheless, he was the Nets' most recognized player and a hero to many. His fans, however, did not get to see him quite as closely as I did. Outside of his friendly demeanor, my overriding image of John was the sight of him after a pre-season game, relieving himself at a urinal, butt-naked, thirty-five pounds overweight, a beer in one hand, eyes watery and straining against the smoke rising from the cigarette dangling from his lips. That, of course, was not the photo that appeared in the Nets media guide, so his hero status was safe with me. But it was a powerful sight. The picture of the pro athlete as "hero."

Charles Barkley was correct when he said that he was not a role model. While Barkley's comments were roundly criticized by the athletic establishment as being irresponsible, his point was quite provocative. It is difficult to find much positive in the values that sport teaches today. Thus, we should no longer blindly glorify and emulate athletes simply because they can dunk a basketball. Charles Barkley should not be any more responsible for setting a good example for children than anyone else and certainly not more than a young person's parents or teachers. The fact is, role modeling is not about professional athletes, but about ourselves. We should neither ask nor expect athletes to do it for us. It's not fair. It's not effective. And it's not smart. Barkley's point was that he was only an athlete, paid to perform athletically and to win games, nothing more, nothing less. And he is correct; what's there to emulate about that?

Our New Gladiator Class

While it is said that sport merely reflects the values of a society, the reverse is also true. The values, attitudes, and behaviors demonstrated in organized sport and of those who play, coach, and administer them greatly influence societal values, attitudes, and behavior. In other words, the relationship between cultural and athletic values is symbiotic.

As a result, today's culture of sport has led to a profound change in our value system as it relates to the types of talents and skills we look upon as being important. From the pee-wee level up, success in sports is aggressively encouraged and richly rewarded. With our chests puffed out in obvious pride, we cheer for, and brag incessantly about, our sons' and daughters' improved times and latest point totals, while we half-heartedly smile, clap politely, and more or less tolerate our children's interests in music, theater, or painting. We are far more excited when our sons choose to emulate the basketball skills of the former NBA player Waymon Tisdale, as opposed to his accomplishments as a bassist and band leader with several recordings on the market. We speak with much more pride about our children hitting a game-winning shot than we do about them getting an A on a big math test. Not only have we placed star athletes on pedestals as role models, but we want more than anything for our sons and daughters to become one. This, despite the fact that we think athletes are dumb.

My purpose is not to suggest that organized athletics cannot be educational and a character-building activity for participants. Sport undoubtably has the potential to contribute to the personal development of athletes and can supplement the mission of our educational institutions. To do so, however, not only must we view sport that way, but it must be structured and conducted with those purposes in mind. The sad reality is that we have come to view professional sports as an achievement of the absolute highest magnitude. We not only believe, but also actively promote, the notion that if you are good in sports, nothing else matters. When youngsters show an early aptitude for athletics, every other interest, skill, or proficiency—education being the most notable—must assume a back seat in the name of athletic development. The huge amount of money and public notoriety generated by success in sports leads many, especially the young, to think that playing games is far more important than education. This notion is not only counterproductive intellectually, educationally, and culturally, but it is self-destructive. Forget the Nobel Prize winners or the Phi Beta Kappas. We want gladiators! Forget thoughtfulness. Forget intelligence. We want big hits! Forget reading and math. We want touchdowns and slam dunks!

The *New York Times* journalist Robert Lipsyte is an astute observer of sports' role and effect on society. According to Lipsyte,

> A new American class has emerged, beyond gender, social standing or race. Call it a gladiatorial class. Families, schools, towns wave twelve-year-olds through the toll booths of life. Potential sports stars—who might bring fame and money to everyone around them—are excused from taking out the trash, from learning to read, from having to ask, "May I touch you there?" No wonder so many of them grow into the confused, sometimes self-destructive "role models" whose sexual abuse trials and drug busts have become the new clichés of the sports pages. . . . The truth is that most athletes are still conservative and obedient to authority, yet trapped by their upbringing in a perpetual state of adolescence. (Lipsyte 1992, 55)

Our obsession with sports is so grotesquely distorted that we are willing to let our sons and daughters travel down a path where the chance of "success" as we define it, is not only incredibly small but, even if "successful," will result in a career that is over, on average, by the age of twenty-five. Not only do we allow it, we actually shove them down that road. As Lipsyte suggests, we are placing our children up before the crowd as gladiators. And we are proud of it!

Again, there is nothing inherently wrong with involving our children in organized, competitive athletics if our expectations of their involvement are realistic and balanced. It is, however, our concept of "success" in athletics that is problematic. For an athlete to have a "successful" career, he or she must have played professionally in the "big leagues." Anything less represents "failure." The prevailing attitude of our sports-obsessed culture is that an athlete isn't really "successful" unless he or she plays professionally. Yet, even given those expectations, we continue to promote Lipsyte's "gladiator" class.

Unfortunately, while we say the value in sport is in the participation itself, we don't really believe it. We have been so blinded by the bright lights and big money of big-time sports, we can no longer appreciate the many positive things it can do for our children, short of playing professionally. We can't simply allow our children to play a game to have fun. We have to make them into "gladiators." And if they display talent at an early age, we begin the process of placing all of their developmental eggs in one basket in the hopes that they just might be one of those lucky ones who beats the odds, one of those "lucky," but dumb, gladiators.

Slam Dunking in the Information Age

The purpose of this chapter has been to raise questions regarding whether the lessons taught and values promoted through athletics are in fact positive as they relate to helping our nation meet the rapidly changing business, economic, intellectual, and social demands of the twenty-first century. The information-based, high-tech, global economy of the future will require all of us to be better educated. The challenges we face in educating our children and maintaining our economic status as a world power are simply too great to invest in activities that are educationally counterproductive. Our economic strength as a nation depends upon our ability to respond to these educational challenges. Thus, it is imperative to critically assess our nation's educational priorities and outcomes, including organized athletics and its tremendous influence on those priorities and outcomes. No nation can become great without a well-educated populace. No nation can remain strong without an uncompromising commitment to developing its people.

Organized sport is not educational simply because it is sport or simply because we claim it to be. Rather, it is the environment within which sport participation occurs that influences the educational, moral, and ethical development of participants and influences our society's values regarding education. Sport kept in the proper perspective, where the process of participation (education) is not subjected by the game's result (winning), can be extremely positive. Sport that is overemphasized in relation to other fields of endeavor, or that undermines educational priorities, is harmful. As much as we love sports, we must value education and the development of the mind more.

For over one hundred years, we have embraced, largely without question, the notion that organized athletics supplement academic development and are a positive influence within our educational institutions. That assumption can no longer be accepted without question. The challenges facing our educational system and our society are too significant to continue to accept without question those existing assumptions regarding athletics' educational benefits.

Over the last century, organized athletics played a significant role in the development of our country. Sports helped to strengthen our bodies and mold our character in a way that met the needs of a young country emerging into a world military and industrial power. But we are now entering a new age, an age where intellect, education, and the ability to manage and communicate large amounts of highly technical information will power our growth and continued development as a world leader. Intellectual muscle, not gladiatorial feats, will be the currency of the future. Against this backdrop we must reconsider whether our tremendous investment in athletics continues to be a sound one.

Thus, we must ask the following questions. Is our obsession with, and investment in, organized sport endangering the educational and economic health of our society by promoting values and encouraging behavior that run counter to sound educational principles? By embracing the principles and behaviors of a gladiator class, have we become less able to meet the intellectual challenges of the new millennium? In short, will a nation full of dumb jocks and passive fans fare well in the fast-paced, information-based, global economy of the twenty-first century?

THE ATHLETE AS COUCH POTATO

Each March, America is overcome by "madness." Throughout the country, sports fans, both casual and hard-core, focus their attention on the NCAA men's basketball tournament. In bars and bakeries, at the dinner table and over phone lines, people catch the madness. Office pools are organized and parties are thrown as television screens everywhere are tuned to "the Big Dance," as teams from Boise to Bloomington; Athens, Georgia, to Athens, Ohio; and New York to New Mexico compete for the national championship. Over three consecutive weekends, the original field of sixty-four teams is whittled down to one, crowned NCAA National Champion the Monday evening following Final Four weekend.

> **When I feel athletic, I go to a sports bar.**
> —Paul Clisura

Dubbed "March Madness" for the unpredictable nature of the contests as well as for its catchy commercial ring, it is the perfect television event. Longer than the Super Bowl's one-day, one-game extravaganza, shorter than the three-month marathons that are the NBA and the NHL playoffs, and more inclusive than the World Series, where only two cities are rep-

resented, it has captivated our nation's televised sports consciousness as no other event. That enormous appeal is why CBS
paid the NCAA $6 billion for the rights to televise the tourna-
ment for eleven years. But rather than the unpredictable nature
of the games or its commercial appeal, the term *March Madness*
is appropriate for another reason: everyone is *watching* it. If
everyone is watching, no one is participating. Instead, fans are
sitting in front of the television set stuffing themselves with junk
food and beer, watching what amounts to a meaningless physical contest between teenagers who are billed as students but who
are, in reality, paid mercenaries.

March Madness is also significant because it is the best example of the evolution in the way we have come to "participate"
in sports. This shift is problematic because our heavy cultural
investment in sport is justified largely upon the belief that it promotes a healthful lifestyle. Those who regularly exercise and participate in sports are more likely to live a longer and more
healthy life. The Greek ideal of sound body, sound mind is, in
fact, sound, as medical research on this claim is irrefutable.
Unfortunately, March Madness has little to do with this Greek
ideal. To the contrary, March Madness encourages behavior that
has a *negative* impact on physical health.

Before televised sports, if a parent wanted to spend a "sporting
moment" with his or her child, the parent and child might have
gone to the backyard and played catch. Today, it is just as likely
that such moments will be spent watching one of the hundreds of
televised sporting events each week. Despite claims of the positive effect on the health of our populace, organized sport in America has become more about watching elite athletes perform rather
than being active one's self; as likely to be associated with lying
on the couch with a six-pack of beer than with working up a sweat
through vigorous exercise. As sport has grown in popularity, more
people are sitting idly, watching the athleticism of the few. With

the dramatic increase in outlets through which to consume sports (there are now several twenty-four-hour-a-day sports channels), the idea of what it means to "participate" in sports has changed.

There is, however, value in watching sports, the most obvious of which is that it is fun, an escape from the ordinary. Watching sports can also be spiritually exhilarating, drawing us together and making us feel that we are a part of a larger force—a team. Whether pulling for your city's professional football team in the Super Bowl or your alma mater's basketball team in the Final Four, such moments allow us to be a part of something much larger than ourselves, to connect with others. This benefit was aptly described by Douglas Putnam in his book, *Controversies of the Sports World:*

> In a world overflowing with self-doubt and broken dreams, the ongoing parade of athletic triumph is a source of optimism. But sports offers more than aggression, violence and the chance for those who lead ordinary lives to experience joy at the achievements of others. In the course of a single contest, a full season, and a lifetime, sports fans can encounter comedy, tragedy, glamour, and high drama. They can also develop a kinship with people who share their devotion, a deep and durable bond that many of them can not achieve readily in any other aspect of their lives. (Putnam 1999, 166)

But there are also significant disadvantages to spectatorship as articulated by James Michener in his 1976 book, *Sports in America:*

> The disadvantages of mere spectatorship are numerous and compelling. The health of the inactive watcher, whether in a stadium or before a television, suffers. He tends to accumulate tensions that are not discharged. While sitting and watching he contributes nothing to the common good and does not do those constructive things he might otherwise have done. Passiveness in sports encourages passiveness in social life and in politics. The mere spectator never shares in the positive rewards of performance and competition. Watching tennis at age fifty is infinitely less productive than playing it. The mere spectator fails to develop whatever innate talents he has and cheats himself of sport's true joys. (Michener 1976, 86)

With the recent explosion of television coverage of sports, this question is even more relevant than when Michener commented on it in 1976. Is such intense community interest in spectator sport, as opposed to education, poverty, or the arts, in our collective best interest? What price are we paying for our shift from active participation to passive consumption of sport? The purpose of this chapter is to examine that evolution from active to passive participation. We will consider organized sports' impact on the health of both the athletes and those watching the athletes. Integral to the discussion will be television's effect on the values promoted through, and perceptions of, sport in our culture.

Television and the Demise of a Culture of Participation

Television has been hailed as a tremendous vehicle for educational advancement, bringing images and information to millions of homes and schoolrooms that heretofore had been inconceivable. Critics, however, claim that its hypnotic and numbing effect on viewers has a negative impact on the creativity and development of children and adults. As is usually the case, the truth lies somewhere in between. Television is only a medium and, as with any medium, its overall influence depends on the way it is utilized. While this argument may be true as it applies to alternative styles of education or to information access, it is not true as it applies to sports. In the case of education, television simply permits access to information in a different and, in many cases, more-efficient manner. Whether being taught in a classroom or through a video format, the purpose is the same—to access information. Television, however, has dramatically changed not only how we experience sport, but also what we value about sport.

Prior to television, our involvement in sport was primarily through participation. By playing games, we learned various personal and interpersonal skills, while improving our health. Today, far too many Americans' only involvement in sports is watching them. Our society's collective involvement in organized sport has changed from being overwhelmingly physical and active to primarily passive and stationary. Television has lured us from the playing fields to the sidelines. It has taken us out of the game. Rather than being in the middle of the action, we are now spectators. We are watching more and sweating less. Meanwhile, our nation is becoming more obese.

According to the U.S. Department of Health and Human Services, the prevalence of obesity in the United States continues to increase. According to the Center for Disease Control's Third National Health and Nutrition Examination Survey (NHANES III), conducted from 1988 to 1994, 14 percent of children and 12 percent of adolescents were overweight. Among adults, 33 percent of men and 36 percent of women were overweight. Previous NHANES results indicate that the prevalence of overweight had increased from 1976-1980 to 1988-1991 from 7.6 percent to 10.9 percent for children, 5.7 percent to 10.8 percent for adolescents, and 25.4 percent to 33.3 percent for adults (*Morbidity and Mortality Weekly Report*, March 7, 1997, 199). While it is difficult to prove a direct correlation between televised sports and increased obesity, it is undeniable that people are watching more television and that a large portion of the television programming they watch is sports related. The irony of this shift is that, as a society, we invested in organized sports largely because it is supposed to promote and encourage a lifestyle of active participation for better health.

Some argue that television has been great for sport in America, popularizing it by exposing more sports to a wider audience of spectators. While that may be true, sports have always been available to anyone who wished to participate. All you had to do was to step outside your door and start running or grab a stick and a ball and start playing. It is the type of sport activity that television has popularized—watching rather than playing—that is so troubling. We are becoming a nation of spectators, not in spite of, but in large part *because* of, sport. As a result, sport is losing what heretofore has been its most direct and vital benefit; improving the health of our populace.

Televised sport's negative effect on individual participation goes beyond time spent in the "couch potato" position. Televised sports can actually intimidate us into not wanting to participate, even after we turn off the television set. There has been more than one potential tennis player who decided against playing the game for fear of looking foolish because he or she would not be able to play like Pete Sampras. It is much safer, far more comfortable, and there is less likelihood of embarrassing yourself to stay seated on the sidelines and simply watch Pete Sampras.

Despite the fact that television ratings for some specific events have declined (likely more a product of an ever-increasing menu of televised sporting events to watch rather than a decline in the popularity of sports), we will continue to spend more time watching sports. Although it is impossible to quantify exactly how much more, there are several factors suggesting that such an increase is inevitable. Television viewership in general continues to increase. It is reasonable to assume that sports viewing will increase correspondingly. Due to improved technology, such as cable, satellite, and pay-per-view, as well as the increasing use of VCRs to tape games that previously might have been missed, there will continue to be more options for viewing. There are more television time slots during which sports can be viewed. There was a time when sports were available only during prime time and Saturday and Sunday afternoons. Now sports are available on television twenty-four hours a day, seven days a week. Networks can now target specific games for specific regions, thus raising interest and overall viewership. Finally, with increasingly diverse sporting events on television, the X-Games and Australian Rules Football, for example, new viewers will be lured to the tube. All this, in addition to the fact that the availability of sports-related information and programming on the Internet is set to explode.

Despite apologists' claims of the health benefits associated with sports participation, the fact is, the main goal of the majority of the sports industry is not to encourage active participation but to lure us into passive spectatorship. The primary purpose of any televised sporting event is not to bring the game into your living room. Rather, televised sports is simply a vehicle through which to sell products and merchandise, from razor blades to automobiles. Who pays to have sports events broadcast? Companies with products to sell. They sell their products through commercials that air during timeouts and half time. Companies sell more product by getting the viewer to watch more of their advertisements. To expose potential consumers to more of their commercials, companies, in conjunction with television networks and sports organizations, design and package sports television programming to not only lure potential consumers to watch the rest of today's game, but tomorrow's as well. And the next day's big game, next week's bigger game, and next month's biggest of all games.

The purpose of televised sporting events is to entice the viewer into watching more televised sporting events. For proof, count the number of times a future game is hyped during a broadcast. The message is, "Hey, this is a big game, but wait till you see the game we're going to bring you next week! Don't miss it!" One game after another . . . over and over and over again . . . season after season after season . . . year after year after year.

Everyone in the sports industry is working toward the same goal—earning more money from sports consumers by enticing them to sit in front of their televisions for longer periods of time. Players want more money. Owners need more money to pay their players and still leave some profit for themselves. Owners know that without high ratings, the television networks won't pay as much for the rights to broadcast their team's games. The networks want good ratings so they can charge companies higher advertising rates. And the companies want more people watching so they can sell more product. Televised sports is not about sports at all; it is about getting consumers to sit in front of the tube for increasingly longer periods of time so they are exposed to more advertisements designed to convince them to buy more goods and services.

While hailed as having a major positive impact on the promotion and development of sport in America, television has done more to destroy what should be its most compelling benefit. Because sports organizations and the television industry have duped the public into thinking that watching sports is a form of "participation," sports is no longer about improving health and learning through active involvement but rather about passively watching and being a fan. There is little benefit in sitting on the sidelines. Watching a game will not improve your health or teach positive character traits. Consequently, the sport experience promoted through television is an empty one, with few significant or meaningful benefits other than those of a financial nature realized by team owners, television networks, or corporate sponsors of the event.

Again, I am not anti-sports. I have spent my fair share of time in front of the television set watching games. I have enjoyed it. I appreciate sport's beauty and believe strongly in its potential to improve the health and character of participants. But enough is enough! How much time are we willing to spend on an activity that offers little of lasting or meaningful significance? We need less observation and more participation. How many times must we be lulled into a mindless stupor, eyes glazing over, aware only enough to reach for another beer and a handful of chips? How much more moronic, sport statistic, mumbo-jumbo analysis from play-by-play commentators and ex-jock color men must we subject ourselves to? It is mind numbing. Don't we have anything better to do? Read perhaps? Learn to play a musical instrument? Exercise? Spend some quality time with our children or spouse? Perform volunteer work? The fact is, we'd all lead much richer, more interesting, and more productive lives without sports television.

Distorting Sports Values

Television has also distorted our perspective and values relating to athletics. Specifically, the value and importance placed upon a particular athletic activity or event is determined by whether it gains television exposure. We have come to believe that if a sporting activity is not on television, it isn't very important.

Why, for example, do we believe that the Final Four is more important than the pick-up basketball game at the local YMCA? Other than its brief entertainment benefit, watching the Final Four on television has virtually no lasting value. (If you do not agree, answer this: Who participated in last year's Final Four? The year before? And the year before that? The fact is, by the time next year's Final Four rolls around, you will have most likely forgotten who participated in this year's. After a while, the games, the players, and all of the subplots become the same. And the Final Four is alleged to be the most compelling of televised sporting events!)

In terms of common perception regarding the relative value of a sports activity, a pick-up basketball game, because it will never be carried live on CBS, is not very significant. If everyone who sits in front of the television watching the Final Four went down to the local gymnasium and actually played the game, sport's contribution to our culture would increase dramatically. Unfortunately, when provided the opportunity to choose between watching the Final Four and spending that time actually playing the game, far too many choose inactivity. It is, after all, easier to watch than to sweat. And televised sports has made it easy for us to make that decision.

Further, television has severely undermined our value system relating to sports. The emphasis upon getting on television is so strong that players, coaches, leagues, college athletic programs, and now even high school programs will do most anything to get a close-up on the tube. Such measures include cheating to recruit the players necessary to win which, in turn, makes the team more attractive as a television commodity, athletes "mugging" for the camera, hopeful that such antics will be deemed worthy of an ESPN highlight, and college athletic programs compromising academic and institutional integrity to win-at-any-cost. There was a time when organized athletics was about participation, learning, teamwork, and sportsmanship. Today, it is about getting on television.

Television has also distorted the standard by which we judge the "success" of an athlete. Currently, an athlete hasn't "made it" until he or she appears on television. Nothing could be further from the truth. Two of the most successful athletes I know have never appeared on television because they "only" play noon-time pick-up basketball, one at a small gym in Kansas City and the other at the 92nd Street Y in New York City. What makes Arnold Grossman and Guy Pinte such successful athletes is that they are still playing the sport at the ages of sixty-nine and sixty-four, respectively—and they're playing it with people forty years younger! If you consider active participation in sports to be of primary importance, Grossman and Pinte are two of the most "successful" athletes of our time. Because sport in America has become something entirely different—more about appearing on television or signing a multi-million-dollar contract than about participating—their achievements will forever be trivialized.

Television has changed the nature of sport in our society from sport based upon the values of participation to the in-activity of spectatorship. This, undoubtedly, is a development with significant negative implications for the health and welfare of our populace.

Sport for the Elite

The distortion of the value and purpose of sport in our culture has lead to the evolution of a sports system that is badly out of step with our nation's health needs. Children and adults are watching more and playing less, not only because of a significant increase in the availability of sports television programming, but also because of the structure of youth, interscholastic, and college athletic systems. Specifically, our nation's system of organized sport is designed to accommodate individuals who demonstrate exceptional athletic potential at the expense of those who don't or haven't yet.

This "elitist" structure is perhaps the most disturbing element in the evolution of sport in America. If we believe sport to be a character-building activity, an activity that prepares youth for adulthood and instills in them important values and discipline, why is our system of organized athletics not structured to encourage maximum participation? Rather than maximizing opportunities to become involved in and reap the positive personal and health benefits of organized athletics, our current system weeds out, at earlier and earlier ages, all but the most-talented athletes and, in the process, discourages participation by all but those who display extraordinary potential.

If sports are so important, why do so few participate? According to a study of ten thousand students in eleven American cities sponsored by the Athletic Footwear Association, sports participation and the apparent desire to participate decline steadily through the teen years. The reason participation declines is primarily because it is no longer fun. According to the study, the number-one reason youth played sports was to "have fun." Benefits cited by participants included improving skills, staying in shape, taking satisfaction from one's performance, and competing against others. "Not having fun" was the second most important reason, after "losing interest," for quitting sports. For those who drop out, "not having fun" was defined as "pressure to perform," to win, and to practice too much. In short, the sense of play seems to have left the youth sport experience. Interestingly, winning, the most publicized and pursued goal of sports, at least from the adult viewpoint, was a poor motivator for most junior and senior high students, never ranking higher than seventh as a reason to participate (Athletic Footwear Association, 1990). Not surprisingly, according to the National Federation of State High School Associations, less than 21 percent of high school students are involved in even one school sport.

Our country's organized sports enterprise has failed to promote the idea that sport for pure exercise is positive, fun, and healthy. Rather, athletics must be about winning and developing future all-stars and pros. This athletic elitism, beginning in youth sports leagues with the selection of all-star traveling teams of ten-year-olds, continues through high school and college. The result is that the best perform while all the others watch. In this system, there is no encouragement for involvement in sports simply to stay physically fit or to have fun. It is all about preparing the team or the team's star to get to the "next level." Children pick up on the exclusive nature of these programs and often stop playing when they realize that they are not one of the elite.

The irony of structuring a youth athletic system that weeds out those who do not show extraordinary potential is that there is absolutely no correlation between athletic performance prior to the ages of thirteen to fourteen and performance as a high school or college athlete. Michael Jordan, for example, was cut from his high school basketball team as a fifteen-year-old sophomore. And there are hundreds of other world-class athletes who were late developers. Further, research suggests that before the age of twelve, most children do not have the ability to understand and conform to team concepts. Unfortunately, coaches, parents, and the youngsters themselves do not realize that this is completely normal in the developmental process. Jay Coakley, a sports sociologist, described this inability to understand team concepts in his book *Sport in Society: Issues and Controversies* as follows:

> Parents and coaches often forget . . . that most children under the age of 12 do not have the cognitive ability to fully grasp the meaning of strategy in team sports. Anyone who has ever watched two teams of 8-year-old soccer players understands what this means. Many children under the age of 12 play what might be called "beehive soccer"; after the opening kick there are 20 bodies and 40 legs within 10 yards of the ball. And they follow the ball like a swarm of bees following its queen. Everyone's out of position and they stay that way for the majority of the game. Meanwhile, many adults on the sidelines loudly plead with their kids to "stay in position" or "get back to where you belong!" But one of the problems in many team sports is that positions change depending on where the ball or other players are. Therefore, the only way players can really determine where they belong is to mentally visualize the relationships between teammates and opponents over the entire field. This ability to visualize all these relationships and think in terms of an overall social system is not often developed before the age of 12. (Coakley 1986, 238)

In such a system, how many thousands of children are forced out of our youth sports programs or simply turned off by athletics in general by the time they are twelve years old? If sports participation is so valuable, why would we tolerate sports programs that systematically eliminate thousands of children from ever getting the chance to fully develop as athletes or to ever develop a love of exercise and sports? What impact does our elitist sport system have on the development of positive lifelong exercise and health habits of our populace? And just who is youth sports supposed to be for anyway? Youth sports is allegedly about the physical, emotional, and educational needs of children, when, in fact, it is about the egos of adults. Children play sports to have fun and, in doing so, positively impact their health. It is the adults who impose their standards of competition, winning, and developing future pro and Olympic athletes on children's games.

If there is any institution through which the ideal that organized sports' most important benefit lies in active participation can be realized, it is through our school systems. There are three programmatic formats through which our schools can affect the health of virtually every child in America: physical education classes, intramural sports, and intercollegiate or interscholastic athletics. Inasmuch as the health and physical fitness of our nation's youth should be a societal issue of utmost importance, the effectiveness with which our school systems are fulfilling this function should be as well. The fundamental question regarding the role of athletics in our school systems is whether the current relative emphasis placed upon these three types of physical fitness activities is such that it best serves our nation's health and physical fitness needs. In other words, what is the most-effective and cost-efficient way in which our school systems can promote good health and physical fitness habits in our nation's youth? More specifically, the question is whether our nation's health interests are being met by the increasing emphasis in terms of time, effort, emotion, and money that is being spent on interscholastic and intercollegiate athletics as opposed to physical education requirements and intramural athletics.

In their book *Lessons of the Locker Room*, Andrew Miracle and Roger Rees highlight the relationship between interscholastic sports and the physical fitness needs of our nation's youth.

> Lessening the status of school athletics would reduce this role conflict between the two activities of the teacher/coach, and allow such teachers more time to concentrate on educating the student body on the importance of physical activity. If the present status of fitness among school children is an indication, their education in this domain has been sorely neglected. While it would be wrong to blame high school sports for the low fitness levels of our nation's youth, the cult of sport has not promoted the idea that physical activity is healthy and enjoyable for everyone. This is hardly surprising since the elitism of interscholastic athletics has meant that the best perform while the rest watch. There is nothing in this model that encourages children to become physically fit themselves, or to learn about and enjoy the process of fitness. (Miracle and Rees 1994, 214–15)

This imbalance is also evident at the college level. For example, it is not uncommon for an intercollegiate athletic department to have a budget of $20 to $60 million for a program that involves 400 to 500 students. Meanwhile, an intramural program, serving the remaining 10,000 to 40,000 students, operates on a fraction of that. Such a disproportionate allocation of resources raises questions regarding the purpose of organized sport on our campuses. Is it to provide entertainment and develop future professional athletes or is it to improve the health of students and to develop in them, positive, lifelong fitness habits? Which of these purposes serves us better as a country? Which of these purposes has a broader, longer-lasting, positive influence on our culture?

Organized sport, in and of itself, is neither positive nor negative. The determining factor of whether sports are educational, enjoyable, and a positive influence is the way they are structured. If the desired outcome of organized athletics is for participants to have fun, develop character, gain confidence, and improve health, they must be organized and conducted with those purposes in mind. Unfortunately, the primary emphasis of our system of organized sport is to develop only those athletes who show signs of being future stars, with the end result (winning and playing professionally) as the driving motivation rather than the process itself (participation, learning). If participation in sports is so valuable, why have we chosen to invest so heavily in such a small percentage of "elite" athletes while the vast majority of our children, teenagers, and adults sit idly and watch?

Ironically, it is our taxpayer dollars or student fees, whether at the high school or college levels, that increasingly pay for elite athletes and programs. On far too many college campuses, multi-million-dollar athletic facilities for use only by the football team are constructed while general health and intramural facilities and equipment crumble. Gym class requirements are being reduced in high school. "Nationally, only 29 percent of high school students had daily physical education in 1999, down from 42 percent in 1991. Two years ago, Virginia stopped requiring physical education in elementary schools. In 1996, Massachusetts did so for high schools. By 1999, only 61 percent of Massachusetts high school students had gym class even one time per week, down from 80 percent five years earlier" (Rothstein 2000). Meanwhile, the basketball or football team budgets go untouched. In short, from the pee-wee leagues to our nation's campuses, encouraging a healthful lifestyle through organized sport and exercise is simply not a priority.

Sacrificing Your Body for the Gold

But what about the health benefits for those who play organized athletics? According to the Women's Sports Foundation, moderate exercise can cut the risk of heart disease in women by 40 percent. Recent studies also indicate that long-term exercise may protect against breast cancer. Further, weight-bearing exercise and strength training helps maintain healthy bones, muscles, and joints, all of which protect the body against osteoporosis (brittle bones) (Women's Sports Foundation 2000). The evidence is clear; exercise, in moderation, along with diet, are the two most important contributors to good health.

But the case for the positive health benefits of participation in organized, competitive athletics may not be as clear-cut as they may seem. While participation in elite, organized sport requires exercise, it is anything but moderate. In far too many cases, the physical demands and expectations required of competitive athletics border on being abusive and physically damaging. Because the rewards for winning—wealth, adulation, and fame—have become so great, athletes are more than willing to place their lifelong physical health at significant risk for these immediate and fleeting rewards. Coaches and athletic administrators, chasing the same rewards, do nothing to dissuade the athlete from doing so, in many cases actively encouraging such short-sighted and unhealthy behavior. Those who are responsible for the physical training, fitness, and general health of athletes—coaches and athletic administrators— are far more interested in winning ballgames than they are in the long-term health and physical welfare of their players.

That such an attitude exists in professional athletics is not a concern. Professional athletes are paid millions of dollars for placing their bodies at risk. At the professional level, there are no secrets and there is no hypocrisy; athletes are a commodity, a piece of meat, a widget in a factory assembly line. Most athletes at this level are adults, able to make their own decisions and fully capable of understanding the consequences of their actions.

Unfortunately, the pros are not the only place where such a training environment exists. As with most of the attitudes, practices, and beliefs that permeate throughout the athletic culture, those about training and injuries filter down from the pros to all levels of competition, including pee-wee leagues. But unlike in the pros, allowing or pressuring an athlete to place his or her future health at risk to satisfy the competitive ego of a high school, college, or youth coach is difficult to justify.

All athletes are pressured to play hurt. In most cases, coaches simply ask, "Can you go today?" While a simple enough question, it is the tone in which it was asked—expectant rather than concerned—that makes athletes feel guilty if they answer, "No." The pressure, however, can be much greater. On one occasion in college, our head trainer suggested to the team doctor the need to "do whatever we need to do to get him [me] ready to play in the next game." Whether he meant therapy, or an injection of painkilling drugs, I do not know. From my perspective, however, doing "whatever it took" clearly meant an injection. All this for a game that had little impact on our post-season standing. The team doctor later reassured me that a painkilling injection was out of the question. The fact that he felt the need to reassure me only confirmed what

I thought the trainer was suggesting. I listened to the game from a hospital bed—the only game I missed during my college career.

Coaches deny that they pressure athletes to play hurt. While they may not do so directly, it is made abundantly clear to the athlete that they must "suck it up" and play, regardless of whether they are physically fit to do so. Coaches want their best players on the field at all times. Consequently, players often feel the pressure to play while hurt. Consider this quote from a student-athlete, which appeared in Ken Denlinger's *For the Glory*, an account of the experiences of football players at Penn State University.

> I blame them for my hamstring. For forcing me back to practice. Not really forcing me but suggesting that I should be out there. Not coming up to me and saying: "You're not going to go today." But coming up to me and saying, "How do you feel? Why don't you go out and try some things on it?" You can't say that to a freshman. Maybe a fifth year guy or a fourth year guy who's gone through the system. But you can't go up to a guy like me, because of course, I'm going to say: "I'll give it a shot." (Denlinger 1994, 27)

And this account from Dave Meggyesy, a former seven-year veteran of the NFL, on his "healthy" experience while at Syracuse University.

> One of the justifications for college football is that it is not only a character-builder, but a body-builder as well. This is nonsense. Young men are having their bodies destroyed, not developed. As a matter of fact, few players can escape from college football without some form of permanent disability. During my four years, I accumulated a broken wrist, separations of both shoulders, an ankle that was torn up so badly that it broke the arch of my foot, three major brain concussions, and an arm that almost had to be amputated because of improper treatment. And I was one of the lucky ones. (Meggyesy 1971, 60)

The NCAA's refusal to eliminate spring practice in the sport of football best exemplifies how little concern there is for the general health and fitness of student-athletes at major college programs.

According to statistics compiled through the NCAA Injury Surveillance System, the injury rate for spring practice is significantly higher (more than double) than the fall practice injury rate. "This result is even more alarming, when it is considered that the 15 spring practices are spread over 29 days, leaving plenty of recovery time (as compared to the fall), and that five of the spring practices are designed as non-contact" (Wilson and Bunce 1996, 4).

More alarming is the fact that the types of injuries sustained during spring practice are more severe. The concussion injury rate is more than double that of the fall. The anterior cruciate injury rate is more than three times that of the fall. Injuries requiring surgery occur in spring at a rate of more than three times that of fall practice. One cannot help but question the wisdom of exposing student-athletes to a chance of injury in the off season that is significantly higher than that of the regular season. If a major priority of organized athletics is to promote the health and fitness of participants, spring practice in the sport of football would be eliminated or, at the least, radically altered to lessen the likelihood of serious injury.

There is, however, very little movement to eliminate spring football because the very purpose of the sport is to hurt your opponent. Coaches and fans alike repeatedly urge players to "hurt 'em" or "kill 'em." Many defensive players openly admit that their goal is to "take out" the opposition's quarterback. And there have been instances where coaches have rewarded players financially for doing so. Crowds thirst for particularly violent hits, and so do members of the media, as such hits are repeatedly replayed on the evening sports highlights. In short, it is not only exciting, but rewarding to maim your opponent. And this is just football. What about boxing!

Injuries are a part of any athletic competition. As an athlete, you accept that fact; it comes with the territory. But there is a difference between sustaining an injury and being forced to play while hurt or continuing an activity in which the rate of serious injury is unacceptably high, particularly in the case of youth, high school, or intercollegiate competition. There are very few individuals who have seriously competed in college and professionally and, increasingly, high school athletics, who have not sustained injuries that will have a lifelong effect. Thus, the claim that organized sport has a positive effect on the health and fitness of participants is misleading.

Celebrated Child Abuse

The most perverse example that the health benefits to participants is of little concern to coaches and administrators of organized sports occurs in women's gymnastics and figure skating. In these sports, the road to Olympic gold is littered with hundreds, and quite possibly, thousands of girls who left their childhood, prospects of lifelong good health, and psychological stability in the gymnasium and ice rink as the sports grew riskier and more demanding each year. Today's routines require more jumps, higher and more dangerous dismounts, and trickier routines to impress judges. "The physical skills have become so demanding that only a body shaped like a missile—in other words, a body shaped like a boy's—can excel. Breasts and hips slow the spins, lower the leaps, and disrupt the clean, lean, body lines that judges reward. 'Women's gymnastics' and 'ladies' figure skating' are misnomers today. Once the athletes become women, their elite careers wither" (Ryan 1995, 7). The 1976 U.S. Olympic gymnasts, for example, were, on average, seventeen and a half years old, stood 5 feet 3 1/2 inches tall and weighed 106 pounds. By 1992, the average U.S. Olympic gymnast was sixteen years old, stood 4 feet 9 inches tall and weighed 83 pounds.

The health problems that can result from a young girl who is pressured to maintain such a petite body type are frightening. In her book *Little Girls in Pretty Boxes*, Joan Ryan chronicles the extraordinary training demands and the price that young gymnasts' bodies and psy-ches must pay for a shot at Olympic gold. Eating disorders are ram-pant. After administering a shot to ease the pain of an injured hand and X-raying a gymnast's hips and back due to a sciatic nerve prob-lem, a doctor was alarmed to discover twenty-two old stress fractures in her back caused by years of gymnastics training. This was in addi-tion to the girl nursing a stress fracture in her left ankle for eight months. To deal with the uncommonly high number of injuries, these teenagers pop anti-inflammatory drugs and Advils like candy, chasing them with gulps of Maalox. To lose weight, they consume large quantities of diuretics and laxatives, vomit after every meal, or simply do not eat.

> In staving off puberty to maintain the "ideal" body shape, girls risk their health in ways their male counterparts never do. They starve themselves, for one, often in response to their coaches belittling insults about their bodies. Starving shuts down the menstrual cycle—the starving body knows it can not support a fetus—and thus blocks the onset of puberty. It's a dangerous strategy to save a career. If a girl isn't menstruating, she isn't producing estrogen. Without estrogen, her bones weaken. She risks stunting her growth. She risks premature osteoporosis. She risks fracture in all bones, including her vertebrae, and she risks curvature of the spine. In several studies over the past decade, young females who didn't menstruate were found to have the bone densities of postmenopausal women in their fifties, sixties and seventies. Most elite gymnasts don't begin to menstruate until they retire. Kathy Johnson, a medalist in the 1984 Olympics, didn't begin until she quit the sport at age twenty-five. (Ryan 1995, 9)

A large percentage of elite gymnasts are children, often training thirty to forty hours a week, beginning as early as age ten. Since these extreme measures are in the name of winning, we justify them as building character and sacrificing for excellence. Or, we simply turn our heads. If such pressure and physical demands were placed upon children in any other context, not only would we say that they are physically unhealthful, but that they constitute child abuse.

Child abuse in sports goes beyond forcing youngsters to play hurt. Children can also be abused verbally, emotionally, and sexually. In his book *Why Johnnie Hates Sports*, Fred Engh, president of the National Alliance for Youth Sports, cites a study by the Minnesota Amateur Sports Commission, indicating that abuse is running rampant in our sports programs. "The MASC study found that when children were participating in sports:

- 45.3 percent of the youngsters surveyed said that they had been called names, yelled at, or insulted;
- 21 percent said they had been pressured to play with an injury;
- 17.5 percent said they had been hit, kicked, or slapped;
- 8.2 percent said they had been pressured to intentionally harm others;
- 8 percent said they had been called names with sexual connotations;
- 3.4 percent said they had been pressured into sex or sexual touching.

All forms of abuse are destructive and detrimental to a child's growth and development, but emotional abuse seems to be the most common form of abuse in youth sports. When an adult places unrealistic expectations on a child, such as winning every game, scoring the most points, or playing without making any errors, that is emotional abuse. While this type of abuse is often more subtle than others, it is equally devastating. When emotional abuse is delivered during growth periods, the expectations and standards may haunt the children for a lifetime. These are the ones who are going to be chronically unhappy with their lives, always unsatisfied and unfulfilled because they never did quite enough. Failure will dominate their existence and devastate their spirits." (Engh 1999, 140–41)

Joan Ryan characterized what she observed in elite gymnastics and figure-skating programs as not only child abuse but "celebrated child abuse."

> In the dark troughs along the road to the Olympics lay the bodies of girls who stumbled on the way, broken by the work, pressure, and humiliation. I found a girl whose father left the family when she quit gymnastics at age thirteen, who scraped her arms and legs with razors to dull her emotional pain and who needed a two hour pass from a psychiatric hospital to attend her high school graduation. Girls who broke their necks and backs. One who so desperately sought the perfect, weightless gymnastics body that she starved herself to death. Others—many—who became so obsessive about controlling their weight that they lost control of themselves instead, falling into the potentially fatal cycle of bingeing on food, then purging by vomiting or taking laxatives. One who was sexually abused by her coach and one was sodomized for four years by the father of a teammate. I found a girl who felt such shame at not making the Olympic team that she slit her wrists. A skater who underwent plastic surgery when a judge said her nose was distracting. A father who handed custody of his daughter over to her coach so she could keep skating. A coach who fed his gymnasts so little that federation officials had to smuggle food into their hotel rooms. A mother who hid her child's chicken pox with makeup so she could compete. Coaches who motivated their athletes by calling them imbeciles, idiots, pigs, and cows. (Ryan 1995, 4–5)

So, is child abuse too strong a term for what often transpires in some of our youth sports programs? Apparently not.

Wanna Play the Game? Ya Gotta Do Drugs

Despite the fact that the health risks associated with performance-enhancing drugs are clear, their use among athletes is epidemic. Hormones such as testosterone, which allows the body to recover quickly from strenuous exercise and is used to build muscle mass, can cause heart disease, liver cancer, and impotence. Erythropoietin, which increases the number of red blood cells without having to "dope" using one's own blood, can cause the blood to thicken to the consistency of yogurt. This can lead to a clot, heart attack, or stroke. Athletes also inject themselves with human growth hormones that stimulate the intra-cellular breakdown of body fat, allowing more to be used for energy. Use of these types of hormones can cause muscle and bone disfigurement such as a jutting forehead or elongated jaw as well as heart and metabolic problems.

The use of these drugs is so widespread that for the athlete who wants to compete at a world-class level, it is practically a required part of the training regimen. Examples of athletes testing positive for performance-enhancing drugs are far too numerous—from Canada's Ben Johnson to football players at all levels to what was seemingly every athlete on the 1998 Tour de France. Sports officials know they are fighting a losing battle in their war against these drugs as testing methods and procedures are perpetually one step behind the chemical and biological advances of those who produce and help athletes mask their drug use.

It would be bad enough to say that the use of these drugs is all in the name of winning, but the value system and the sense of priorities of sports officials and coaches are so warped that it goes beyond merely wanting to win. Evidence that emerged during the Salt Lake City Olympic bid scandal suggested that the International Olympic Committee and other sports federations, far from being stalwart defenders of the purity of athletic competition, often turn a blind eye to the use of these drugs by athletes. Critics contend that the IOC, for example, has sometimes discarded positive drug test results for fear that they would tarnish the image of the Olympic Games.

> There are many powerful factions within the current system, and most of them would be hurt badly by the exposure of widespread drug use: the corporate sponsors of the Olympic Games and other competitions that would lose the participation of many qualified world-class athletes, the athletes themselves, past and present, who would face shame and denigration for their tainted accomplishments, the enforcement bodies that

would appear to have failed for so many years in their drug control efforts, and the doctors, trainers, coaches, and manufacturers who profit from the sale and use of performance-enhancing drugs. (Putnam 1999, 125)

Obviously, the rampant use of performance-enhancing drugs is not just about athletes wanting to win, but it is also about leaders in sport wanting to preserve a clean reputation so their organization can continue to generate money, despite the potential cost of lifelong, major physical harm and even death of athletes.

The rewards of making it in college and professional sports are entirely too seductive for anyone to expect adolescent males to resist them. That is why the issue of performance-enhancing drugs is so conceptually straightforward. As long as there remain disproportionately valuable prizes for those who win games, people who play them will break the law and endanger their health. There are simply no effective countervailing influences in the sporting world even to make possible the elimination of, say, anabolic steroids. Taking such drugs is considered a matter of course in college wrestling, weightlifting, and football, and they are used as well by high school athletes in these sports. Because performance-enhancing drugs contribute substantially to producing physical size and strength, even well-known side effects—impotence, liver damage, emotional instability—deter few athletes. (Gorn and Goldstein 1993, 245–46)

Violence, Drinking, Long-Term Participation, and Team Doctors

Of significant interest in the debate regarding the long-term health benefits of participation in competitive athletics is that there is no indication that athletes who have competed at a high level of competition are more likely than nonathletes to maintain a reasonable level of physical fitness after their competitive athletic careers are finished. While research in this area is meager, there are several factors that might be of influence. First, many highly competitive sports are not activities which one is able to continue to participate in after the athlete's organized playing days are over. How often do you see a group of adults playing a game of full contact, eleven to a side, football in the park? After competing at a high level of play, athletes often feel that any lesser competition simply will not satisfy their tremendous competitive urge. If one has climbed a mountaintop, it is difficult to get excited about a molehill. Finally, due to injuries sustained while playing competitively, ex-athletes, bodies battered and broken from years of playing while injured, are often relegated to being just that, an ex-athlete not only unable to engage in rigorous exercise, but also unable to perform even the most basic of physical functions normally.

A 1990 Ball State study commissioned by the National Football League Players Association (NFLPA), which covered the previous fifty years of league history, revealed that among 870 former players responding, 65 percent had suffered a "major injury" while playing—that is, an injury that either required surgery or forced them to miss at least eight games. The study also reported that the percentage of players incurring such injuries had increased alarmingly: from 42 percent before 1959 to 72 percent in the 1980s, after stadiums had switched from grass to artificial turf. Two of every three former players disclosed that their injuries had limited their ability to participate in sports and other recreational activities in retirement, and more than half also had a curtailed ability to perform physical labor. Of those who played during the seventies and eighties, nearly half (50 percent and 48 percent, respectively) reported that they had retired because of injury—up from 30 percent in the years before 1959 (Nack 2001).

Curt Marsh was an NFL lineman from 1981 to 1986. Marsh allowed team doctors to shoot him up repeatedly with painkillers and cortisone. After seven years in the league, Marsh had a scoped knee, bulging disks, and a right ankle that had been destroyed when a team doctor apparently mis-diagnosed and mistreated a broken talus bone. By 1994, after the thirteenth operation on it, the ankle was a hopeless ruin and doctors cut off Marsh's leg eight inches below the knee. After more than twenty operations, including one to replace his left hip and another to replace his right scheduled, Marsh is imminently qualified to speak of the harsh physical realities of playing in the NFL. "When I came to my first NFL camp, it was like I was a tall, cold can of beer. They popped the top and all that energy and desire and ability poured out. I gave of myself with the same passion that I had in high school and college. When I was empty, when I had no more to give, they just crumpled me up and threw me on the garbage heap. Then they grabbed another new can and popped him open, and he flowed out until he was empty" (Nack 2001, 62).

Further, the psychology of elite athletic competition, where the entire worth of an athlete's career is judged by whether he or she "makes it" in the pros, takes its toll on the athlete's love of the game. Many leave the game bitter, as if the game had failed them. It is not the game, but rather, the win-at-all-cost culture of the game that failed them. The incredible pressure placed upon athletes by the unrealistic expectation that the only "successful" athlete is one who plays professionally, results in athletes ending up "burned out" on a sport that, at one time, they loved unconditionally. I experienced basketball burnout. For three years after my competitive playing days were over, I wanted little to do with the sport. While I eventually rediscovered my love for the game, many other elite athletes do not.

And the thought that athletes are clean-living role models for a healthful lifestyle is, apparently, a myth. According to a study in the May 1998 issue of *Journal of American College Health*, far from being health-conscious role models, college athletes tend to binge drink and get into more alcohol-related trouble than other students. The study, the largest yet linking participation in college athletics and increased alcohol use, covered 51,483 students on 125 campuses. It found that college athletes consumed on average 7.34 drinks a week—78 percent more than students who were not athletes, who averaged 4.12 drinks. Team leaders drank even more, 8.25 drinks per week. Further, students who identified themselves as team leaders reported higher rates of hangovers, impaired academic work, trouble with police, drunken driving, violence, and sexual misconduct resulting from the use of alcohol and other drugs.

Although the study did not attempt to target reasons for drinking, it is safe to say that being a part of the athletic culture is a major influence. Athletes live in a world in which they work hard and play hard. As an athlete, you believe your body is stronger than those of nonathletes. As a competitor, you are trained to test your body's limits. To think that type of behavior and mindset is something that can be switched on and off is naive. The attitudes and behavior that are encouraged on the field carry over off the field. In many cases, such behavior is not healthful.

Athletics' purpose has become so distorted that even the motives and function of team doctors can be called into question. Team doctors are supposed to be the guardians of the athlete's health and physical well-being. But for whom do they work? To whom do they answer? Who hires them? The doctor is hired and paid by the athletic director in high school and college and by the team owner in professional sports. The team doctor's job is to get athletes back in the lineup as soon as possible so they can help the team win. "The problem goes beyond the willingness of athletes to play injured, or of trainers to use painkillers as a quick fix. The whole ethos of modern sports dictates that the body can be manipulated to achieve rationalized goals. The use of drugs—recreational drugs to alter moods, performance-enhancing drugs to increase strength and endurance, analgesics to enable pain to be endured—grows out of the larger assumption that our bodies can be objectified in the most extreme ways in order to attain the desired end, victory over an opponent" (Gorn and Goldstein 1993, 248).

Sports for a Healthy America?

As a culture, we have long accepted the notion that organized sports contribute positively to the physical health of both the individual athlete and the collective populace. But could it be that organized sport in America has evolved to where the physical well-being and lifelong health of the participant is simply not a concern, that all that matters is winning and advancing to the next level of play, regardless of the long-term health consequences?

Has athletic training become so intense and specialized, driven by a grossly distorted idea that the absolute greatest achievement that our sons and daughters could ever obtain is to be a professional athlete, that its long-term effect on the body is negative, particularly when ex-athletes have to live with their bodies for more than fifty years after their competitive playing days are over? And what is the impact on the health of our general populace of an "elitist" sports system where an ever greater proportion of the money, facilities, and attention is being lavished upon the few who show pro potential? With television dramatically altering the way in which much of the American public is "involved" in sport, we are undoubtedly watching more, which raises the question of whether we are playing less. We must ask whether our interests and priorities are best served by a sports industry that is driven by the interests and money of television and corporate sponsors, and geared, not to encourage us to get out and play the game, but rather, to stay on the couch and watch it. While it is difficult to establish a definitive link between our nation's increasing obesity and the evolution of sport from a participatory to observatory activity, one must raise the question.

Given these questions, it is imperative that we ask whether, from a health perspective, our personal and societal investment in organized sport is a positive one. Perhaps our nation's general health needs are better met through other exercise and athletic programs. The health benefits associated with exercise and athletics are not exclusive to highly organized, ultra-competitive youth, high school, college, or Olympic sports. Positive health benefits can be derived from involvement in exercise and fitness programs that are less competitive and less expensive, such as intramural sports, wellness programs, or local club teams. For sport to maximize fully its potential to positively influence the health and fitness of our populace, the focus of our investment in sport should be upon involving the maximum number of participants rather than on spending an increasingly large commitment of time, money, effort, and emotion on only those athletes who might have the potential to play major college or professional sports. In short, we must begin playing more and watching less. But to do so, we must consider whether our nation's long-term health is best served by organized athletics as they are currently conducted, marketed, and consumed.

GIVE ME
YOUR MONEY!

You know the story.

You open the morning newspaper and see a picture of the owner
of your local professional sports
team next to an article entitled
"Owner Demands Concessions."

The owner complains about how difficult it has become to compete against teams from larger markets. Citing escalating player
salaries, increased travel costs, and a stadium that, despite being
built only twenty years ago, is outdated, the owner cries out for
help from the community. He explains that to maintain a competitive team, a new or remodeled stadium, with multiple corporate
skyboxes and special seating, is necessary. The additional revenue
from the skyboxes will not only help pay for quality players but
will also demonstrate the city's commitment to being a big-time
city, a winner. The owner also implies that if financial help is not
forthcoming, he will be forced to move to a city more sympathetic
to his quest to build a winning team.

Community leaders and politicians, determined not to be
remembered as being responsible for the city losing its team and,

as a result, its identity as "major league," begin to turn the wheels of power to meet the owner's demands. Various forces are brought together in a broad, well-organized campaign to sell the public on meeting this alleged crucial civic challenge. The team's public relations machine swings into full gear, making grand claims regarding the team's positive impact on the region's economy and civic identity. The new stadium is positioned by business leaders as the key component of a revitalized inner city, the anchor of a broader urban renewal effort, attracting other businesses to the area including restaurants, bars, shops, hotels, and housing. Sportswriters and the news media, who would have far less to talk and write about if the team left, challenge fans not to let "their" team leave town. An economic impact study is released. The figures on the "economic activity" that the new sports complex will generate are impressive, projecting that the city will recoup its investment many times over.

A group of politicians and civic leaders call a press conference to announce an economic incentive plan designed to keep "our" team "where it belongs." Momentum for the project gains steam, playing upon community and civic pride to drown out the critics' calls for caution and more analysis. The owner lets it be known that other cities have expressed interest in the franchise, thus raising to a higher level, calls for municipal action to save "our" team. Sports reporters add fuel to the fire by pointing out that other cities that did not respond to similar demands lost their franchise. The initiative begins to take on a life of its own as a referendum is placed on a ballot for a vote. A loosely organized group of community activists struggle to highlight the fact that the city's schools are in shambles, its roads and infrastructure are crumbling, and businesses are moving to the suburbs. Their calls to reconsider the plan and invest the money in civic projects of a more critical nature are barely heard. The team owner reassures the public that the project will pay for itself. The referendum is approved or, if

not, politicians figure out a way to end run the process and millions of taxpayer dollars are spent to subsidize another wealthy
owner and group of millionaire ballplayers with no guarantee that
the identical scenario will not occur five or ten years later.

Heard that story before?

Organized sports programs and franchises have been portrayed
as having a significant positive financial impact upon those institutions, cities, or states that sponsor them. Professional franchises are
characterized as being a central economic component of a vibrant
community. And we are lead to believe that not only do athletic
programs generate a positive revenue flow to the college or university that sponsors them, but that they are also an indispensable
institutional fund-raising resource. Most of these claims are based
upon hopeful projections and unchallenged myths as much as fact
because, until recently, there has been very little hard financial data
with which to accurately assess them. With stadiums full, merchandise flying out of vendors' booths, and television ratings and
rights fees rising with no apparent end in sight, the public believes
that the city or university is receiving a handsome return on their
investment in their team.

But are they?

The purpose of this chapter is to raise questions regarding the
economic impact of sports franchises and college athletic departments on the cities and universities that sponsor them, using a
growing body of economic research: hard data rather than commonly accepted claims. For example, what kind of economic and
educational return on investment are we getting as taxpayers, alumni,
and students on our professional teams and college athletic programs? Is it enough to justify the tremendous amount of resources
we allocate to them in the form of money, emotion, and public-
image risks we assume? Is it sound civic or educational policy to
make decisions involving millions of public dollars based upon on
unsubstantiated claims, half-truths, and commonly accepted myths

regarding organized sports' economic impact? With our communities and educational institutions facing significant challenges in the form of poverty, crime, illiteracy, educational reform, environmental degradation, and the task of preparing our workforce to compete in the global, information-based, markets of the twenty-first century, has the price tag on our sports obsession gotten too steep?

Ain't Nothin' but a Business

Perhaps it was in 1957, when the Brooklyn Dodgers moved to Los Angeles, that the first dim rays of realization began to dawn on the public that professional sports was, before all else, a business. Since then, television contracts have grown, seasons have lengthened, strikes, lock-outs and walk-outs have occurred, salaries have escalated, and sneaker companies have become entities of major influence in the sports marketplace. From skyrocketing ticket prices to athletes with criminal records being signed to win championships, the idealized notion that professional sports is about something more than winning and generating revenues has all but vanished.

More than anything, however, it has been the increasing frequency with which professional sports franchises are moving or, if not moving, holding cities "hostage" by threatening to move, that is crushing our sentimentality, fueling our cynicism, and waking us to the fact that there is no such thing as a home team anymore. The team you call "yours" today may relocate to Tucson, Memphis, or Kansas City next week. In the NFL, for example, the Colts moved from Baltimore to Indianapolis, the Rams from L.A. to St. Louis, that is, of course, after the Cardinals moved from St. Louis to Phoenix. Oakland moved to L.A., then back to Oakland. The Browns, from Cleveland to Baltimore to become the Ravens. This, all within the past fifteen years. New franchises pop up in Jacksonville, Charlotte, and Cleveland, although how long they will remain in those cities is anyone's guess. Despite the fact that they play their "home" games in the New Jersey Meadowlands, both the Jets and the Giants refer to themselves as being from New York. And in baseball, the Yankees, the Bronx Bombers, those Yankees of Ruth, Gehrig, Berra, DiMaggio, Jackson, and Rizzuto, those Yankees with twenty-six World Championships to their credit, are threatening to do the same. There has even been talk about selling the right to attach a corporate name to Yankee Stadium. Yes, Yankee Stadium, the House that Ruth Built, may one day become Frito-Lay Park or General Motors Field.

What is going on here?

The answer is business—money; more specifically, our money. Players want more of it. Owners want more of it. Television networks want more of our money as do sneaker and apparel companies. And all will go where they can get it. Franchises and players move so often that you need a scorecard to tell what teams and cities are in a league. Professional sports is no longer about loyalty or creating a bond between a team and a city. And loyalty will become even less important as the days of the family-owned professional franchise are numbered as the cost of buying a team escalates rapidly. The Cleveland Browns sold for $530 million and a year later, a deal to sell the Washington Redskins for $800 million was tentatively agreed to before it fell apart. Corporations may soon be the only entity able to afford what will soon be a $1 billion price tag for many teams.

Yet, despite the increasingly expensive price we must pay for our sports fix, we continue to shell out our hard-earned cash to satiate our addiction. Worse, we continue to justify our investment largely on idealized notions about sports' positive civic impact.

Perhaps we have simply become numb to the business of sports. The numbers have become so outlandish, almost surreal, so large that they no longer mean anything, as if it were Monopoly money. The reporting of the signing of the first $100-million-per-year player will likely be greeted with not much more than a yawn at most breakfast tables across the country. The fact is, professional sports has always been about business. What team owner or player, whether at the turn of the century in 1900 or at the dawning of a new millennium in 2000, doesn't want to make as much money as possible? In short, professional sports' link to any higher moral or civic purpose has been, and will continue to be, tenuous at best, if at all.

Why is it, then, that when an owner holds our cities hostage, extorting taxpayer money to get a better stadium deal, we refuse to evaluate the proposition on business terms? Why do we cling to romanticized notions of community spirit and identity, while ignoring fiscal reality and civic responsibility? It is obvious that team owners and, increasingly, corporations that own teams, have long ago abandoned such idealized notions, intent upon driving the most lucrative economic package possible. Why shouldn't we, the taxpaying public, demand that our politicians and business leaders do the same?

Economic Shell Games

While it is difficult to gauge the influence of a pro sports franchise on community spirit, determining economic impact is easier. When all of the fantasized notions regarding civic attachment and responsibility are stripped away to reveal the bare economic reality of pro sports teams and the stadiums and arenas they play in, the picture is not pretty. Team owners' claims regarding the economic benefits of having a professional sports franchise are greatly exaggerated.

For example, the addition of a sports franchise to a city's entertainment menu does not generate a significant amount of *additional* entertainment spending. Most families' entertainment budgets are constant. Simply because another entertainment option is offered does not mean that consumers will raise their entertainment spending accordingly. After the rent and bills are paid and the children are clothed and fed, there is only so much for entertainment. Parents won't forego their children's annual medical check-ups or decide against buying them winter coats so they can afford the three hundred dollars it takes to attend a professional game.

If families begin to spend their entertainment dollars on professional sports, what are they no longer spending it on? Concerts? Movies? Going out to dinner? While a significant amount of money is being spent at the ballpark or stadium and in the surrounding restaurants, bars, and concession stands, what is portrayed as *additional* entertainment dollars generated by a team or sports complex is, largely, a *redistribution* of entertainment dollars from one part of the city to another. In short, the meal eaten at the stadium club or the sports bar across the street was likely a meal that would have previously been eaten at a restaurant in another part of town.

This is not to suggest that a professional sports franchise will not generate revenue for a local economy. Out-of-town fans attend games. Visiting teams and their entourages stay and eat in local hotels and restaurants. These dollars represent new entertainment income for the local economy as a direct result of a professional sports franchise. It is this category of economic activity that is the most meaningful indicator of the return on investment a city or region will receive on a professional sports franchise. Most economic impact studies, however, at least those commissioned by the team or local community leaders who favor keeping or attracting a team, calculate economic impact using total projected dollars (including the "redistributed" entertainment dollars referred to above) rather than the more meaningful total of *new* revenue. In most cases, the new economic activity generated is not very significant—certainly not significant enough to warrant the appropriation of large sums of public dollars to attract or retain a team of millionaire players owned by a wealthy businessman.

There are three ways in which the construction of a sports complex aids the local economy. First, the direct spending required to build the complex. Second, the spillover of economic activity into other local businesses such as restaurants, hotels, and bars. Finally, there is the effect of enhancing the reputation of the city as a good place to live and do business, thus increasing the likelihood of companies wanting to locate in the area. In his book *Playing the Field: Why Sports Teams Move and Cities Fight to Keep Them*, Charles C. Euchner, assistant political science professor at the College of Holy Cross, summarizes a growing number of studies indicating that it is becoming increasingly clear that stadiums and pro sports teams do not reap the economic dividends that we have been led to believe.

For example, a 1988 study by economist Dean Baim found no direct economic gains to cities as a result of having a professional sports franchise. Of the fourteen cities in his study, only one, Dodger Stadium, showed a positive value and two other facilities, Mile High Stadium and Anaheim Stadium, showed less-definite gains. It is interesting to note that Dodger Stadium was privately built and both Anaheim and Mile High stadiums "reflect a minimal investment by municipal authorities" (Euchner 1993, 66). It is also quite likely that the chance of stadiums benefitting cities economically is even more remote today as the costs of stadium construction have skyrocketed since the late 1980s. Further, the competition between cities for franchises has intensified dramatically, resulting in a corresponding increase in the amount of economic concessions being asked for by owners.

Euchner cites another study by Robert Baade and Richard F. Dye indicating that for every $1 million of debt for a stadium, two large crowd event dates per year are necessary. Thus, a city that assumes $100 million of debt to build its stadium would have to schedule two hundred events per year for the stadium to pay for itself. Today, cities are assuming much more than $100 million of debt to construct their stadiums. For example, in exchange for agreeing to move the Cleveland Browns to Baltimore, the owner Art Modell got Maryland taxpayers to fork over $200 million for a downtown stadium. At the same time, Modell gets to keep all the revenue generated by the stadium! In other words, the city of Baltimore will get nothing from its investment of millions of public tax dollars. And with the difficulty in calculating cost overruns in building a stadium or arena, a city often ends up spending far more than it originally budgeted. The original cost estimate for Baltimore's Camden Yards was $60 million, but ended up costing in excess of $100 million. The renovation of Yankee Stadium was originally projected as costing $24 million but ended up with a $120 million price tag.

The second alleged benefit of sports facilities is that they stimulate additional economic activity. Euchner suggests that the estimates of the economic gains resulting from this multiplier effect are overstated as there is little evidence that the money generated from these related services stays in the city. For example, stadiums are designed for the quick entry and exit of suburban fans with automobiles. Sports teams pay high salaries to their athletes, who often do not live in the city. Many of the services (concessions, cleaning, advertising, etc.) are contracted out to companies from outside the city. Thus, it is likely that the supposed multiplier effect associated with a professional sports team or stadium project is overstated.

Finally, sports franchises are said to provide a city with a major league reputation which serves to enhance its prospects of attracting other businesses. Again, Euchner cites research by Baade and Dye concluding that this effect was positive in only one of the eight cities studied. While a company may consider whether a city has a major-league franchise when deciding where to relocate, a multitude of other factors will carry more weight, such as tax incentives offered, school systems, health care facilities, cost of living indexes, housing costs, crime and poverty rates, and overall business climate. Having a pro sports franchise can help, but does it help a city enough to warrant the tremendous public expenditures it takes to attract one? Doubtful.

Most economists who seriously study the economic impact of sports stadiums and franchises agree they are not a good civic investment. The economists Andrew Zimbalist of Smith College and Roger G. Noll of Stanford University edited a book on stadium financing for the Brookings Institute titled *Sports, Jobs, and Taxes*. In it, Zimbalist, Noll, and fifteen collaborators study the issues "from all angles" and contend that, "a new sports facility has an extremely small (and perhaps negative) overall effect on overall economic activity and employment. No recent facility appears to have earned anything approaching a reasonable return on investment" (Zimbalist and Noll 1997). Zimbalist and Noll say that "even the most successful publicly funded new stadium, Oriole Park at Camden Yards in Baltimore, has had a net gain to the Baltimore economy of about $3 million a year, not much return on a $200 million investment" (Gross 1999).

Even if a city agrees to an owner's demand to build a new stadium, there is no guarantee that in a decade or so, the issue won't resurface. For example, twenty years ago, the Minnesota Twins declared that they could no longer play outdoors because of the weather. Thus, Minnesota taxpayers helped pay for a new arena, the Metrodome. Now, the Twins claim they need a more "authentic" outdoor baseball environment to attract more customers so they can make more money to remain competitive. It never ends.

The sad civic reality is that while a pro team or a new stadium may produce a winner for the city on the field or court, from an economic standpoint, they are perennial losers.

Stadiums and Urban Renewal

Some argue that it is unfair to judge the impact of sports teams and their facilities on such narrow economic indicators. Large sports complexes, they claim, can revitalize a city, attracting other businesses and development. While there may be a measure of truth to this assertion, a sports complex is simply one element of a much larger urban renewal arsenal. For example, Baltimore's Camden Yards has been hailed as the key in revitalizing Baltimore's harbor waterfront area. The fact is, the city had been revitalizing the area for a decade before the stadium was built, with an aquarium, restaurants, shops, and hotels. In St. Louis, Busch Stadium was simply one component of a broader effort to rebuild the riverfront area, centered around the building of the Gateway Arch in 1965. And New Jersey's development plans for the Hackensack Meadowlands were modified to include Giants Stadium and other sports facilities. In many cases, the projected economic development and urban revitalization benefits never materialize, the Houston Astrodome and Rich Stadium in Buffalo being two examples (Danielson 1997, 109).

In most cases, sports complexes represent simply one component in a city's redevelopment plan; perhaps it is the icing on the redevelopment cake, but it is one part nonetheless. Sports complexes should not be looked upon as the foundation of an urban renewal effort because they are not sound economic investments. Stadiums are not used very often. Football only stadiums are generally used fewer than thirty times per year. Further, the types of jobs connected to sports complexes are seasonal and generally low paying with little long-lasting economic impact.

The overblown estimates of a professional sports franchise's economic impact on a local economy distorts public debate regarding the appropriation of public dollars to retain or attract a professional sports franchise. As much as we believe that pro sports are big business, they are not. According to Mark Rosentraub, associate dean in the School of Public and Environmental Affairs, Indiana University at Indianapolis, if sports teams were classified by their gross revenues, they would be considered small- to medium-sized businesses. In his 1997 book entitled *Major League Losers: The Real Cost of Sports and Who's Paying for It*, he makes the following observation.

> Relying on *Financial World's* estimates of team revenues, it is likely that only two teams in 1994 or 1995, the New York Yankees and the Dallas Cowboys, had or would have had direct annual revenues of more than $100 million. (The baseball strike reduced the actual revenues of the Yankees.) . . . Firms with annual budgets of $60 million or $100 million are certainly vital, vibrant, and valued in terms of the development of any region's economy. But businesses of this size are quite small when compared to other organizations in urban areas. For example, few would consider urban campuses of state universities to be engines that drive a city's economy. Yet, in budget terms, they are quite a bit larger than even the most successful sports teams. The budget for Indiana University-Purdue University Indianapolis (IUPUI), with its enrollment of 25,000 students and excluding its health center, is in excess of $300 million. (Rosentraub 1997, 139–40)

Rosentraub also analyzed the impact of professional sports teams in terms of total payroll dollars per county within which the team was located. He found that, "professional sports never accounted for more than .08 percent of the jobs in any group of counties. Professional sports payrolls were largest in the largest counties; even there, though, this grouping accounted for just one-half of 1 percent of the private sector's total payroll" (Rosentraub 1997, 142). In Chicago, for example, "the five pro teams generate less than 1% of the personal income in the city" (Murphy 1998, 41).

While we see sold-out stadiums, read about athletes signing multi-million-dollar contracts, and are told of the creation of jobs, the generation of tax revenue, and the overall economic development potential by team owners, a pro sports franchise's impact on a local economy is minimal. "Almost always, the purported benefits in terms of jobs, tax revenues, and general economic development are overstated, and the costs understated. And with the rapidly rising price tags for sports projects, particularly those located in central business districts, economic benefits have become even harder to realize. Selling these increasingly expensive sports palaces to those who will pay for them, however, leads advocates to ever more grandiose claims of economic riches and revitalized cities" (Danielson 1997, 109–10).

In short, a professional sports franchise or stadium has less economic value than a widget factory. A manufacturing company generates tax dollars instead of using them to subsidize the extravagant lifestyles of millionaire owners and players. A manufacturing company also produces long-term, well-paying jobs as opposed to the seasonal, minimum-wage jobs generated by a stadium or pro sports franchises.

The amount of money we spend on stadiums and arenas is staggering, in terms of dollars spent and, most shockingly, in terms of percentage of the total price tag. Andrew Zimbalist estimates that "taxpayers will supply about 75% of the $10 billion that will be spent on new stadiums between 1990 and 2006" (Zimbalist 1999).

> The agreement reached between the Los Angeles Rams of the NFL and the city of St. Louis in 1995 provides an excellent example of how lucrative stadium financing can be for a team. The city of St. Louis, St. Louis County, and the state of Missouri agreed to assume the entire $290 million cost of a new indoor stadium for the team, the 67,000-seat Trans World Dome. The sale of Personal Seat Licenses (PSL) to fans eager to see a pro football team in their city produced $70 million, which the Rams used to pay for relocation expenses and a practice facil-

ity and to absolve debts owed to the city of Anaheim, California, their previous home. The Rams' rent in the Trans World Dome is a modest $250,000 for each year of the thirty-year lease. During that time, the team will receive 100 percent of all food and drink revenue as well as 100 percent of the revenue from luxury boxes and club seats, with a guarantee from the corporate community of St. Louis that 85 percent of those boxes and seats will be occupied for the next fifteen years. Seventy-five percent of all in-stadium advertising revenue will belong to the Rams, as will the $1.3 million paid by Trans World Airlines for the right to name the stadium. Finally, the team was given 1,200 parking spots in the stadium parking lot for each game and a merchandise store near the Trans World Dome, built and paid for by the city. The total value of the financial package to the Rams is estimated to be $700 million. (Putnam 1999, 155–56)

It is bad enough that cities are investing in pro teams and stadiums that are not producing a reasonable return on investment. Far worse, however, is the fact that communities are pumping incredible amounts of money into such facilities when pro teams are perfectly able to fund such projects on their own or with minimal public financial support. "In Washington, Miami, Charlotte, and San Francisco, owners have built state-of-the-art stadiums on their own nickel. And it is a little ironic that as sports revenues reach record heights, owners cry poverty. (Note that until the 1960's, when the sports business was much more modest, owners almost always built their own ballparks. Curious, that!) In fact, they simply don't want to build their own ballparks—and you wouldn't either. If New York wanted to build you a half-a-billion-dollar house and let you keep the rent, would you say no? Of course not. But then, for most of us, that's not an option. You have to be seriously rich already to get the chance to scarf that greedily at the public trough" (Murphy 1999).

In the final analysis, professional sports teams and the stadiums and arenas they require are a poor civic investment. That being the case, as responsible citizens, we must seriously consider whether professional sports teams and stadiums are the best use of limited public dollars.

Athletics and the University

Concern regarding making ends meet financially has been as much a part of the history of American higher education as the classroom lecture. Contrary to the prevailing notions about its ability to contribute to the well-balanced education of student-athletes, it was the never-ending search for new revenue streams that was the driving force behind the formal incorporation of athletics into higher education. As public interest in college football grew in the late nineteenth and early twentieth century, leaders of financially strapped colleges and universities saw athletics as a means to generate much-needed resources in the form of money and visibility.

Regardless of whether a successful sports team generated additional resources and political favor for a university—points that remain in dispute to this day—college presidents *believed* that a successful football program legitimized their institution as a major university. Athletics was formally incorporated into higher education's structure because academic leaders believed that a successful athletic team could serve an important public relations function for the university, which in turn, would result in increased financial support. This, along with the alleged "educational benefits" that accrued to participants, made the marriage of athletics and higher education seem reasonable. From these beginnings, this belief has evolved to the point where it is now accepted as an unchallenged "truth."

With coaches signing six-figure contracts, 100,000-seat football stadiums sold out, CBS paying $6 *billion* for the right to televise the NCAA men's basketball tournament for the next eleven years, and institutions receiving $5 million or more for participating in a football bowl game, it is no wonder many think college athletic programs are rolling in the dough. Coupled with the occasional report of an athletic department writing a $100,000 check to the institution's library to purchase books, it is no surprise that the public believes that athletic departments not only generate a huge financial surplus, but direct a portion of that surplus to the institution's general education budget. Even athletic departments that operate at a deficit purportedly contribute to the educational mission of the university in the form of exposure generated through television and the media. Such exposure enhances the institution's stature and generates public interest in the university, resulting in increased applications, alumni donations, and favor with legislators and the surrounding community.

The facts, however, paint a different picture.

According to a biannual NCAA-sponsored report, *Revenues and Expenses of Intercollegiate Athletic Programs: Financial Trends and Relationships,* when institutional support (salaries, cash, tuition waivers, etc.) is not included on the revenue side of the financial ledger, most Division I college athletic programs lose money. For example, in 1993, only 30 percent of the 207 Division I programs (there were 301 total Division I programs at that time) reporting generated more revenue than they expended. Further, only 51 percent of the 85 Division I-A schools reporting generated a profit (the total number of Division I-A programs, those with major college football, was 106). According to the 1995 report, the financial outlook was even more negative. That report revealed that only 28 percent of the 206 Division I programs reporting, and only 46 percent of the 89 Division I-A programs reporting, generated a profit. In the NCAA's most recent report, in 1999, only 23 percent of all Division I programs and less than half (46 percent) of Division I-A programs generated a profit. In short, without general institutional support, less than one in four Division I athletic programs would be solvent.

A more-detailed accounting (from Fulks 2000) of the financial statistics from these reports follows:

	YEAR	PROFIT	DEFICIT	EVEN
Division I-A	1999	46%	54%	0%
	1997	43%	56%	1%
	1995	46%	52%	2%
	1993	51%	49%	0%
	1989	55%	40%	5%
Division I-AA	1999	14%	86%	0%
	1997	9%	90%	1%
	1995	13%	85%	2%
	1993	15%	81%	5%
	1989	33%	52%	15%
Division I-AAA	1999	5%	95%	0%
	1997	10%	89%	1%
	1995	18%	82%	0%
	1993	17%	81%	2%
	1989	27%	71%	2%

Further, it is likely that the future financial outlook will be increasingly negative as institutions are being mandated to appropriate equal athletic funding for women according to the provisions of Title IX of the 1972 Educational Amendment Act.

Nevertheless, there is more to the issue of athletics as a sound institutional business investment. The National Association of College and University Business Officers (NACUBO) conducted an analysis of college athletics' finances in a report titled "The Financial Management of Intercollegiate Athletics Programs." The analysis, published in 1993, brought to light additional concerns regarding university accounting procedures as they apply to athletic operations. The report concluded that current costs, as high as they are, may yet not be telling the entire financial story. Specifically, the report questioned the practice of institutions paying many indirect or overhead costs generated by the athletic department.

> Interviews with personnel in 18 institutions across all athletics divisions showed that only one of these data elements, amortization of facilities, could be calculated with any degree of accuracy, and even then this could be done only by the four Division I-A institutions in the study. Given this difficulty, it seems likely that many indirect or "overhead" expenses attributable to athletics activities are borne by the university as a whole. In institutions that require other programs or divisions to bear their share of indirect costs, allowing athletics to escape this burden creates a basic inequity. (NACUBO 1993, 20)

Andrew Zimbalist, an economist at Smith College and one of the nation's foremost authorities on the financing of college athletics, identifies many ways universities engage in creative accounting to hide the true cost of an athletic program. For example, athletic scholarships might be attributed to the general financial aid budget. Portions of athletic recruiting might be charged to general university overhead or to the admissions office. Coaches' salaries and benefits may be allocated to the general salary pool or may be paid for by a booster club, and facilities costs may be paid for by the state. Expenditures for the construction and maintenance of sports facilities, as well as for security, sanitation, and infrastructure may be allocated to buildings and grounds, general debt service, or campus security. Athletic departments often count as revenues the subsidies from student fees, transfers from the university budget, or appropriations from the state budget. (For example, New York State contributed $4.3 million to the University of Buffalo's athletic department for the academic year 1999–2000 [*Chronicle*, December 10, 1999, A-56]). Further, athletic departments often receive large alumni gifts that may come at the expense of giving to the institution's general fund.

Further clouding the financial future of intercollegiate athletic programs is the fact that revenue sources—in particular, licensing and sponsorships—are not as lucrative as we have been led to believe. Generally, universities receive only about 8 percent of the wholesale price of the sale of items (hats, shirts, etc.) bearing the university logo. "As logo use was commercialized on the basis of a school's athletic success, the practice of sharing licensing income between the general budget and athletics emerged. While some sharing still prevails at most schools, there has been a clear trend for greater and greater shares of licensing income to go to athletics" (Zimbalist 1999, 136).

Accordingly, we can easily conclude that were athletics' accounting held to a common business standard where all direct and indirect expenses are charged against revenues, significantly less than 23 percent of all Division I institutions would report an athletic department profit. In short, the vast majority of athletic programs do not support themselves, a far cry from the commonly accepted belief that they generate significant resources for the college or university. "This finding is not surprising in colleges that designate varsity sports as part of the educational budget and make no claim to seek massive crowds. It does warrant concern, however, when one looks at institutions that have established varsity football and/or basketball as major, self-supporting activities intended to produce revenues, with large arenas and stadia and with television audiences" (Thelin and Wiseman 1989, 15).

Other than for a few elite programs, the claim that athletic programs make money for the university is simply untrue. Yes, athletic programs generate revenue. And yes, occasionally we read about an athletic department writing a check to the university's library or general scholarship fund. But what is not as readily reported is that major college athletic programs also spend a tremendous amount of money, particularly in the sports of football and basketball.

According to the NCAA's *Revenues and Expenses of Intercollegiate Athletic Programs: Financial Trends and Relationships,* in 1985, the average Division I-A football program budget was $2.39 million with the largest being $6.0 million. In 1999, the average Division I-A football program budget had more than doubled to $5.26 million with the largest being $15.9 million. Men's basketball program expenses, though far less, are still significant. In 1985, the average budget of a men's basketball program at a Division 1-A institution was $620,000, with the largest being $1.68 million. By 1999, the average budget had jumped to $1.58 million with the largest reported budget being $6.16 million (Fulks 2000, 27). While many football and basketball programs operate at a profit, there are a sizable number that do not. In 1999, 36 percent of Division I-A football programs and 81 percent of I-AA programs reported an operating deficit. The same study revealed that in men's basketball, 29 percent of programs at Division I-A institutions, 69 percent at Division I-AA institutions, and 63 percent at Division I-AAA reported an operating deficit (Fulks 2000, 30, 48, 66). These numbers are significant as football and basketball programs are alleged to generate a positive revenue flow, which helps pay for other sports, such as tennis, golf, and various women's sports, that do not. Contrary to popular belief, many football and basketball programs do not even pay for themselves.

And, as in the case of the various hidden costs of athletic departments generally, the financial realities regarding football and basketball programs are likely to be more dire than portrayed in the above-mentioned statistics. For example, many budget analyses do not apportion non-sport specific costs among the sports themselves. Expenses such as facilities maintenance, administrative salaries and benefits, travel, entertainment, tickets, advertising, and utilities, for example, are often lumped into a department-wide figure. This, despite the fact that the majority of such expenses are attributable to football and basketball.

Athletics as Good University Public Relations?

Athletic directors and even college presidents often downplay these deficits, indicating that athletics consumes a very small percentage of the overall institutional budget. While the amount of institutional dollars spent on athletics may be small, the impact of this spending is great. Athletics is by far the largest and clearest window through which the public views the university. According to an NCAA-sponsored survey, 53 percent of the total American public, 65 percent of men and 43 percent of women, follow college sports (National Collegiate Athletic Association 1991, 22). "Of all the column inches written about the University, I would estimate that 75 percent is regarding the athletic program," Scott Selheimer, director of sports information at the University of Delaware, told Bob Torpor in an interview in the March 1995 issue of *Marketing Higher Education* (Torpor 1995, 6). With such visibility comes increased public scrutiny. Spending on athletics reflects, at least in the public's eye, institutional priorities to a greater degree than any other university entity. If public opinion evolves to a point where the negatives associated with major college athletics (i.e., recruiting scandals, coaches being paid more than presidents, the compromising of academic standards, and so on) cannot be rationalized away based upon athletics' financial and institutional advancement benefits, universities will become even more hardpressed to justify expensive athletic programs.

In most cases, the link between the athletic department and the institution in financial matters is weak. For example, many bigtime athletic programs are run as independent, profit-driven, auxiliary enterprises. Despite the claim from athletic fund-raisers that they work closely with the institutional advancement office to raise funds for the university, such cooperation is usually superficial. The separation and mistrust that exists between most academic and athletic communities means that virtually all athletic department fund-raising efforts are directed at raising money specifically for sports, rather than for the institution generally. Money generated and raised by the athletic department is spent by the athletic department. It is rare when an athletic department donates money to the institution because there is no excess revenue to donate. Even in those cases where an athletic department receives a financial windfall in the form of a bowl payout, much of that revenue is split among conference members, and what is left is often spent paying for the travel, lodging, and entertainment expenses of athletic department employees and "friends" to attend the game and the festivities that surround it.

Further, there is no conclusive evidence that proves a successful athletic program results in increased alumni giving or applications. The research simply does not support this assertion. In the case of increased applications, one has to wonder what kinds of students would attend a school just because it has a good football or basketball team. College is far too expensive to imagine a parent funding such a folly. And will such students improve the academic profile of the student body and enable the school to become more selective? Will the supposed increase in applications also lead to a higher yield (i.e., in the percentage of admitted students who end up enrolling at the school). According to an internal study at the University of Massachusetts, apparently not.

> The period fall 1988 to fall 1990 did not include outstanding basketball years. In 1991, UMass was a semi-finalist in the NIT and in the four years since has been featured consistently on national television, has been ranked consistently in the top twenty and has gone to the NCAA tournament. . . . It is clear that after double digit declines in out-of-state applications from fall 1988 to fall 1991, we experienced two years of double digit increases in fall 1993 and 1994. It has been suggested that this bump in applications might be related to, among other things, greater awareness of the University beyond Massachusetts, at least partially as a result of the success in basketball.

It has been reported that the University of Connecticut experienced a similar application increase after their very successful Elite Eight season in 1991, with a 26% increase of out-of-state and a 6% increase in in-state applications. Despite the growth of applications correlated with UConn basketball success, the conclusion was that there was no impact on yield (enrollment divided by admittances). With the numbers of applications up, it would also be expected that the quality of students enrolled might increase because of a larger pool upon which to draw. The Connecticut experience indicates no change in the quality of students. In the UMass figures there was a decrease in the SAT scores of applicants and enrolled students for both in- and out-of-state students. In fact, this [1995–1996] was the first year that the SAT scores of out-of-state students fell below in-state. None of this suggests that team success carries beyond the application stage. In fact, in the year following the "Dream Season," UConn applications dropped back to earlier numbers. Their conclusion was that there was no lasting impact on the admissions numbers. (Zimbalist 1999, 170–71)

Similar conclusions can be drawn in the area of fund-raising. For example, "in 1986, the year after Tulane shut down its basketball program in the wake of a point shaving scandal, donations to that school leaped by $5 million. Wichita State raised $26 million in a special drive in '87, the year in which it dropped football" (Wolff 1995, 25). The primary reason athletic success has little impact on general university giving is because a large number of athletic boosters are not alumni. Such boosters' connection to or interest in the school extends no further than the gymnasium or the football field. Hence, they donate exclusively to the athletic department as they have very little interest in the institutions's academic reputation or programs.

Even in the case of alumni, there is little connection between a winning football team and giving. In fact, according to a study by the Mellon Foundation involving comprehensive information about the entering classes of 1951, 1976, and 1989, at thirty-two institutions of all sizes, "one of the more striking findings derived from this year-by-year analysis is that at the most intensive level of play (NCAA Division I-A), winning appears to have had, if anything, a modest negative effect on the overall amount of alumni/ae giving. The evidence suggests that the majority of the former students at those schools who were not themselves intercollegiate athletes may give less, not more, when the football team does better" (Shulman and Bowen 2001, 223).

While it is possible that a successful athletic program can be a factor in alumni giving and student applications, it is unlikely that it has much of a long-term effect. While an institution may experience an immediate, short-term jump in applications or financial support (more than likely earmarked specifically for the athletic program rather than for the institution generally) after a particularly successful football or basketball season, most institutions will continue to attract quality students who, when they graduate, will donate money to their alma maters, with little regard to the quality or even existence of a highly competitive athletic program.

John DiBiaggio, former president of Michigan State University, sums up athletics' effect on university fund-raising as follows: "No data support the oft-heard claim that wins on the field or on the court bring in more private dollars or more state and federal funding. Losses do not result in decreased financial support either. To be sure, wins can and do often bring in more support for athletic programs. But the myth of institutional dependency on athletic revenues— therefore on athletic victories—needs to be aggressively refuted" (Zimbalist 1999, 168).

We're the Suckers

If professional sports franchises and college athletic programs are not the financial gold mines they are played up to be, who pays the price for these fiscal extravagances? Who pays the multi-million-dollar salaries of our professional stars? Who pays for the tax concessions provided wealthy owners and for the construction costs for stadiums? Who pays college athletic programs' deficits?

We do, whether we ever attend or watch a game or even like sports. We're the suckers.

We pay in the form of skyrocketing ticket, parking, and concession prices. For example, the average ticket price for an NBA game is $40.82, not far behind the NHL ($42.79) and NFL ($42.86). Only Major League baseball seems reasonably affordable at an average of $15.26 a ticket. That, of course, is before parking, concessions, and a souvenir. It adds up quickly for a family of four. We pay in the form of higher advertising rates, needed by television networks to pay escalating rights to televise sporting events. Companies pass on those increased advertising costs to the consumer. We pay in the form of the damaged integrity of our educational systems resulting from athletic scandals and admitting athletes who are academically unqualified. We pay in the form of increased cable television rates. For example, in January 1998, ESPN agreed to pay $600 million a year to air NFL games on Thursday and Sunday nights for the next eight years, which was two and a half times what ESPN and TNT paid together to divvy up the games the previous season. Most cable operators expect that ESPN will have to increase the monthly fee it charges local cable operators by 20 percent for the next few years to recoup its investment. Those who subscribe to cable packages that include ESPN will have to pay for ESPN's largess, regardless of whether they ever watch sports (Mohl 1998, 1).

When a sports star holds out for more money, or a league goes on strike, it is the fan who will eventually pay. When an owner writes that big check to his star player or when CBS pays the NCAA $6 billion for the broadcast rights to the Final Four, it is coming out of our wallets. Owners, commissioners, agents, and athletes are not involved in sports for our collective entertainment benefit, they are involved to make money. They know that we, the public, will spend increasingly large amounts of money for the "privilege" of going to a game or vegetating in front of the television to cheer "our" team on to glory. We have been duped into thinking that the professional franchise in town is "ours," that we have a stake in it. We don't. The fact is, there are no more "home" teams. Owners will take their teams to whatever city pays the most. Thus, our arrangement with our sports teams, no longer based upon loyalty and commitment to the people of a city or region, is simply a business transaction. The sooner we let go of our idealized notions about what a sports team can do for our town or university, the better. Sports aren't "played" anymore, rather, they are packaged, marketed, and commercialized as a money-making entertainment enterprise. It is time we face this reality and start making civic and educational policy decisions in an economically responsible fashion.

James Michener raised the question of misplaced civic priorities relating to athletics back in 1976, long before organized sports' financial "boom times."

> Should a well-run society divert so high a percentage of its gross national product into sports, when there are so many other aspects of our national life that cry for attention? A recent study has shown that we spend about one hundred billion dollars a year on sports and recreation, considerably more than we spend for national defense. If this vast sum went for the improvement of the national health, fine. If it encouraged our citizens to be active participants and to avoid physical and mental deterioration, fine. And if it encouraged young people to build patterns of living that would serve them throughout life, fine.
>
> But if a great deal of this investment is merely subtracted from the creative process of the nation, and siphoned into the hands of a few essentially brash young men and women, the consequences can only be destructive. Our nation may be generating deep resentments in establishing and promulgating such unbalanced priorities. (Michener 1976, 462)

Since Michener posed these questions, our investment in organized sports has increased dramatically. Of great concern is whether we will ever recognize the danger in such misplaced public priorities. Many wonder, including Douglas Putnam, who wrote in *Controversies of the Sports World*, "In the end, it does seem to be vanity that lies at the root of the stadium finance game, and there is an ample supply of that quality among the nation's major cities and the millions of sports fans who live in them" (Putnam 1999, 158).

Despite the oft-claimed economic justification used to explain our country's tremendous investment in sports, the facts reveal this assertion as not simply a myth, but a dangerous myth. Thus, the fundamental question regarding our society's financial investment in organized athletics is as follows: With our communities and educational institutions facing significant budget shortfalls, decaying infrastructure, and declining services, can we afford to continue to spend enormous amounts of community tax and education dollars on organized sports?

SPORT AND UPWARD MOBILITY

During the 1997 season, Major League baseball celebrated the fiftieth anniversary of Jackie Robinson breaking its color barrier. In virtually every account of this event, sport was credited as one of the most progressive and discrimination-free enterprises in our society. Advocates have long claimed that sport is a unique entity in this regard because in athletics, your worth is determined by one factor; performance on the fields of play. Sport has been hailed as our country's only enterprise where everyone—black, white, red, or green—can compete on equal footing. "Sports represents pure meritocracy, where people earn what they get under conditions of perfect equality. There are no slaves and masters in baseball, no peasants and lords or gentlemen and commoners, just .200 and .300 hitters" (Gorn and Goldstein 1993, 111).

As we were told repeatedly during the coverage of this milestone baseball and civil rights event, Robinson's achievement lead to doors of opportunity being opened in many other organizations and industries. While the significance of this accomplishment should never be diminished, the days of mere participation in sports by blacks as being symbolic of some greater racial tolerance and progress are long gone. While everyone may be competing on equal footing on the fields of play, beyond them, sport is no more effective at promoting equal opportunity than any other American institution.

Onto the Fields, But out of the Boardrooms

It is likely that the popular notion of sports as a powerful vehicle for promoting racial tolerance and upward social mobility in other fields is more a product of sports' visibility within our culture than from any overwhelming evidence. The fact is,

> Colleges and professional teams were notoriously slow in opening up their rosters. It wasn't until July, 1959, when the Boston Red Sox brought up Pumpsi Green from the minors after protests from the NAACP, that every team in baseball had at least one black player. The National Hockey League did not integrate until 1957, with the debut of Canadian Willie O'Ree. The Professional Golfers Association kept a written "Caucasian clause" in its bylaws until 1961. It wasn't until 1962, when the all-white Washington Redskins traded for Bobby Mitchell that every team in all of the major sports had at least one black player. (Entine 2000, 223)

Consider the sports establishment itself. Minority advancement and opportunity has occurred almost exclusively on the fields and courts. Meanwhile, the white athletic establishment maintains its vice-like grip of power off them, from the manufacture and sale of sporting goods to the coaching, administration, and ownership of teams. It is ironic that sports is sold as being effective in promoting equality, opportunity, and upward mobility, yet meaningful "upward mobility" hasn't occurred within the athletic establishment itself.

For example, according to the NCAA *Minority Opportunities and Interests Committee's Two-Year Study of Race Demographics of Member Institutions,* excluding the historically black colleges and universities, in 1999–2000, less than 3 percent (2.9) of NCAA directors of athletics and only 4.4 percent of NCAA men's and 4.4 percent of women's head coaches were black. In the revenue-producing sports of football and men's basketball, only 8.6 percent of head coaches were black, and that number rose to only 13.7 percent in Division I (NCAA 1994).

These shortfalls are particularly damning considering the high percentage of minority student-athletes participating in athletics, particularly in the revenue-generating sports of basketball and football. According to the 2000 NCAA Division I Graduation Rate Report, 25 percent of scholarship student-athletes entering Division I athletics programs from the 1990–1991 through the 1993–1994 academic years were African Americans. The numbers are particularly high in football (50 percent), men's basketball (59 percent) and women's basketball (37 percent) (NCAA 2000–2001).

While our sports teams are one of the most-integrated entities in our society, the integration or upward mobility promised through athletic participation hasn't been upward at all. Minority representation in decision-making front-office positions in college programs and professional sports teams is dismal. The number of minority owners of professional sports teams is nonexistent in the NFL, the NHL, the MLB, or the NBA. According to the Elias Sports Bureau, of all the head coaches hired in the NFL since 1989—the year Art Shell became the first black head coach in pro football—through the conclusion of the 1997 season, black head football coaches had a regular season winning percentage of .555, while white head coaches had a .486 percentage. Not one of the three black coaches under contract at the conclusion of the 1997 season—Dennis Green of the Minnesota Vikings, Philadelphia's Ray Rhodes, and Tampa Bay's Tony Dungey—had a losing record. Neither did Shell, who was 56-41 with the Oakland Raiders. Yet, despite such success, blacks are rarely hired as head coaches.

The fallacy of the "sports as a vehicle for upward mobility" claim is brilliantly articulated by Alan Sack and Ellen J. Staurowsky in their 1998 book, *College Athletes for Hire: The Evolution and Legacy of the NCAA's Amateur Myth*:

> At first glance, the dominant role of blacks in collegiate sport would seem to provide further evidence that sport is indeed an elevator to success. A closer look, however, reveals that the universities have been far more concerned with exploiting the athletic talent of the black community than with nurturing its academic potential. Affirmative action programs on behalf of minority college students are currently under attack across the nation. Yet affirmative action programs that give preferential treatment to athletes remain sacrosanct. The message this sends out is that America's colleges and universities are more concerned with producing winning teams than with seeking out and educating future black lawyers, doctors, and corporate executives. (104–5)

Obviously, there have been many individuals who have utilized sport as a means to achieve upward mobility, but far more "chase the dream" far too hard and long. What makes the upward mobility myth particularly harmful is that it appears to be most deeply rooted in the black community. Unfortunately, it is the black athlete that our nation's athletic/educational enterprise fails most miserably. "Of black high school athletes, 51% believe they can reach the promised land of the NBA, NFL, or Major League Baseball. In reality, only 1 in 10,000 will. Pursuing the dream, 25% leave school functionally illiterate. Of black college athletes who play football and basketball, 44% believe they will make the pros. Only 3% will. African-American football and basketball players graduate at half the rate of white football and basketball players" (Lapchick 1996, 72).

Despite the widespread illusion of sports as a vehicle for upward mobility, the reality is that those who benefit most from the labors of athletes are the corporations and businesspersons who own the teams. At season's end, when these individuals—almost exclusively white businessmen—return home, a large number of athletes end up as casualties of the system. While the sports establishment dangles illusions of fame, fortune, and upward mobility before millions of star-struck youth, a large percentage being black, only a handful realize the dream because sport is not about opportunities for upward mobility—it is about business; it is about making money. In short, "the same system that promotes that 'opportunity' is endless for all—in particular African American male student-athletes— does not even graduate and/or hire diverse individuals within the organization of sport" (Harrison 2000, 37).

Some argue that organized sport has actually lagged behind other American institutions in promoting upward mobility of blacks into positions of leadership and influence. Michael Lomax, assistant professor of sports management at the University of Georgia, writes, "In the three decades since the passage of the 1965 Voting Rights Act, the number of African American elected officials increased dramatically, from barely 100 to over 8,000. The number of African American mayors jumped, from virtually zero in 1965 to more than 400. African Americans have been well represented in presidential cabinets, on school boards and in city councils, and in statehouses across America. Yet, this kind of upward mobility in middle- and upper-management positions in college and professional sport has not occurred" (Lomax 2000, 22).

It is far more likely that those who use sport to better their lot in life do so not because sport is any better vehicle to achieve life-long success than say, business or the arts, but rather because they are good people—determined, talented, and perceptive enough to realize that athletics is simply a means to an end. A determined and talented youngster will find a way to succeed whether through athletics or some other field. Such individuals will apply the same work ethic and positive character traits to whatever occupation they pursue. While sports can channel an individual's energy toward a specific goal or career, so do many other disciplines. Good, smart, and determined people will achieve long-term success because they are good, smart, and determined people, not necessarily because sports instilled these character traits in them. In short, the portrayal of sports as a particularly effective vehicle through which to achieve upward mobility is exaggerated.

The Politically Neutered Athlete

In Jackie Robinson's day, blacks were barred from many institutions and establishments. Under such circumstances, competing in athletics with whites was significant. But are sports responsible for significant social advancements in areas that really matter today? Hardly. The notion that current athletes are on the vanguard in pushing for meaningful social change is highly questionable. The modern-day athlete seems far more concerned about securing his or her next big contract than influencing any meaningful social change. While the claim that sports opens doors for social change and advancement may have rung true in the 1950s, it rings hollow today.

John Hoberman, author of *Darwin's Athletes: How Sport Has Damaged Black America and Preserved the Myth of Race*, provided a vivid analysis of the dynamics of athlete involvement in difficult social change in an article titled "The Price of Black Dominance":

> To be sure, what black athletic heroes such as Joe Louis and Jesse Owens did for African-American morale during the Jim Crow era should never be underestimated. But the social value of such performances during the subsequent era of integration has frequently been overestimated, and especially regarding the black stars of the 1990's. . . . There are many black athletes, for example, who could have bailed out the NAACP when it faced bankruptcy a few years ago. The fact that not one of them responded to this nationally publicized financial emergency is one index of the decline of the black athlete as a significant social actor on the stage of American race relations.
>
> So which social or political roles are appropriate for the black athletic stars of the 1990's and beyond? Where are the barriers they might breach on behalf of racial progress? Who are the inheritors of Joe Louis and Jackie Robinson and Muhammad Ali? The absence of such figures is

one result of the commercialization of the black athlete over the past generation. Whereas Jackie Robinson faced a society that did not want him, fifty years later Michael Jordan confronted an advertising market that could not get enough of him. His apolitical status came to be taken for granted as the entirely sensible price of a commercial operation that netted over $50,000,000 a year on the basis of his crossover appeal. His domestication for white audiences was definitively certified by a film in which he engaged in comical colloquies with familiar cartoon characters. As the late Arthur Ashe once pointed out, "advertisers want somebody who's politically neutered." (Hoberman 2000, 53)

Ashe could not have been more correct. And Michael Jordan could not have provided a better example of today's politically neutered athlete when he was pressed to endorse Harvey Gantt, a black candidate running against the ultra-conservative Jesse Helms for a U.S. Senate seat in North Carolina in 1996. Despite rather intense public pressure, Jordan, a native North Carolinian, chose not to endorse Gantt in the racially charged, closely contested race, allegedly explaining his decision by pointing out that "Republicans buy Nikes too." Somehow, it would be hard to imagine the likes of Jackie Robinson, John Carlos, Tommie Smith, or Jack Johnson being unwilling to utilize their visibility and stature in the black community to take a personal stand in so important a matter.

The day following his team's loss to the Philadelphia '76ers in the seventh game of the NBA Eastern Conference semi-finals, the Toronto Raptors' star Vince Carter was criticized for attending his college graduation ceremony at the University of North Carolina the morning of the game. In a column in the *New York Times*, Jere Longman offered the incident as a particularly telling example of the "politically neutered" athlete and the hypocrisy surrounding the sports as a vehicle for educational advancement, independence, and upward mobility. "In truth, amateur and professional leagues want their players pliant and obedient, not particularly well educated and free thinking. Why do you think Michael Jordan was so popular? Sure, he was great, but just as important, he did not offend, as he was more beholden to his corporate sponsors than to any convictions. We want our athletes smart and articulate, but unwilling to offer contentious opinion. Or to take independent actions, such as attending graduation the day of a game" (Longman 2001).

Athletics to Maintain the Status Quo

Closely related to the notion of sport as a vehicle for upward mobility is the claim that sport has been effective in influencing broad, positive social change. When a city, state, or our country rallies around a group of racially diverse athletes working together in pursuit of a common goal, it would seem that there would be a carry-over of good will and trust off the fields of play. The result would be increased opportunity and advancement for blacks and other minority groups in education, medicine, and business. There is, however, simply no proof of such a carry-over effect, particularly when the athletic establishment's record regarding upward mobility for minorities is so dismal. If there were any segment of the business community where meaningful minority advancement into major ownership and decision-making positions would exist, it would be within the field of athletics itself. Unfortunately, the claim that sports is a major engine of broad social change and continues to have a significant influence in opening doors of opportunity for blacks in corporate America's boardrooms and executive suites is grossly overstated. Athletics' influence on the upward mobility of blacks and other minorities and its impact as an agent of meaningful social change are minimal at best.

Certainly, there are examples of players on racially diverse teams working side-by-side toward common goals. Athletics' influence in eliciting meaningful, long-lasting change in the area of civil rights, however, is not as strong as we would like to, or have been led to, believe. The fact is, the athletic culture is very conservative, presenting the views and values of the establishment. There is ample evidence that America's elite has used athletics as a tool to reinforce class distinctions and maintain the status quo by thwarting, rather than promoting, meaningful social change. Throughout the history of sport in America, exclusion, not inclusion, was usually the motive for the creation of various sporting clubs, leagues, and organizations.

> Even before the Civil War, baseball leagues and athletic clubs built high walls of class and ethnic discrimination; a man's status as an accomplished sportsman—in yachting or tennis, for instance—often was achieved within rigidly limited social situations. . . . For many athletic-club members, the movement's mission was to promote not just health but social status. Besides building new facilities and hiring instructors in fencing, swimming, handball, gymnastics, boxing, even baseball and football, the clubs' larger goal was to promote sports for the elite, to employ athletics as a marker of class distinction. (Gorn and Goldstein 1993, 112, 133)

As discussed in the Introduction, American school sport was modeled on school athletics in Britain. To the British, the rough-and-tumble nature of sport, coupled with moral principles such as teamwork, self-sacrifice, obedience, and loyalty that it instilled, offered a means of "controlling" the boys and preparing them for a life of service and leadership. "Under the guidance of athletics, the public schools provided the training necessary for the British gentleman to go out and fulfill his God given right to govern the inferior races in the far-flung corners of the British Empire. . . . Through sports, the boys would develop character, which would later be used in imperialist domination" (Miracle and Rees 1994, 35).

Similar interests fueled America's industrial leaders' influential support of the incorporation of athletics into the American school system. "Just as in the English public schools, the rough and unorganized recreational activities of the students became institutionalized and were used by American school authorities to control the boys. Under the guise of building character, athletics, particularly team games, became compulsory for all students" (Miracle and Rees 1994, 40). In justifying organized sport, there has always existed an undercurrent of control and a desire on the part of the society's elite to maintain the cultural status quo. Indeed, the primary character-building benefits of sport—obedience, self-control, self-sacrifice, teamwork, discipline, loyalty, and so forth—all suggest values that discourage, rather than promote, independent thinking. Such a philosophical basis hardly suggests an environment within which change could easily occur, particularly difficult social change.

In fact, the evolution of the distinction between amateur and professional athletics owes far more to maintaining class distinctions and preserving the power of the society's elite than to anything to do with receiving pay for play. In *Sports and Freedom: The Rise of Big-Time College Sports*, Ronald A. Smith writes,

> Amateurism in sport was a nineteenth-century upper-class concept created by the English. It was an elitist attitude contrived to keep the lower classes from mixing with their social superiors on the athletic field. It was an undemocratic, non-egalitarian concept designed to make amateurism appear to be superior to professionalism. It ran counter to the social and political forces of the nineteenth century, calling for freedom of opportunity regardless of class position. It was, therefore, a reactionary policy to preserve for the traditional power and social elite control over an important area of upper-class life—sporting activity. (Smith 1988, 162)

Athletics came into prominence in America in a time much different than today. Women had yet to earn the right to vote and blacks had virtually no rights. America was run by wealthy white males and, as is the case of any group in power, their primary interest was to maintain their grip on society's privilege. Not only did America's great industrialists of the late nineteenth and early twentieth centuries see athletics as a way to develop loyal and submissive workers to man their factories, they also saw athletics as a way to spread what they saw as true "American values." In short, the values of sport reflected those of the elite.

Wholesome athletics certainly were part of a social control movement designed to channel people, especially working-class immigrants
and youth, into safe activities. By the end of the [nineteenth] century,
many reformers believed that sports could be a socially stabilizing force
that would help Americanize foreigners, pacify angry workers, clear the
streets of delinquents, and stem the tide of radicalism. Sports could
deflect tension away from an oppressive social structure and channel
energy into safe activities that taught the modern industrial values of
hard work, cooperation, and self-discipline, and thereby help secure
social order. (Gorn and Goldstein 1993, 104)

Using organized athletics to exert control and to maintain the
social status quo has continued throughout the history of sport in
America. The reaction of the athletic establishment to the widespread student unrest in the late 1960s and early 1970s, for example, illustrates how coaches and athletic administrators represented
and fought for what were considered "establishment" viewpoints.
Specifically, their response to student protests of the Vietnam War
and the efforts of black athletes to fight racism in sports, referred
to by the establishment as the "revolt" of the black athlete, is hardly
an example of the athletic establishment promoting progressive
social thought. Athletes who displayed any interest in or spoke out
against the war or the discrimination of the black athlete were
branded "rebels" or "uncoachable" and were often dismissed from
teams. Athletes were simply not permitted to speak out against the
status quo, question authority, grow a beard, or have long hair. Athletes were expected to be clean-cut and model their behavior
according to the dictates of the conservative athletic establishment; hardly an environment for encouraging social awareness in
the individual or an example of a progressive social organization
for society to emulate.

In an excellent historical account of college football, entitled College Football: History, Spectacle, Controversy, John Sayle Watterson notes
the NCAA's reaction to a series of black rebellions that broke out
on various campuses in 1968, many of which involved athletes in

football. "After a year of threats and boycotts by African-American players, the NCAA approved a resolution at its convention in January 1969, allowing its coaches and athletic directors to cancel the athletic scholarships of players who refused to obey rules and regulations set by the athletic department" (Watterson 2000, 321).

These examples demonstrate that the morality taught by the athletic establishment has been one that emphasizes tradition, strict discipline, blind respect for authority, and other conservative values. And there is little evidence to suggest that such attitudes and expectations have changed in any significant ways. One needs to look no further than the lack of blacks in meaningful leadership positions in management and ownership and the ongoing resistance to providing equal opportunity for women in athletics, particularly at the college level, for more evidence of this reality. Neil Isaacs's point in his 1978 book, *Jock Culture, U.S.A.*, holds true today, "that even in the sporting world, where blacks have had their most conspicuous success (outside of a few other specialized areas of show business, [and now the military (added by author)], the establishment has kept them out of the establishment" (Isaacs 1978, 91–92).

The issue of equal opportunity for women in sports provides more evidence of the prevailing attitude of resistance to change that permeates the athletic establishment. Close to thirty years have elapsed since the passage of Title IX in 1972, the federal law prohibiting sex discrimination by educational institutions receiving federal funds. Yet, the vast majority of colleges and universities still do not comply with the law. This should come as no surprise as the NCAA (long controlled by athletic directors and men's football and basketball coaches at the nation's major universities), with its formidable lobbying power, held up Title IX's application to college athletic departments for years, arguing primarily that enactment would cause undue financial hardship for university athletic departments. And it was not until 1991, ten years after becoming the governing body for women's athletics that the NCAA formally adopted gender equity as a basic principle of the organization. Today, women continue to lag behind men in every phase of athletic opportunity, receiving fewer scholarships, fewer coaching and administrative opportunities, fewer participation opportunities, and smaller operating budgets. Again, rather than promoting positive social change, the athletic establishment has resisted such change, in many cases vigorously.

Apologists cite the thousands of athletes who volunteer to speak to, and work with, youth, particularly disadvantaged youth as examples of influencing positive social change. Unquestionably, athletes, due to their high visibility, can have a positive impact in this regard. The key to having a positive impact on youth, however, is not necessarily who is involved, but rather the *commitment* of who is involved. For example, over time, a committed college student, whether a musician, artist, computer geek, or fraternity or sorority member, will have a far greater impact on a young person than cursory involvement of a star athlete. While a junior high or high school student might take notice of a well-known athlete more quickly than an unknown college student, what will eventually make a difference in that child's life is having someone interested in, and involved with, his or her life on an ongoing basis. Ultimately, the child does not care whether it is an athlete or a computer geek, as long as that someone is genuinely interested in, and committed to, making a difference in that child's life. This is not to suggest that athletes should not get involved, but rather that we should let go of the notion that athletes are more effective in influencing social change and more equipped than others at making a difference in the lives of youth.

While there is the very visible example of change in the form of athletes on the courts and fields, off them, sport is far from a model for such change in the more meaningful arenas of management, coaching, and ownership. Progress in these areas has been far too slow and resistance to change has been far too consistent to cast sport as a greater vehicle through which to achieve positive social change than any other institution or industry. In short, the claim that sport in America serves as a powerful vehicle for positive social change is largely an illusion.

Athletics and Educational Equality?

Education is seen as a basic right in America. This belief is a fundamental American value arising from the notion that education is the key to opportunity and the ability to achieve equality. It was for this reason that James Meredith demanded to be accepted for enrollment at the University of Mississippi. It was why, in 1957, nine young black children risked their lives to gain access to previously all-white schools in Little Rock, Arkansas. And, it was why Thurgood Marshall, when chief counsel for the NAACP, concentrated so heavily on civil rights cases that dealt with education. In America, the notion that access to equal educational opportunity is a precursor to future social and financial opportunity, advancement, and equality is strong. Equally as strong is the widely accepted belief that athletics is our educational system's most-effective vehicle through which to provide the disadvantaged— blacks in particular—educational opportunities which later translate into upward mobility and social equality.

Unfortunately, this is simply another myth perpetuated by the athletic establishment to help justify its uncomfortable relationship with the academic community. While athletic scholarships provide opportunities for many blacks who otherwise could not afford to attend college, this supposed concern over the educational well-being of these student-athletes is mired in hypocrisy. Despite the romanticized notions regarding athletics as a vehicle for social advancement, the only equality of opportunity that exists in sports is the equal opportunity to help a school or pro team win games and generate revenue. The athletic establishment is not interested in long-term educational development and equality of opportunity, but rather short-term wins and revenue projections. Despite the athletic community's propaganda to the contrary, the increased number of blacks on predominantly white campuses is more a product of an institution's desire to build winning sports programs than a sincere push for educational opportunity and subsequent upward mobility.

For example, after Sam Cunningham scored three touchdowns to help the University of Southern California rout the University of Alabama football team, Paul "Bear" Bryant reportedly walked off the field muttering, "He just did more for integration in the South in sixty minutes than Martin Luther King did in twenty years." The crowd, after witnessing Cunningham's dominant performance, allegedly besieged the Alabama coaches with cries of, "Get us one! Get us one!" Bryant did. And, despite his openly racist attitude, four years after losing to a team with five black starters (Texas Western) in the 1966 NCAA Championship game, Adolph Rupp brought his first black basketball player to the University of Kentucky (Lapchick 1991). The integration of these college rosters had nothing to do with education or social advancement, but everything to do with winning.

The issue of the education of black student-athletes cannot and should not be viewed as a separate issue than that of the education of blacks in general. The question of whether the tremendous amount of attention and resources spent upon black student-athletes as a means of integrating predominantly white college campuses is flawed, particularly if the substance of that education is based upon the desire to establish and maintain athletic eligibility rather than earning a meaningful degree (Bilberry 2000). As Nathan McCall suggested, such an approach simply reinforces the myth that the road to educational and economic equality for blacks rests on the football fields and basketball courts rather than in the English class and the chemistry lab. If there is a serious concern on the part of education leaders and society to educate young blacks, those resources and attention would be better spent on black students who demonstrate academic, rather than simply athletic, potential.

In my book entitled *Sports in School: The Future of an Institution*, I asked two recently graduated African American Division I-A football players to each contribute a chapter regarding the interplay among race, athletics, and education. Both suggested that the notion of educational opportunity through athletics was more myth than reality, noting that providing a black youngster a scholarship does not, of itself, constitute a meaningful educational opportunity. Their concern related to the issue of expectations. Specifically, both argued that the "educational opportunity" afforded through an athletic scholarship is an illusion if what is expected of black athletes academically is lower than what is expected of white athletes and other students generally.

> "The most pressing issue regarding race in athletic programs conducted within our country's educational systems has nothing to do with anything that occurs on the fields of play," wrote Darren Bilberry. "Rather, it is the myth that athletics has been used to provide black youth with educational opportunity. Ironically, the greatest force working against student-athletes being able to transform athletic achievement into educational advancement are the low expectations and resultant behavior of the very people who promote athletics as a provider of meaningful educational opportunity for thousands of African Americans—coaches and other members of the athletic and educational establishment.
>
> Black student-athletes are routinely admitted to colleges with lower academic credentials than the general student body. While most universities have special admissions criteria through which students who do not meet regular admissions standards can be admitted, it is no secret that at most schools that sponsor major college athletics, a disproportionately large number of those "special admits" are black student-athletes in the high visibility sports of football and basketball. (Gerdy 2000)

After outlining the harsh realities of trying to be taken seriously as a student at Vanderbilt University, Derrick Gragg wrote:

While the purpose of this essay is not to dwell upon these well-documented transgressions, they must be mentioned because they have a very direct effect upon the issue of the integration of the black student-athlete into the mainstream high school or college community and, later, into mainstream society. These acts of exploitation, whether they be academic, ethical, or having to do with lower expectations or the perpetuation of racial stereotypes, all seem to occur more often to black student-athletes than white. These perceptions and abuses serve not to integrate, but to further isolate the black student-athlete, not only from the general student body, but from other student-athletes as well. Thus, the claim that athletics is an effective way in which to promote the integration of blacks into the educational or societal mainstream is suspect at best. (Gragg 2000)

In short, black athletes are expected to fail academically. And, in large part, as a result of those expectations, they often do.

An Affair with a Succubus

In theory, an athletic scholarship is an educational opportunity which, if utilized, can lead to upward social mobility. Reality suggests, however, that athletic scholarships are just that—an opportunity to play athletics, created as a means of paying athletes to perform athletically in a way that was reasonably acceptable to the academic community. While many athletes have taken that scholarship and turned it into real educational opportunity, the question is, how many of those would have succeeded academically without an athletic scholarship? It is more likely that those who are motivated would succeed academically without athletics, not because of athletics, as we continually are led to believe.

Simply put, the notion of athletics as a vehicle for upward mobility—that achieving athletic success will automatically translate into success later in life and career—is overblown. As Robert Lipsyte suggested, athletes are our society's gladiators. Their societal value lasts only as long as they can perform superhuman physical feats for our entertainment.

To think that businesses are going to hire athletes in a meaningful capacity simply because they were a good athlete is a myth. Businesspersons run companies to make money. They are not in the business of hiring people who are commonly perceived as having few skills outside of scoring touchdowns or dunking basketballs. When you choose sides for a pick-up basketball game, are you going to choose the 6'8" power forward who can play or the 5'10" fat kid who spends all of his time in the library? You pick the 6'8" guy who can play because you want to win. With athletes being perceived as nothing more than gladiators, in the job market, they are the 5'8" fat kid competing against a lot of 6'8" power forwards who can play. Businesspersons are in a high-stakes game, and they want to win too.

The stereotype of the athlete as a dumb jock or, more precisely, that success on the fields of play, with its requirement of great physical strength, somehow equates to being less intellectually accomplished, has plagued black athletes in particular.

> Black intellectuals from W. E. B. DuBois to Harry Edwards have warned that the black community's historical romance with athleticism is like an affair with a succubus. "Far from being a positive force in the development of the black masses," Edwards has written, "integrated big-time sport in its present form is perhaps a negative influence." Edwards has campaigned over many years with eloquence and anger that big-time sports is a "form of cultural exhibitionism" with black athletes acting as minstrel actors who had shuffled from the "cotton fields to the playing fields" for the entertainment value of white America. Sports, he asserts, exerts a Novocain effect on the "black masses" and provided the black fan with the illusion of spiritual reinforcement in his own life struggles. "The only difference between a black man shining shoes in the ghetto and the champion black sprinter," Edwards has charged, "is that the shoe shine man is a nigger, while the sprinter is a fast nigger." Although written in the seventies, when there were far fewer opportunities for blacks outside sports, no one should be fooled into thinking that the opportunity gap has disappeared entirely. Even today, despite a remarkable surge in the salaries of all athletes, there remains a plantation-like imbalance between the domination of blacks on the field and their dearth in the

executive suite. As a consequence, says the Harvard scholar Henry Louis
Gates Jr., black pride has become more or less "tethered to the stereotype of innate physical superiority." (Entine 2000, 334–35)

The notion of sport as a vehicle for upward mobility and opportunity is a complex one, encompassing issues of race, education,
and class. And while there have been many who have, through athletics, improved their standing in life, the notion that sport is an
institution that vigorously promotes equality, social justice and
advancement, and upward mobility is largely an illusion. The athletic culture is extremely conservative, authoritarian, homogeneous
in the currency of ideas and thought. The old coaching adage, "If
you are not with us, you are against us," still holds sway in the
locker rooms and front-office suites. And, if you don't look like us,
well, you best stay on the field where you belong. The athletic culture is the culture of the elite, of conformity, of the way its always
been done, of the establishment, where difference is mocked and
free thought frowned upon or squashed outright. As a result, athletes are looked upon as dumb jocks and gladiators, with no long-
term value to society once their ability to thrill and entertain on
the playing field is gone.

So while the fiftieth anniversary of Jackie Robinson's breaking
of the color barrier in baseball was held up by the athletic establishment as a shining example of the significant role it played in
helping blacks, women, and other minority groups break free of
the horrible grip of discrimination, in far too many ways, organized athletics remains shackled to its elitist and discriminatory
past. It is time for the athletic community's self-congratulatory
rhetoric to give way to recognition of current reality. For too long,
the athletic establishment has received a free pass on the issue of
discrimination in the areas of the most important and long-term
consequence simply because what the public knows of athletics
is what it sees on the fields and courts of play. Meanwhile, the

imbalance between real opportunity on the courts and fields of play and our nation's corporate boardrooms remains. The first step in making athletics an institution that fully embraces social justice and through which upward mobility can truly be realized for more than a few must be to recognize the fact that organized athletic programs in America were created in large part for two reasons: to promote sports for the elite and as a way to secure social order and standing over the underclass. Rather than continuing to blindly accept, and thus perpetuate, the myth that organized athletics is a colorblind meritocracy, we must acknowledge the depth of athletics' discriminatory past and begin to move forward to a different reality.

"GET OVER IT!"

As we enter a new millennium, many of our American institutions are being scrutinized to determine their societal relevance in the next century. From our schools to our welfare system, old ideas, institutions, and philosophies are being examined, revised, or discarded, replaced by new ones more acceptable to the age with the fundamental standard of evaluation being utility. Do these institutions continue to serve the public in relevant and timely ways?

Organized sport is an important American cultural institution. As such, we as individuals and, collectively, as a society, must critically assess its impact on our culture. If it is deemed to have an overwhelmingly positive impact on our society we should invest more heavily in sport. But if many of these supposed positive benefits are disproved, as individuals and as a society, we would be well-served to reconsider that investment.

Again, I would like to be clear. I love sports. I love playing them. I love watching them. I believe they play an important role in our lives. I do not advocate the elimination of organized sport in America. This is neither wise nor realistic. It is, however, critical that we honestly evaluate its impact on our culture and, if appropriate, restructure our societal investment in organized athletics accordingly.

The issue, then, is balance and perspective, not elimination. Sport's potential to contribute to our society in a positive manner is enormous. If kept in the proper perspective, sport provides compelling entertainment, contributes to a healthful lifestyle, and builds character in participants. The problem, however, is that as a society we have lost perspective regarding the role that organized athletics should play in our culture. Organized sport in America has simply become too big, too important, with too much money, ego, and media attention attached to it. As a result, it has grown to a point where it demands too much of our time, money, and emotion. In short, sports are not nearly as important as we have come to believe.

Albert Einstein said, "The significant problems we face cannot be solved at the same level of thinking we were at when we created them." No statement could ring more true as it applies to the challenge we face in restructuring our societal investment in sport. Changing sports' cultural impact will require a radical change in thinking regarding its purpose and structure. Specifically, we must rethink the role of organized sport on a personal level and on a public-policy level. While change of any sort, particularly societal change of this magnitude, is difficult, the consequences of continuing to ignore sports' negative cultural impact are too great. To that end, the following suggestions are offered as a means of helping us to refocus our priorities relating to the role of organized sport in our culture. They are offered in the hope that they can be used to fulfill organized athletics' tremendous potential to impact our society in positive, meaningful, and timely ways.

If It Is to Be, It Is Up to Me

It is easy to succumb to the notion that there is nothing that can be done to stem sports' seemingly insurmountable tide of growth and influence. In this case, however, that assumption is not true. You can do something. Not only can you do something, but the effects of your actions can be direct, immediate, and life changing.

To start, turn off the television. Stop watching. Instead, read, learn to play a musical instrument, or study a foreign language. Spend more time with your children or spouse. Exercise. Do anything but watch. Or, at least, watch much less.

You can stop attending games. Attend a concert or the theater instead. Rather than spending hundreds of dollars taking your family to a major-league ballpark, take them to a museum or a cultural festival. Travel. Stop buying sports memorabilia and sportswear. Dis-invest in sport to where it assumes a more-balanced role in your life. Such decisions are highly personal. The changes themselves will be very difficult. But kicking any addiction requires difficult personal decisions and behavioral changes. I am not suggesting a total disassociation from sports. You do not have to go "cold turkey" to make a meaningful change in your life and the lives of your loved ones. I am simply suggesting that obsessive sports-related behavior can be modified to allow the development of other interests and relationships resulting in a fuller, more balanced life experience.

You also have the ability to make a profound impact beyond yourself and your immediate family. For example, rather than simply shaking your head when a youth league coach yells at a ten-year-old for dropping a fly ball, let the coach know that such behavior is inappropriate. Challenge the coach who doesn't allow the least-talented player on the team to play for fear of losing a pee-wee soccer game. Become a youth coach or get involved in your local youth sport board where you can work more directly to structure sports programs that meet the developmental and educational needs of the children who play them rather than the ego needs of the adults who supervise them. For example, spearhead an effort in your town to eliminate elite travel squads for ten-year-olds. Ten years old is too young for any travel team, let alone an elite one! Insist that the games be given back to the children.

And stop expecting athletes to be positive role models. Whether they be family members, or members of the community, there are others more worthy of your children's attention. Undoubtedly, these people are more accessible than star athletes and, as a result, are more able to make a positive, long-lasting impact on your children. Athletes are merely people who are physically gifted, with little in their background or training that would prepare them for the awesome responsibility of being a major influence on any children but their own. Athletes owe us nothing more than an honest performance on the field or the court. It is not their responsibility to raise our children.

You can change your life. You must, however, choose to do so. Go to the scorers' table and check out of the sports obsession game. Check yourself into a different game, one that offers more meaningful benefits of more lasting significance.

This highly personal approach to sports reform applies to another problem area that has received scant attention in this manuscript—gambling. Upon finishing the first draft of this book, a friend whom I had asked to read it could not believe that a book about the destructive influence of sport in our culture barely mentioned the "evils" of sports gambling. "How can this be considered a thorough treatment of the issue of sports in our culture without addressing the issue of sports gambling?" he asked.

Undoubtedly, gambling is a huge problem in sports. It is also a huge societal problem. And, yes, a gambling addiction can ruin a person's life. Other than declaring gambling illegal, there is little we can do about it. Making gambling illegal, for example, would simply drive all of the sports gambling underground. While the concern regarding the incredible amount of sports wagering in America is justified, the fact is, other than professional league and college officials' efforts to educate their players and referees regarding the pitfalls of becoming involved in gambling activities (for fear of point shaving or game fixing), there is little that can be done from a collective standpoint to address the problem.

Like watching an excessive amount of televised sports, or being hopelessly attached to your local pro team, gambling on sports events is a personal decision. If gambling represents some kind of flaw, it is a personal flaw, the failings of the individual rather than a systemic failure. People are going to gamble, whether on a state lottery, on slot machines in Las Vegas, or in the NCAA tournament pool at the office. If you are concerned about the negative consequences of sports gambling, don't do it. It is your choice. While my brief missive on gambling meets my friend's concern, I am certain that it falls far short of those concerned about the potential for gambling to ruin lives or damage the integrity of athletic contests. But no amount of hyperbole is going to change the reality; people are going to gamble on sports events. The issue is whether you allow it to negatively impact your life; that decision is yours and yours alone.

Giving Youth Sports Back to the Kids

It is no secret that there are significant problems with organized youth sports programs. Incidences of parents screaming at nine-year-old children over a missed basket or a misplayed fly ball are commonplace. Youth-league umpires are regularly abused and increasingly attacked. Brawls have erupted after youth-league soccer games. Obviously something is wrong.

What is wrong with youth sports is the adults. Youth sports programs are no longer about meeting the educational, developmental, and recreational needs of children but rather about satisfying ego needs of adults. Adults have imposed their values and priorities about sports upon their children's games, from the organization of player drafts to the imposition of structure, organization, and rules to a disproportionate emphasis placed on winning. This, despite the fact that children, more than anything else, want to play sports, not to win, but simply to have fun. It is the adults who are destroying youth sports. That being the case, it is time to give youth sports back to the children.

But how will our children manage without adults supervising their athletic activities? Quite well, thank you! Studies contrasting spontaneous youth play versus youth sport organized by adults indicate that children, if left to their own devices, will successfully organize, administer, and manage their own games. They will choose sides and mediate disputes. They will set their own rules. In some cases, those rules may change from game to game. But they will be rules that work for the children. Children will handicap their games to ensure they are evenly matched, interesting, and fun. Such organizational, mediation, and interpersonal skills are valuable characteristics that children are not permitted to develop when they are forced by adults to play the "adult," supposedly *right*, way.

A perfect example of the stark difference between "pick-up" and "organized" adult-run youth games is the typical situation where there is one very superior athlete in a baseball game. In the "organized" game, the adult coach will have that child pitch. The child proceeds to dominate the game, striking out most of the batters he or she faces, while the children in the field stand like statues waiting to field a ball that has virtually no chance of being hit to them. By the end of the game, many players have never handled the ball. If left to their own devices, the children in the "pick-up" game will agree amongst themselves that the dominant player either not pitch or pitch with his or her opposite arm. In basketball, the dominant player may be allowed only a limited number of shots or may be required to shoot with his or her "off" hand.

Children make adjustments in their games to ensure that the game will be interesting and fun, and thus, continue. Their purpose in getting together to play is, after all, to have fun. If the game is not fun, children will quit playing and, if enough quit, the game will end. That being the case, they must work to make the game interesting and enough fun so everyone will want to continue to play. Without adult-enforced structure, rules, and expectations, there is nothing holding the game together other than the children actually wanting to play it. And what holds the game together is being involved and having fun. In short, the game would not exist if it were not fun. In youth leagues organized by adults, the adult-imposed goal of winning replaces the goal of maximizing fun and participation.

Another significant difference between these two types of games is the way in which the outcome of the game is treated. In adult-organized games, the result of the contest is recorded as a win or a loss, regardless of the closeness of the game or the performances of the individuals involved. In the pick-up game, while the result may be discussed on the walk home, it is usually considered insignificant and quickly forgotten as the children focus more on the actions of the individuals and the fun they had. Clearly, the children have their priorities straight regarding sports as it is the process (participation and having fun) rather than the end result that is most important.

How do we restructure youth sports programs to give the games back to the children? "De-organize" them. Children should not be permitted to participate in structured youth sports programs as we currently know them until they reach the age of thirteen. Prior to that, they should participate only in "de-organized" youth sports activities. In such "de-organized" activities, no more than 25 percent of the playtime should be devoted to fundamental skill instruction. The remaining time should be turned over to the kids for them to play pick-up games . . . with no parental or adult involvement! Other than a safety official, adults should not be permitted to coach, instruct, or even watch. The real joy of youth sports comes from playing with friends, far from critiquing and criticizing adults.

Leave the kids alone! Let them pick their own teams, make their own rules, and mediate their own disputes. The only rule that they must abide by is that everyone plays.

In other words, to make youth sports "about the kids," athletic activities should resemble "pick-up" games. In my childhood, we organized, scheduled, administered, and refereed our own games. We would meet at a designated time or simply go door to door to see who was interested in playing a game. For safety reasons, parents today are hesitant to allow their children to roam the neighborhood unsupervised, searching for a basketball game. Under this proposal, children would be provided a safe playing environment, but would be allowed to manage their own games and, as a result, begin to develop those personal skills—organization, conflict resolution, leadership, management, and mediation—that make participation in athletics valuable. Other than specific playing skills and techniques, children learn very little from adult-organized athletics. While adults may cringe at denying children their "expert" coaching advice, the fact is, children's interpersonal skills will develop more if they are left to manage their own games. Without adult supervision, the games will be closer, more interesting and, most important, more fun. It is time to get adults out of youth sports. It is time to let the kids have their games back.

But the games must be returned to the players at all levels of play. For example, why do coaches, from pee-wee leagues to the college level, insist on calling every play and dictating how every minute of every practice is spent? Why not provide the opportunity for a high school or college quarterback to think for himself and exhibit leadership and decision-making skills by calling his own plays? After all, we claim that sports builds those skills. Or, what would be so detrimental in allowing a player to develop and implement a practice schedule or even be responsible for making travel arrangements for a road trip? Before full-time, paid coaches became a fixture in college athletics, students organized and administered all aspects of their programs without adult supervision. Today, other than actually playing in the game, adults perform virtually every task associated with youth, high school, and college athletics.

What are the consequences of the domination of adults over games allegedly designed for young people? There is evidence that athletic participation may not be developing the leadership skills we have long claimed that it does. Again, according to William G. Bowen and James J. Shulman, while those who play college sports feel that leadership is important in their lives and felt this way before college,

> Surprisingly, this greater inclination toward leadership is not reflected very clearly in any measure of actual leadership that we can identify. . . . Overall, College and Beyond (term used to describe students in their study) graduates who were athletes (and who went on to earn advanced degrees) seem slightly less likely than other C&B graduates to work in public affairs. Former athletes are no more likely than other C&B graduates to provide leadership in the marketplace via service as CEOs. . . . It is not clear what accounts for this disjunction between the subjective importance attached to leadership by athletes and the actual pattern of leadership that is displayed. Perhaps part of the explanation is as simple as the tendency for any group to believe certain "mantras." One such mantra is that athletics teaches leadership. Reiteration of such beliefs may outrun their translation into actual conduct. (Bowen and Shulman 2001, 197–98)

The fact is, if organized athletics is ever going to meet its promise of developing the leadership, organization, and decision-making skills of participants, parents, coaches, and administrators must place their egos on the shelf and give the children and young adults the freedom to exercise and develop those skills. Ultimately, what difference does it make whether a junior high school quarterback calls for a pass on a third and three situation when the coach would have preferred to call a draw play? Or, whether a basketball squad comes to a decision amongst themselves during a timeout to set up for a three-point shot rather than dumping the ball into the low post? We claim that sports is for the kids, yet they have absolutely no ownership of the activity because the adults are making every decision for them. It is no longer their game. We need to give it back to them.

The Preparation of Coaches and Administrators

Coaches and athletic administrators justify their involvement with young people on the basis that they are educators. The playing field or court, they say, is their classroom and the lessons taught there in discipline, teamwork, and sportsmanship are just as important as the lessons being taught in the lecture hall, the chemistry lab, or at home. Ironically, there are virtually no educational standards or criteria for becoming a coach; all one needs is a whistle. In the case of athletic administrators, while training programs exist in the form of bachelor's and master's degrees in sports administration, the focus of those programs is upon the business, marketing, and operational issues rather than on the educational issues and expectations relating to the job.

From the pee-wee to the major college level, the attitudes and behaviors of coaches have a direct impact on the personal, educational, and athletic development of the athlete. In the case of athletic administrators, while their impact may not be as direct, it is, nonetheless, profound, as they have tremendous influence over the goals and tone of the athletic programs they supervise. Given such influence, the issue of the preparation and continued professional development of those who coach and administer athletic programs is absolutely critical.

The environment within which sport activities occur has a tremendous impact on the athletic, personal, and educational development of youth. It is at the youth sport level that the future high school or college athlete is first introduced to organized sport and that direct parental involvement is greatest. The attitudes and expectations regarding organized athletics instilled in the ten-year-old are carried throughout a lifetime. It is the attitudes and actions of the adults and parents that most directly determines the quality of a child's youth sport experience.

Perhaps the single most-important factor in conducting youth sports programs that are beneficial and most important, fun, for children is the preparation and education of coaches. Unfortunately, the majority of America's youth coaches are people with no formal preparation in fitness training, child development, or first aid; their only coaching credentials are that they are parents, they like youth, or they have an interest in a particular sport. As mentioned previously, there can be significant negative implications when unprepared coaches are placed in such positions of influence. That being the case, the adoption and implementation of education programs using agreed-upon standards of coaching competencies is critical. Such standards have been developed through state and national youth sports organizations.

Further, such programs must also be developed for college coaches as they, too, justify their position on campus on the basis of their being educators. Specifically, there is a dire need for an increased emphasis on the academic preparation of coaches as well as the implementation of professional development programs that incorporate components that relate directly to the educational mission of the institution as well as to the academic and personal development of the student-athlete.

The issue of the education, preparation, and professional development does not apply solely to coaches. While knowledge of the management and fiscal intricacies of running an athletic department are important, athletic administrators' preparation must also foster an appreciation and understanding of the role of athletics within an educational setting. The institutions most responsible for such preparation are colleges and universities that offer degrees in athletic administration. That being the case, such degree programs must increase the emphasis placed on curricular elements that provide students with a better understanding of the relationship of athletic programs to the educational process as well as of the goals and mission of the educational institutions of which they are a part. Such a shift in focus of the preparation of future athletic administrators will serve educational institutions well as they search for ways to more fully integrate athletic programs into the educational community.

In short, with such a strong influence over the lives of young athletes and the programs in which they participate and with such a tremendous potential to have an impact on the goals and mission of the educational institutions of which they are a part, the preparation and professional development of coaches and athletic administrators is of utmost importance.

Establish Minimum-Age Limits for Professional Sports

Our nation's child labor laws are designed to protect children from being exploited for economic gain. Just as it is unlawful and abusive to force a twelve-year-old to work in a paper mill, so, too, is it to allow a child to risk significant, lifelong damage to their health to train for professional athletics or for an Olympic medal. There is no difference between an unscrupulous factory or shop owner illegally employing children in unsafe work conditions and a coach, an athletic official, or even a parent exposing adolescent athletes to physical harm. In both cases, the child is being exploited by adults for economic gain.

What transpires in the name of Olympic Gold in the sports of gymnastics and figure skating, for example, is child abuse. Adults justify the intense athletic training of a ten-year-old as simply allowing the youngster to fulfill his or her dream of Olympic stardom. This rationalization begs the question of whose dream it really is. Is it the child's? Or, is the quest for Olympic Gold, and the fame and fortune that follows, far more important to the coach or the parents? It is not unreasonable to raise such questions, because there is plenty of evidence to suggest that, from pee-wee league to the professionals, organized athletics is not about the dreams, needs, and desires of the athletes, but rather, money, entertainment, and the egos of adults.

Critics will claim that it is unconstitutional to deny someone the right to earn a living, even if that person is fifteen years old. The right does not apply, however, if the work is unsafe. Further, those who are particularly naive may even claim that training for an elite career in athletics is not "work", but fun. That, of course, is foolish. Playing a pick-up basketball game is fun. Training for an NBA career is work. Pushing and punishing your body for six to eight hours a day whether on an assembly line or in a weight room is dangerous work. If you do not believe that intense athletic training, particularly in the case of young bodies that are still maturing, is not dangerous, ask the gymnast whose doctor found twenty-two stress fractures that apparently had not been treated when they occurred or the hundreds of ice skaters and gymnasts who develop anorexia and bulimia, all in the name of Olympic Gold.

Professional leagues or the Olympic movement would suffer minimal damage if the respective governing bodies imposed a minimum age limit for participation of eighteen. The result would simply be that "new" stars would break onto the scene a few years later and, it is hoped, far wiser and more mature. Sports governing agencies would adjust to this change accordingly. For example, gymnasts are thought to be through with their careers by the age of twenty-two because the sport has been transformed to where skills that can only be performed by pre-pubescent bodies are rewarded. The International Gymnastics Federation can just as easily mandate changes in judging to reward skill, experience, and grace rather than the ability to launch through the air like a spinning missile.

The fact is, an unhealthful work environment is an unhealthful work environment and child abuse is child abuse whether it occurs in a factory or a gymnasium. It is time that we recognize the unhealthful and often abusive training practices that children are subject to, all in the name of athletic fame and riches.

Just Get over It!

In the preceding pages, I have drawn many examples from professional sports of what is wrong with organized sports in America. Professional sports are an easy target in this regard. When asked to pinpoint where organized sports has gone "most wrong," is most "out of control," or perpetuates "warped values," most Americans would cite the excesses of the pros. Indeed, professional players, owners, and organizations provide an endless stream of examples of the negatives of organized sports.

If so much is wrong with professional sports in America, why then, in my prescriptions for reform, have I only cited a need to establish a minimum age for professional participation? Shouldn't I be prescribing a long, detailed laundry list to address issues such as astronomical salaries, franchises moving from city to city, exorbitant ticket prices, and the fact that having a criminal record means nothing to a pro team if the athlete can help win games? Absolutely not!

The fact is, professional sports are not the problem and do not need to change. Rather, we are the problem and we need to change. Specifically, our attitudes and expectations regarding professional sports and the athletes who play them must change.

Professional sports are exactly what they are—professional. They are the purest and most honest of all sports. Professional sports are a business with a bottom line of winning, providing entertainment, and making money. That is it. They are nothing more; nothing less. And it is about time that we accept them exactly for what they are and stop trying to attach values and expectations regarding team loyalty to a city or athletes' role-model status and that high achievement in professional athletics represents something more profound and valuable than winning a Nobel Prize.

Perhaps the following analogy might help to clarify this point. I knew a girl in college. Let's call her Ramona. I fell head over heels in love with Ramona. She was everything I envisioned that a woman should be. Unfortunately, Ramona knew that my love for her was blind and that I would do anything she asked and would accept anything she did. She ran all over me. In short, Ramona was trouble with a capital "T." Eventually, certainly far longer than one with any good sense (hey, love makes you do some strange things), I realized that she wasn't at all as I had imagined that she ought to be. While disappointed in discovering that the real Ramona was no good for me, I had to place my emotions in check and back off the relationship. It was time for Ramona and me to "just be friends." It hurt. But I eventually got over it.

Our cultural problem relating to professional sports and a major cause of our All-American addiction is the fact that we continually project onto professional athletes and organizations, ideals, values, and expectations that meet our individual needs. Should athletes be role models, and should professional organizations be unfailingly loyal to the city in which they reside? In an ideal world, yes. Should professional sports mean more than simply winning and generating a profit? Certainly. Do many professional athletes conduct themselves with dignity and class, and are some organizations loyal and responsible corporate citizens? Absolutely. But should we, the average fan, *expect* such behavior and commitment from professional athletes and organizations? Absolutely not! It is foolhardy. The only thing more foolhardy is to become upset or disappointed when athletes or owners do not meet our lofty expectations. The fact is, the only thing pro athletes owe us is to give their maximum on-the-field performance.

Like my love affair with Ramona, we have got to get over our love affair with professional sports.

Similarly, we must get over our infatuation with college sports, but for another reason. College sports is a game played by kids. We should enjoy the games and support our favorite school, but at the same time, we should always remember that college sports are played by kids who, after the game, must return to class, or at least they *should* be returning to class.

While on one level, we need to disinvest in college sports, on another level, what transpires in college athletics is extremely important. Herein lies the key distinction between college sports and professional sports. If we expect any leadership, vision, or initiative to come from professional sports in regards to reestablishing a healthful, well-balanced, common-sense perspective regarding the role sports should play in our culture, we are whistling in the wind. Reform of our cultural consensus regarding the appropriate role of organized athletics will not come from the professional ranks. Regardless of how much we may wish for or hope for leadership from professional sports in this regard, the fact is, they have no compelling reason to provide any. All the "players" in the professional sports equation—from the television networks, to the leagues, to the advertisers and the corporate sponsors—are interested in only one thing: making money by selling a product, which is accomplished by generating big television ratings. For proof, look no further than the short-lived Extreme Football League, a joint venture between the WWF's Vince McMahon and NBC, created for the sole purpose of attracting the very desirable demographic for corporate advertisers, males, eighteen to thirty-four years of age.

College sports, however, are intimately tied to our nation's educational system. An important component of higher education's mission is to provide moral, educational, and cultural leadership in addressing the societal issues of the day. For this reason, unlike professional sports, it is entirely appropriate to expect our nation's colleges and universities to provide leadership in combating our All-American addiction. This is a subject that will be addressed more specifically in the following chapter.

The individual sports lifestyle changes articulated in this chapter are important because they could have an immediate and significant impact. The "de-organization" changes in youth sports are important because such programs represent an individual's first exposure to organized sports and, thus, are likely to leave impressions that last a lifetime.

The decision to "get over" our infatuation with professional sports is a highly personal one, but one which can yield immediate and significant results. You do not have to wait for a blue-ribbon commission or a task force to produce a report to initiate sports reform. You can develop your own reform plan and guarantee immediate results. While these changes can have a profound impact on our personal All-American addictions, the prescription with the greatest potential for a broad and long-lasting impact on our collective addiction rests in our educational system, the subject of the following chapter.

MIND OVER BODY
IN THE
INFORMATION AGE

> Instead of pouring new knowledge into people's heads, we need to help them grind a new set of eyeglasses so we can see the world in a new way.
>
> —J. S. Brown

American education has tacitly endorsed, and our society celebrates, a culture that accepts the notion that it is an educational institution's responsibility to provide the very best in facilities, coaching, and support so that elite athletes have every opportunity to develop their athletic abilities to the fullest. There is nothing inherently wrong with wanting to provide the resources and support to help an individual develop fully as an athlete. The problem, however, is that while this goal has become the primary purpose of the athlete's educational experience, the academic and personal development of the individual has become an afterthought. It is as if we have come to believe that if during a star athlete's years in school, he or she *happens* to get an education, it is a bonus. This, as opposed to a system that has as its fundamental expectation that a young person develop fully academically, intellectually, socially, and personally while he or she *happens* to play athletics. It is the athletic development that must be a pleasant byproduct of the educational process, not the other way

– 208 –

around. We simply can no longer tolerate a system that demands athletic excellence but accepts educational mediocrity, for no matter how small a group of students.

For example, if we believe in the health and character-building benefits of exercise and athletic participation, why is it that schools and universities are spending an increasing amount of money and resources on interscholastic and intercollegiate athletic programs, while the development of physical education, intramural, and well-ness programs remains a low priority? If the benefits of athletic participation are so great, shouldn't the opportunity to take advantage of them be available to all? Shouldn't participation in comprehensive physical education, intramural, and wellness programs, designed to develop an appreciation for the benefits of lifelong exercise and athletic participation, be required? Our schools and universities invest a tremendous amount of tax and education dollars on activities designed for a select few. Meanwhile, the lifelong health and fitness needs of the vast majority of students go largely unmet. In terms of public health and education, such an approach amounts to a very poor return on investment in organized athletics.

Given the critical role that education must play in meeting the many challenges facing our society, it is unconscionable that we continue to expend valuable resources, effort, and emotion on activities that do not supplement the goals and missions of our schools and universities in direct and meaningful ways. That being the case, serious consideration must be given to radically altering how athletics is utilized as a tool to advance America's health and education interests.

Take, for example, the sports our school systems teach and emphasize. Schools should emphasize sports that can be enjoyed for a lifetime, such as swimming, tennis, recreational basketball and soccer, aerobics, and jogging. It is ironic that our schools spend the most money on football, a sport that the vast majority of participants will never play again after they leave school. From a public

health standpoint, how can we continue to spend such a disproportionate amount of money and emotion on sports for an elite few,
sports that have as their primary purpose, to provide entertainment,
while the health and physical fitness needs of the majority of our
students go unmet?

If community and education leaders were committed to using
athletic participation as a tool to improve public health, school systems would be strengthening, rather than weakening, physical education requirements and would be appropriating increasingly scarce
public education dollars to programs that emphasize broad-based,
lifelong participation rather than elite football or basketball teams.
At the college level, athletic programs with budgets in excess of $50
million that provide athletic opportunities for less than 5 percent of
the student body would simply not exist. The health benefits associated with participation in a competitive athletic program can be
achieved by participating in recreational activities, ranging from
intramural teams, physical education classes, and individual sport
activities such as jogging or swimming, and at a far lesser expense.

How about Music?

There is also the larger question of athletics' effectiveness as an
educationally justified extracurricular activity. For example, a strong
case can be made that music programs yield a far greater return on
educational dollars invested than do elite athletic teams.

"Music programs?" critics will ask. "Playing the flute won't build
character like getting knocked down on the football field. And
nothing teaches teamwork better than sports."

To think that one can acquire traits such as perseverance, teamwork, communication skills, and discipline through athletic participation alone is woefully misguided. You do not need to get a bloody
nose to learn about perseverance. Mastering a musical instrument, for
example, takes an incredible amount of perseverance, discipline, and

hard work. Playing in a five-piece band requires the same teamwork skills necessary for participation on a basketball team. There is no difference between working together to achieve a desired sound than working together to win a ballgame. To play a song well requires the same commitment, cooperation, and discipline as executing a touchdown pass. While it takes more physical strength, conditioning, and agility to dunk a basketball, the traits necessary to be a successful athlete—discipline, hard work, perseverance, teamwork—are identical to those required to be a successful musician. In short, both music and athletics can contribute significantly to the "character" development of participants.

Music, however, offers something that highly competitive, organized sports do not—a direct link between participation and intellectual development. A growing body of evidence indicates that arts instruction can significantly strengthen students' academic performance.

For example, "Students in two Rhode Island elementary schools who were given an enriched, sequential, skill-building music program showed marked improvement in reading and math skills. Students in the enriched program who had started out behind the control group caught up to statistical equality in reading and pulled ahead in math" (Gardiner, Fox, Jeffrey, and Knowles 1996). A University of California (Irvine) study showed that after eight months of keyboard lessons, preschoolers showed a 46 percent boost in their spatial reasoning IQ (Rauscher, Shaw, Levine, Ky, and Wright 1994). Data from the National Education Longitudinal Study (NELS) of 1988 showed that music participants received more academic honors and awards than non-music students, and that the percentage of music participants receiving A's, A's/B's, and B's was higher than the percentage of nonparticipants receiving those grades (National Center for Educational Statistics 1990).

Coaches and athletic administrators, citing the large percentage of black athletes in their programs, often argue that athletics is more effective than any other extracurricular activity in positively influencing minority students. Simply because a high percentage of athletes in high school and college athletic programs are black does not mean that coaches and athletic administrators have cornered the market on influencing these students to achieve academically and socially. For example, a study of 811 high school students indicated that the proportion of minority students with a music teacher role model was significantly larger than for any other discipline. Thirty-six percent of these students identified music teachers as their role models, as opposed to 28 percent English teachers, 11 percent elementary teachers, 7 percent physical education/sports teachers, and 1 percent principals (Hamann and Walker 1993). The athletic establishment also claims that "at-risk" students respond particularly well to the discipline and structure provided by athletics. Such students also respond well to music programs. A 1992 Auburn University study found significant increases in overall self-concept of at-risk children participating in an arts program that included music, movement, dramatics, and art, as measured by the Piers-Harris *Children's Self-Concept Scale* (Barry 1992).

Most interesting for purposes of evaluating the type of educational investment necessary to prepare our workforce for the future is that "the very best engineers and technical designers in the Silicon Valley industry are, nearly without exception, practicing musicians" (Venerable 1989).

On a somewhat less-empirical level, Plato spoke often of the benefits of music as compared to athletics. Plato elaborated on the value of teaching music when he said, "I would teach children music, physics, and philosophy; but most importantly music, for in the patterns of music and all the arts are the keys to learning" (National Coalition for Music Education 1997). While Plato was not opposed to athletics, he often expressed alarm at the course that athletics in ancient Greece had taken; from the purpose of developing a healthy relationship between the mind and body, to one of specialization and intense training in specific events or sports (sound familiar?). "Plato was clearly in favor of moderate physical education, but on principle he had to be critical of contemporary athletics as uneducational and impractical for the good of the individual and city" (Kyle 1993, 139).

When comparing music to our current elitist, win-at-all-cost youth, interscholastic, and intercollegiate sports programs, athletics comes up short as a vehicle to prepare students to compete successfully in the workplace of the future. Yet, time and time again, when a school district or university is faced with budget cuts, it is far more likely that a program in the arts will be downsized or eliminated while the athletic program remains untouched. From an educational standpoint, such decisions are counterproductive.

James Michener considered the consequences of our intense emphasis on athletic accomplishment over that of other fields of endeavor. "The emphasis on sports is not of itself regrettable—our nation has the energy and money to support the expansion—but when sports are encouraged to preempt financial and psychological support that might be better spent on more worthy projects, society could be drifting into trouble. . . . Eighteenth-century Europe produced musicians because society of that time prized creative talent; twentieth-century America produces athletes because our society obviously treasures sports more highly than creativity" (Michener 1976, 467–68).

As much as we love sports, we must value education more. If it is determined that any element of our educational system undermines educational priorities, we must radically alter that element or eliminate it in favor of programming that promotes positive educational ideals and offers a better educational return on dollars invested. Thus, the fundamental question is as follows: What role should our educational system assume as it relates to the cultural subject matter of athletics? Should its purpose be to develop elite athletes and teams or rather to encourage in our citizenship, through broad participation opportunities, an appreciation for, and development of, good lifelong health, fitness, and personal wellness habits and behaviors? In other words, should the primary emphasis of sports within our educational system be the final score or the process of participation?

As discussed in chapter 5, the societal costs of athletics programs that undermine academic values and institutions are significant and far-reaching. While the negative impact of watching hours upon hours of sports television programming are limited primarily to the individual and his or her family, misplaced priorities relating to the role of athletics within our educational system have a tremendously broad and far-reaching societal impact. This is particularly true in the case of athletics within American higher education.

Higher Education's Leadership Responsibility

For over three hundred years, Americans have looked to our nation's colleges and universities to provide direction and leadership in addressing the critical issues of the day. One only has to pick up a newspaper to gain a sense of the challenges facing our society. Deficiencies in public education affecting everything from illiteracy rates to our ability to compete in a global economy, the disintegration of the family, the challenges of living in an increasingly diverse and technologically advanced society and environmental degradation are all very broad issues facing our country. Crime, poverty, and calls to restore in our young people a strong sense of ethical awareness and civic responsibility are also concerns that must be addressed. These problems are enormous and our society is facing them in an environment of declining resources and increasing costs.

While some may consider it a stretch, the fact is, the way colleges and universities conduct athletic programs influences their ability to effectively address the broader public concerns outlined above. As the public comes to view the hypocrisies of major college athletics with a more critical eye, higher education pays a price, specifically in the form of declining credibility and public trust. Such a decline in public trust diminishes higher education's moral authority to address other important societal issues and challenges. If universities cannot conduct their athletic programs with integrity, by embracing an unyielding commitment to sound academic principles and emphasizing the development of student-athletes as more than simply jocks, how can it be expected that the public believe in its ability to effectively address issues such as poverty and illiteracy? Simply put, our colleges and universities can no longer afford to waste precious resources in the form of public trust and credibility on athletic programs that compromise these principles.

The values that are projected by college athletics programs are critical for another reason. What we do in our college athletic programs, the values we embrace, and the messages that we send filter down to all levels of sport. If our institutions of higher education tacitly endorse activities that undermine educational priorities and achievement at the expense of athletic accomplishment, it provides an example for all to emulate. In short, the public looks to higher education to provide educational leadership, including leadership regarding the role, importance, and purpose of sport in relation to education.

This reality was brought home to me while at the Southeastern Conference. In an effort to increase communication between the conference office and the state high school athletics associations in the states in which an SEC school was located, the directors of those state associations were invited to Birmingham for a brainstorming session. One of the questions posed to the directors was whether the quality and professionalism of their coaches was improving. Their answer was a resounding, "No!" Most disturbing, however, was the reason given for high school coaches being increasingly difficult to manage. Each of the directors cited the influence of college coaches, particularly in the area of bench conduct and decorum, as the major cause of the decline in sportsmanship and professionalism in high school coaches. As one director put it, "Who do you think our coaches are modeling themselves after? They are watching your coaches on television!"

For these reasons, the key to addressing our All-American addiction, at least from a broad societal standpoint, lies primarily at the doorstep of our educational institutions, particularly our colleges and universities.

College Athletics Reform Revisited . . . Again

Concern regarding the marriage of big-time athletics and American higher education is not new. For reasons with which we are all too familiar, to characterize the relationship as "strained" is an understatement. Consequently, periodic attempts to initiate meaningful, long-lasting athletic reform are almost as much a part of the higher education landscape as the classroom lecture. Unfortunately, despite the well-intentioned efforts of many intelligent, virtuous, and dedicated individuals, attempts to reform big-time college athletics in a meaningful and permanent way have yielded few results. Typically, the reform scenario plays out as follows: A series of scandals ignites widespread public indignation over the excesses of big-time athletics. Calls for sweeping reform are heard from many quarters. A commission, full of high-profile educational leaders, is formed to examine the problems and recommend reform measures. A series of changes are recommended, most of which, if implemented, have little, if any, long-lasting impact. Amid much self-congratulatory praise, the public is once again appeased. And life within our college athletic departments returns to business as usual until the next series of scandal reignites the process.

For example, in 1984, the newly created NCAA President's Commission undertook a radical restructuring of its governance and decision-making processes. Over the ensuing twelve years, this group spearheaded a series of reform measures designed to more fully integrate athletic departments into the mainstream university community. The changes included requirements to report graduation rates of student-athletes, increased penalties for violators of rules, financial audit requirements, student-athlete welfare initiatives, increased initial and continuing eligibility standards, a series of measures to ensure more-effective institutional control, and an athletic department certification requirement.

But the NCAA President's Commission was not the only force pushing for athletic reform. In 1989, the John S. and James J. Knight Foundation, a foundation active in higher-education–related issues, created a Commission on Intercollegiate Athletics. The commission viewed itself as an outside watchdog group with a mission to prod the NCAA to stay the reform course by assessing the state of college athletics and to develop its own reform agenda. Consisting of a cross-section of leaders in business, higher education, athletics, and politics, the group served its function admirably, initiating meaningful dialogue on important issues and producing a thoughtful, far-reaching blueprint for reform. The Knight Commission released a series of reports from 1991 to 1993, which served to keep the pressure on the NCAA to reform.

Thus, the formation of the NCAA President's Commission in 1984 through 1996, when the NCAA adopted a restructuring plan that solidified presidential authority within the NCAA governance structure, marked the most comprehensive and sustained effort to reform intercollegiate athletics in the history of American higher education. Never before had there been so many elements and interest groups—college presidents, faculty, politicians, an increasingly aggressive media, and an outraged public—converging around the idea that major college athletics was out of control and that sweeping reform was not only necessary, but also critical for the future health and credibility of higher education. It was a unique moment in the history of American higher education. If meaningful reform were ever to occur, it was then.

That is why it was significant that in 2000, ten years after the release of its original report, *Keeping Faith with the Student-Athlete: A New Model for Intercollegiate Athletics*, the Knight Foundation reconvened its Commission on Intercollegiate Athletics. Knight Foundation leaders feared that what had been the most-sustained effort at substantive college athletic reform had suffered the same fate as all previous attempts—much rhetoric, lots of proposals, a few changes, and life returning pretty much to a state of business as usual. Based upon hours and hours of testimony from a wide range of leaders and experts on college athletics and higher education, along with the empirical evidence compiled by Shulman and Bowen cited in previous chapters, it was believed that the chasm between the athletic and academic communities was actually widening. In short, a convincing case was made that, on balance, college athletics was no better off in 2001 than in 1990 or 1984. It appeared that history had, once again, instructed us that attempts to reform big-time college athletics in a meaningful and permanent way bear little fruit.

The mere fact that the commission felt the need to reconvene suggests that those hopeful days of reform have faded to business as usual . . . or rather, bigger business as usual. Consider, for example, the major tenets of the Knight Commission's 1991 report: presidential control, academic integrity, financial integrity, and independent certification. Other than independent certification, it is difficult to argue that much real progress has been made on the commission's recommendations. While presidents undoubtedly possess more control and authority within the NCAA governance structure, the larger question is whether anyone is truly in control of major college athletics. For example, how much power do presidents wield in the face of television networks, street agents, Amateur Athletic Union (AAU) coaches, rabid fans and boosters, exorbitantly paid coaches, gamblers, and bookies? And can presidents exert much influence over sneaker companies pouring millions of dollars not only into college programs, but into high school and AAU programs as well, a culture that glorifies athletic accomplishment more than academic excellence, and a legal system that is reconsidering the nonprofit status of the entire enterprise? In such an environment, it is hard to argue that anyone is in control. Major college athletics has gotten so big, with so much money and ego at stake, that perhaps even presidents are helpless in initiating significant change.

While the NCAA has emphasized academic integrity by periodically raising eligibility standards, we have seen little improvement in graduation rates. Institutions continue to admit athletes who are not prepared to perform college work, but who, nonetheless, are required to devote an inordinate amount of time to athletically related activities. The fundamental conflict between the short-term, financial, and athletic interests of coaches and athletic administrators and the long-term academic and personal interests of student-athletes remains. And, we continue to sell the false dream of athletic stardom to youth—mostly black—far too often at the expense of academic achievement and the development of personal responsibility. In short, the anti-intellectual culture that permeates the athletic establishment continues to undermine academic values and integrity.

While athletic department fiscal operations are much better managed, the fact remains that there is much more money involved at all levels of the enterprise. As a result, the stakes have continued to rise significantly. With higher stakes comes a greater likelihood of external influence and corruption. Although student-athletes' financial situation has improved with NCAA funds being made available for emergencies and other needs, the public continues to wonder whether they receive fair market value for their services. Obviously, student-athletes do not believe they are compensated fairly, which is why so many of them think nothing of taking payments prohibited by the NCAA. And coaches continue to earn ridiculously large sums of money, much of it from sources outside the institution, raising questions of where their loyalty rests. In short, financial integrity is elusive at best.

My purpose is not to dismiss the great strides the NCAA has made in restructuring the athletic enterprise to fit more comfortably into the culture of higher education, nor is it to dismiss the tremendous influence the Knight Commission had on those improvements. Progress has been made. Student-athlete welfare is now an issue that receives regular attention. Athletic departments are more open to the university community in matters academic and fiscal. Institutions have recognized their responsibility in the areas of institutional control and oversight. Coaches are more aware of the rules and regulations. And, presidential authority is now more clearly delineated and understood. College athletics, at least from an internal standpoint, is much better off than fifteen years ago.

Unfortunately, while internal improvements have been made, external influences have grown as well, but at a much faster pace. The commercialization of college athletics has grown so rapidly that it has overwhelmed what reform progress has been made. In short, initiating meaningful and long-lasting reform of intercollegiate athletics is like trying to lasso the wind.

Unquestionably, most of what transpires in college athletics is positive, at least in terms of sheer numbers of student-athletes taking advantage of the educational opportunity that a college scholarship offers. And most coaches take their responsibilities as an educator seriously. But the sad reality is that all the positive might be outweighed by the negatives associated with the high-visibility, megacommercialized sports of football and basketball. We continue to have far too many scandals in which academic and institutional integrity are seriously damaged; student-athletes are still getting illegal money; coaches continue to get paid far more than presidents; and fears abound that another major gambling scandal is imminent. The negative influence of these two sports on the credibility of higher education remains too pervasive. Thus, the question is whether or not, on balance, college athletics is better off than ten or fifteen years ago and, more important, whether there is any evidence that things will improve anytime soon.

The Fourth Quarter for Reform

Given these concerns, along with the fact that athletics' societal influence has become so pervasive, it is clear that college athletic reform is no longer about the traditional fare of student-athlete welfare, academic integrity, and presidential control. Today, reform is about the cultural values we will pass on to our children and grandchildren. It is about ensuring that we prize and reinforce values such as honesty, intelligence, and civility over athletic prowess.

While most of what transpires in college athletics is positive and the various reform measures initiated by the NCAA over the last decade have been significant, the problem remains that our country has lost perspective regarding the role of organized sport in our culture. We have come to glorify athletic accomplishment far more than academic achievement. And, higher education has, in large part, been responsible for allowing this culture to evolve.

That being the case, if our cultural consensus regarding the proper relationship between sport and education is ever going to be restored, it is up to the higher education community to initiate the process. Perhaps this is an unfair burden. After all, professional sports also bear some responsibility. In an ideal world, perhaps. But as discussed in the previous chapter, there is very little incentive for professional sports organizations to initiate meaningful reform. Changing our cultural consensus regarding the balance between sport and education is largely higher education's responsibility because in the case of the cultural subject matter of athletics, it has failed in its public mission. Higher education has not provided the necessary leadership in establishing a healthy societal attitude regarding athletics.

Thus, we should give serious consideration to the most fundamental issue relating to the role of athletics in higher education: whether higher education, in its efforts to fulfill its public mission of meeting the many challenges facing society, is best served by sponsoring major college athletics as currently structured?

It is critical that we have this conversation because it needs to be made clear to the college athletic community as well as to the public that simply because one hundred thousand people may attend a football game does not mean that athletics is indispensable. People need to understand that higher education was around for more than two hundred years before the first intercollegiate athletic contest and will continue to provide quality education, produce important research, and contribute to the betterment of society with or without athletics. For that reason, it is indeed possible, in the words of Tuft University's president John DiBiaggio, "that we end up being so disenchanted that we choose to abandon this important component of our students' educational experience."

But before expelling athletic programs from the academe, we need to ask whether we can change the direction enough to make athletics the positive cultural force it should be. Perhaps one last effort at reform is warranted. Because athletics has tremendous potential to contribute in positive ways to the goals and purposes of our educational institutions, perhaps it is prudent to see whether the emerging wave of reform initiatives, pushed by groups like the Knight Foundation and the recently formed faculty organization, the Drake Group, take root.

The question is how does higher education utilize athletics' influence to change cultural attitudes and behaviors? This is a tremendous undertaking. The following suggestions are offered as a blueprint for the higher education community to begin what will be a slow and arduous path toward cultural change in this area.

A Reform Agenda

Our current athletic culture measures success on championship banners hung from gymnasium rafters, entertainment quality, and revenues generated. The issues facing higher education and our society are simply too daunting to expect, and thus allow, such a potentially powerful educational tool to be evaluated on such narrow criteria. Athletic department success must be measured in terms of contributions to institutional efforts to meet the many challenges facing higher education and the society it is meant to serve. This must be the new standard of athletic department success.

To that end, everyone within the higher education community, from the assistant volleyball coach to the chair of the board of trustees, must fully understand that, with regard to athletics, we must begin playing by a new set of rules. Then, we must evaluate each and every element of the athletic department to determine how it might be reprioritized, restructured, repackaged, and reprogrammed to improve institutional capacity to utilize athletics as a vehicle to assist higher education in meeting its mission.

This sort of cultural change will require a sustained, comprehensive educational and professional development initiative to reconnect athletic departments to the academic community. All within the higher education community and, in particular, those directly connected with athletic programs, must begin to learn a new set of truths and behavioral expectations, new subject matter. We must distinguish between what we *do*, which is conduct games, and what we are *about*, which is education. Take coaches, for example.

As mentioned in the previous chapter, it is ironic that virtually no educational standards or criteria are required to become a coach. Not until coaches are expected to be, first and foremost, educators, will they begin in earnest, the process of becoming educators. Desired educational backgrounds and occupational credentials for coaches should be identified, emphasized, and rewarded. Once hired, coaches must be provided meaningful professional opportunities to develop more fully as educators. Finally, the evaluation criteria for coaches need to be explicitly geared away from wins and losses and box office revenues. Otherwise, efforts to change their behavior will be fruitless.

Meeting the new standard will also require structural institutional changes. For example, to improve athletics' potential for institutional contribution, the marketing, sports information, and fundraising departments should report to the university's institutional advancement office. This shift does not mean that campus officials would de-emphasize efforts to highlight or raise money for athletics. Rather, those efforts would continue as part of an overall effort to promote and generate resources for the entire institution. And, as the former NCAA executive director Dick Schultz proposed in 1991, "Athletic departments should be funded like any other university department."

Athletics' most powerful resource for advancing broad institutional goals is its tremendous visibility. Unfortunately, in the attempt to maximize financial return, we have given away too much control over the way our "product" is presented and portrayed. College sports is packaged, marketed, and projected as purely entertainment with the opportunity to communicate with the public about education an afterthought, at best.

To better utilize this resource, every point at which the athletic department interfaces with the public—from television and radio games to media brochures to coaches speaking to civic clubs— should be identified and evaluated to determine whether that opportunity can be used to more effectively promote the broad goals of the university rather than the specific goals of the athletic department. I am not suggesting, for example, that we turn our television events into *National Geographic* specials. Rather, that if we spent half as much time and effort developing dynamic and creative ways in which to weave educational images and messages throughout telecasts as we spent promoting next week's "Game of the Century" or the Frito-Lay Play of the Day, higher education would more fully realize the tremendous potential of this, athletics' most powerful resource.

To begin work toward that goal, presidents and institutional advancement personnel should become much more directly involved in the negotiation of television and radio contracts and in content design. Traditionally, these duties have been left to conference commissioners and athletic directors. As is understandable, these individuals have as their leading priority the promotion of their athletic programs, and as would be expected, the content and images projected through these important media resources reflect those priorities. Athletic administrators may resist giving up control over the way "their" product is presented, but the fact is, college athletics is not "their" product. It belongs to higher education. Higher education should view the telecasts of college athletic events as an opportunity to interface with the public in an educational context rather than simply an athletic context. Otherwise, any television contract, no matter how big a financial payoff, is a lost opportunity to further advance higher education's goals and mission.

Similarly, every NCAA rule must be evaluated using the new standard. For example, freshman ineligibility would provide student-athletes an opportunity to be a regular student for a year. Eliminating off-campus recruiting would send the message to coaches that coaching is more than recruiting. Eliminating athletic scholarships in favor of need-based aid would lessen significantly the often-excessive athletic department power and control over student-athletes. Playing seasons should be shortened and out-of-season practice, including spring football practice, should be eliminated. Serious consideration should be given to whether conducting national championships contributes to our cultural obsession with having to have only one winner.

Instituting the new standard will not be easy, nor will it happen overnight. It will require a new level of institutional teamwork and understanding. Coaches and athletic administrators must realize that athletics is not bigger and more important than the university. The academic community must recognize that athletics, with its visibility and influence, can be a tremendous educational resource and that to dismiss it as trivial is to waste it. In short, the way in which institutional return on investment in athletics is measured must change. Only when athletic departments are provided some relief from the pressure to balance budgets can they begin to invest in the changes required of the new standard. Less pressure to balance budgets means less pressure to win and that means more room to make decisions based upon the academic and personal welfare of the student athlete and broader good of the institution. The purpose of the new standard is to provide a framework within which the high-pressure, win-at-all-cost culture of intercollegiate athletics can be ratcheted down a few notches. Again, the goal is not, in the words of the Indiana University president Myles Brand, "to turn off the game, but lower the volume." By doing so, our nation's colleges and universities would better serve their public purpose by providing a leadership example that would allow those who administer, coach, and support sports programs at all levels, including high school, junior high, and pee-wee leagues, to turn down the volume as well.

Before outlining the vehicle through which such change can be initiated, it is important to address the traditional arguments against such change.

First, is our tendency to rationalize the current state of major college athletics as simply a reflection of societal values. That may be true to some extent, but as mentioned repeatedly, the relationship has become symbiotic, with athletics greatly affecting cultural values as well. Regardless, an educator's job is to reinforce positive, not negative values. College athletics' visibility and influence has become so great that it has come to shape societal values and behaviors.

It is also easy to say that the problems associated with Division I football and basketball affect only 2 or 3 percent of student-athletes. But again, because of their visibility and financial impact, the influence of these two sports is wildly disproportionate to the number of student-athletes involved in them.

Finally, I simply do not accept the notion that implementing the new standard will adversely affect Auburn's, Ohio State's, or UCLA's entertainment value in the marketplace. The fact is, the public loves college athletics and will continue to love it even when we slightly modify the packaging. Ultimately, the University of Alabama fan does not care whether the student-athlete who turns the corner runs a 4.5 forty or a 5.4 forty, or whether he was required to sit out as a freshman, or whether he is on athletic or need-based aid, or whether the coach was allowed off-campus to recruit him, or whether he participated in spring football. That fan simply wants him to score a touchdown for Alabama. In fact, college athletics' public appeal would likely grow if some of these changes were made. Most people want their college athletic programs to stand for something more than simply turning a buck, preparing the next generation of professional stars, and winning at any cost. While some may say it is naïve to try to change our society's obsessive win-at-any-cost mentality, I believe it is higher education's responsibility to help establish and support a vision for the right set of cultural ideals. I do not accept the notion that nothing can be done about these problems. We have choices. We can set a new standard.

The issue is balance. Somewhere along the line, our cultural consensus regarding the importance of athletic performance versus intellectual achievement has become grotesquely distorted. And the societal consequences of our loss of perspective are becoming too great. If you accept the notion that higher education's most essential purpose is to provide leadership in addressing the critical issues of the day, its responsibility is clear.

It is a monumental challenge, one that suggests the need for a long-term commitment by the higher education community to see the task through. As evidenced by years of futile attempts by the NCAA to initiate substantive, long-lasting reform, it is clear that such change must be sparked by a source outside of the NCAA through the continued application of public pressure, but the change must be implemented through the NCAA. The most likely source of outside influence would be a body of highly influential leaders in higher education, highly visible and respected business leaders, and a few powerful political leaders, with the sponsorship and political influence of a coalition of educational organizations and foundations behind it. Such a group would provide leadership and direction in framing national dialogue relating to the role of athletics in higher education and would serve as a catalyst in facilitating a strengthening of the links between athletics and the educational missions of colleges and universities. Such a group could push for continued movement on various reform initiatives by identifying and empowering key individuals in the higher education community to come together in a critical mass to move forward on reform. Areas of focus should include presidential authority, academic integrity, the role of television and the media, financial disarmament, and athletics' influence on cultural values. Such a group would serve as a public conscience on issues relating to the conduct of athletics in higher education with hopes of beginning to effect a cultural change in regards to the appropriate role of athletics in our educational institutions by encouraging dialogue, generating relevant research, and continuing to apply pressure on the NCAA for change.

But will it happen? Can it happen? Can significant reform of intercollegiate athletics actually occur?

Athletics can and should contribute to the educational missions of our colleges and universities in vibrant and timely ways. Because their potential to contribute is tremendous, pursuit of such a reform agenda is critical and worthy of the expenditure of the significant time, effort, and resources it will require. But at the same time, we must be realistic about the prospects for meaningful, long-lasting reform. History has told us, time and time again, that such reform is unlikely. Perhaps the beast within the gates of the academy has become so big and powerful that reform is a pipe dream. Given the odds against such meaningful reform, we must be prepared to answer the following, more realistic questions. When does the gulf between the athletic and academic cultures on campus become so great as to be irreparable? What action is required when athletic programs operate so far outside the mainstream university community as to become a counter influence on higher education's goals, culture, and mission?

As expressed in chapter 5, it is arguable that we have reached that point.

Despite the fact that ultimately, it is very likely that the elimination of highly competitive, elite, interscholastic and, particularly, intercollegiate, athletics is in the best interests of our educational institutions, doing so, at least at this point, is simply not feasible. The fear of vast public and alumni outcry leaves educational leaders with little stomach to take on such a thorny issue. But by all indications, the path we are now following will lead to an ever-widening gulf between athletics and the higher education community. If the gulf between the athletics and academic cultures on our college campuses continues to widen; if athletic departments continue to embrace the highly commercialized values of the entertainment culture, higher education leaders will be forced to act, and act decisively. Without a change in direction, the values and purposes of athletics will become so separate and distinct, with so little in common with the values, mores, and purposes of the academe as to be two distinct entities, if not in structure, then certainly in practice and public perception. If major change is not realized in the future, perhaps much sooner than we, at this point, can imagine, it is simply a matter of time before big-time athletics becomes so estranged from the higher education community that we will be left with little choice but to expel it from the academy. Regardless of the impression one might get from the bare-chested, face-painted rabid fan in the stands, most people realize that, ultimately, it is far more important that our colleges and universities develop scholars, advance knowledge, and produce important research than to train future professional athletes and field elite sports teams. And while the public firestorm over such a change would be monumental, the fact is, with time, the public would come to accept the change, and our educational institutions would go on about their business of educating our populace.

American higher education is at an important crossroads regarding athletics. This may be the last opportunity for significant reform, the last chance to tame the ever-growing beast that is college athletics. In short, the clock is running out on college athletics reform.

And if we find that the beast cannot be tamed, what then?

Adopt a Club Sport System

What would happen to our schools and colleges without interscholastic and intercollegiate athletics? What would happen to the athletes? Where would they play? What would coaches do?

Our schools and colleges will survive quite well without athletics. Contrary to what many believe, educational institutions were not created simply to sponsor a basketball or football team.

The life and purpose of a university does not revolve around the athletic department. Despite the impression we may get from newspaper accounts, a school does not close down after the football team loses to a conference rival. The dropping of big-time football at the University of Chicago in 1928, for example, did not harm the university as it is recognized as one of the world's best. While the University of Chicago is the most famous case, it was not alone in dropping big-time football. In *Sports in America*, James Michener cites a study by Felix Springer of the institutional impact of various schools that dropped their football programs during the forties, fifties, sixties, and seventies. Such schools included Chicago, DePaul, Niagra, St. Joseph's, LaSalle, NYU, Bradley, Santa Clara, and many others. Michener summarized as follows:

> What were the consequences of quitting? To an astonishing degree, no visible consequence at all, except that the dropping often served as a catalyst for improving the rest of the athletic program. Alumni giving did *not* stop. Alumni did *not* sever connections with their schools. Student applications for entrance did *not* diminish. And state legislatures did *not* cut yearly grants. In fact, businessmen and legislators alike tended to agree that when the school stopped pouring money down the football rathole, it gave evidence of managerial responsibility; its reputation was enhanced rather than damaged. Springer notes that many schools launched successful fund-raising drives coincident with dropping football, as if having done so were evidence of the school's determination to improve its general posture. (Michener 1976, 271

While our school systems may be less dynamic, and in some ways, less fun without big-time athletics, they will continue to go about the business of educating. In fact, the education of students would likely improve with the elimination of interscholastic and intercollegiate athletic programs, as the focus on academics would intensify.

What would happen to the athletes and coaches? Elite sports activities and training would simply shift to other local sponsoring agencies, similar to the European club sport system. Local organizations and youth groups that receive no public funding would develop and sponsor more comprehensive athletic programs. And, like the European sports clubs, existing professional teams would begin to sponsor their own feeder systems and programs. Each professional league would be forced to develop a minor-league system, similar to the one that currently exists in baseball. In short, the responsibility for developing future professional athletes would shift from our high schools and colleges to private sports clubs and pro teams where it belongs. In such a system, "there is no controversy about what to call them. They are neither student-athletes nor athlete-students. They are students *and* athletes. The spheres of activity are separate and distinct" (Putnam 1999, 212).

Shifting the responsibility for conducting elite sports programs from our nation's schools and colleges to outside sports clubs is clearly in the best interests of the schools, the athletes, and the coaches. Our educational system would be rid of a highly visible source of hypocrisy and scandal. Further, intramural, physical education, and wellness programs could be expanded, resulting in far more students being able to avail themselves of health- and exercise-related resources. With such a change, our educational system would be better positioned to begin the process of serving the broad, long-term, health and exercise needs of America.

This change would also benefit athletes as those who wish to become professionals can immerse themselves entirely in pursuing those goals without the added "burden" of having to go to school. They would be provided with the best in training practices, equipment, and coaching. Coaches would not have to "put up with" their athletes being "distracted" by academics. If athletes wished to go to school, they could on their own time, in the off-season, or after their playing days are over. This would allow them to approach their studies without the constant conflicts of athletic demands and responsibilities. Those students who are in school primarily to play sports serve nobody's best interest. How much can or do they really learn if they are not interested in school? And should we be wasting tax dollars and school resources on those who have no desire to learn?

The only downside of such a shift would be the loss of an entertainment source and rallying point for the school. It is likely, however, that supporters of the institution would display their school spirit by supporting other activities such as music or theater groups. And if the only reason to maintain the current system of elite high school and college athletic programs is a fear of not having enough entertainment, that admission alone highlights how divorced intercollegiate athletics has become from the academic mission of the institution.

While the move to the European club sport system may sound radical, it is not. The fact is, our school systems and universities would survive without highly competitive sports and so would our elite athletes and coaches. Interestingly, America is the only country in the world where athletics is so intimately intertwined with the education system. Could it be that our concept of the role and purpose of school- and university-sponsored athletics is, after a century-long experiment, misguided?

According to Michener,

> Ours is a unique system which has no historical sanction or application elsewhere. It would be unthinkable for the University of Bologna, a most ancient and honorable school, to provide scholarships to illiterate soccer players so that they could entertain the other cities of northern Italy, and it would be equally preposterous for either the Sorbonne or Oxford to do so in their countries. Our system is an American phenomenon, a historical accident which developed from the exciting football games played by Yale and Harvard and to a lessor extent Princeton and certain other schools during the closing years of the nineteenth century. If we had had at that time professional teams which provided public football entertainment, we might not have placed the burden on our schools. But we had no professional teams, so our schools were handed the job. . . . If an ideal

American educational system were being launched afresh, few would want to saddle it with the responsibility for public sports entertainment. (Michener 1976, 237)

While cultural expectations and alumni, booster, and corporate forces against moving intercollegiate and interscholastic athletics out of the educational system will be strong, it is something that we must consider seriously. We have tinkered for too long. In the final analysis, American education will structure itself according to what will best enable it to meet its responsibility to provide leadership in addressing the many challenges facing our society. If organized athletic programs are not supplementing this, the most fundamental public purpose of our educational institutions, in positive and timely ways, then they should no longer be a part of them.

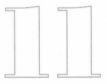

WHAT IF?

Our enormous investment in organized sport has been justified largely on the health and educational benefits to participants. Beyond the individual benefits, are the alleged societal benefits—athletics as an important socialization tool and an economic force, as well as a means of improving military preparedness.

But in the face of Nike commercialism, NCAA Final Four hype, and Dennis Rodman's changing hair colors, it is increasingly difficult to see any connection between athletics and such "higher purposes." Sport in America has become more about money, winning, and ego than about education, sportsmanship, and ethics; more about commercialism, sneaker deals, and trash-talking than about personal development and educational opportunity; and more about being a passive spectator than an active participant. Sport is corporate sky boxes, sneaker deals, television contracts, free agency, salary caps, coaching "packages," academic fraud, trading-card signing shows, sports memorabilia, traveling "all-star" teams of seven-year-olds, win, win, win, sell more product—

hats, jackets, commemorative coffee cups—all-stars, all-world, all-universe. It all adds up to an All-American addiction.

It is interesting to note that the growth of organized sport in America paralleled that of the Industrial Revolution. To the industrialists of the early twentieth century, the relationship between athletics, economic prosperity, and social order was clear. Organized sport was viewed as a means of increasing economic prosperity, improving health and military preparedness, contributing to educational goals, and maintaining social order by instilling in a nation of immigrants a sense of what it took to be "American." But America's economic, military, health, education, and social needs are vastly different from those of a century ago.

While advancing technology played a significant role, it was the muscle and diligence of factory line workers that powered the development of America's vast industrial infrastructure. Over the past two decades, however, the United States has been undergoing a radical transformation from an industrial economy to an information-driven, knowledge-based, global economy, all in an increasingly diverse world. America's entrepreneurial giants of the past century were industrialists like Andrew Carnegie. Today, the likes of Bill Gates and the CEOs of thousands of start-up computer, high-tech, and service companies will power future American economic prosperity. America's ability to strengthen democratic ideals and to compete successfully in the global economy of the Information Age will require not more physical manpower, but better brain power. Thus, the link between education and the future health, prosperity, and economic competitiveness of America is more critical than ever.

America's military demands are also changing. Obviously, there will always be a need for strong, tough foot soldiers. But, as evidenced in the Persian Gulf War and NATO's bombing campaign in Kosovo, our wars are now being fought from thousands of miles away using highly sophisticated technology. With technologically complex fighter planes and weapons systems to operate, the ability to coordinate and integrate vast amounts of information and technology has become a vitally important military skill. Military effectiveness has become so dependent upon technology that soldiers may be better off training in a video arcade than on a football field. War by remote control. While a bit overstated, the point is, even in military matters, it is the ability to understand, process, and execute in matters relating to sophisticated technology—skills of the brain—that are increasingly important.

And our nation's health needs are changing. Health care costs are rising dramatically. This, coupled with an aging population, dictates that preventive care assume a more important role in our nation's health strategy. Regular exercise and ongoing participation in athletically related activities are critical to preventive health care. Thus, our nation and its people must develop an increased appreciation for, and commitment to, lifelong athletic participation and exercise. Unfortunately, our current elitist system of sport does not encourage broad-based involvement. Instead, participation is relegated to a minority of elite athletes. Meanwhile, our population becomes more obese as we watch more and participate less. The long-term health and economic cost of these trends will be staggering.

Commitment to lifelong exercise and athletic participation does not simply occur. It must be taught and nurtured, and eventually, it must become a part of the individual's lifestyle and ingrained in the collective community mind-set. That being the case, it is critical that our society's understanding of the role of sport shift from our current model of elite participation, driven by a win-at-all-cost ethic, to an educationally centered model emphasizing lifelong, broad-based participation. This change in our collective view of the role of organized sport must become a part of our culture. Simply put, a system of organized sport designed to develop elite, highly competitive athletes contributes very little of substance to national health efforts.

Finally, a return to a more-balanced conception of the mind/body relationship becomes essential as we confront the challenge of strengthening our democracy in a society that is increasingly diverse. As John Kenneth Galbraith articulated in his 1996 book, *The Good Society: The Humane Agenda*, education has a vital bearing on social peace and tranquillity in three ways. First, education provides the "hope and reality of escape from the lower, less favored economic strata to those above. . . . For upward escape, either by the individual or by his or her children, education is the decisive agent." Second, education "allows people to govern themselves intelligently. There is no well-educated population that is subject to dictatorship or, at a minimum, is not in a measure of revolt therefrom. Dictatorship of the poor and illiterate, on the other hand, is commonplace." Finally, education is "most of all, for the enlargement and enjoyment of life" (Galbraith 1996, 69–70).

In short, it is the development of the mind rather than the body that will assume more cultural significance as we strive to maintain and strengthen our institution of democracy. Organized sport, with its prevailing culture of violence, individualism, corruption, and anti-intellectualism does little to contribute to the building and maintenance of a civil society.

Simply stated, organized sport in America is in trouble. It has been sold to us based upon a set of assumptions and expectations that are not being met. As a result, it is undermining the ideals of a civil and just society, threatening our future economic competitiveness by subverting educational values and institutions, contributing to a general decline in our nation's health, and diverting valuable public resources from vital civic projects and priorities. Like a team that has sunk to the bottom of the league standings, organized sport in America has turned into a loser.

The Virtues of the Game

Obviously, not everything about organized sport is negative. There are thousands of athletes who are good citizens. There are athletic programs that supplement the goals and missions of the schools and colleges of which they are a part in vibrant and meaningful ways. There are cities and communities that benefit from the presence of a professional sports franchise. Therein lies the conundrum. Despite all of the negatives that have become a part of organized sport, the essence of the games remain pure; the virtues of competitive athletics are still positive and worthwhile. While my concerns regarding the state of organized athletics in America are significant, I continue to love sports. I love to play sports, and I read about them daily. They can be beautiful to watch.

Unfortunately, the money, the hype, the big contracts, the sky boxes, the hoopla, the sneaker deals, and the soap opera off-the-field lives of our superstars all tend to obfuscate the essence of the game. The trappings of sport have become sport itself. The most-glaring example of this evolution is the Super Bowl. Amid the mountains of media hype, the corporate sponsorship excesses, the grotesquely expensive television commercials, and the outrageously elaborate pre-game, half-time, and post-game show extravaganzas, the game itself has become little more than a sideshow for what has become America's most garish entertainment spectacle.

Yet, buried beneath all of the trappings, all of the negatives, the essence of sport, even today's sport, remains. The challenge we face as individuals and as a society is to cut through all of the hype and to begin to appreciate and embrace the essence of the games—the substance. If we genuinely believed in the virtues of the athletic experience, if we were truly interested in promoting the essence of the games themselves, we would understand that all of the trappings of modern-day sport are meaningless. One can experience the beauty and essence of sport without them. Our problem is that we have forgotten that it is the game that should always come first, whether a pee-wee game, an intramural contest, or a pick-up soccer game in the park on a Sunday morning. Fans in the stands and cameras in the sky are unnecessary. You can experience the positive virtues of the game without the prospects of a pro career. The virtues of athletics have nothing to do with big contracts, ESPN highlights, $150 sneakers, all-star teams, and big trophies.

Like a behind-the-back pass that sails out of bounds when a simple chest pass would have done, we have come to worship form over substance in organized athletics. The values of an entertainment culture have supplanted in importance the educational, health, and personal development of the individual. In youth sports, it is the belief that it isn't really sports unless it involves a uniform, a trophy, a personalized picture playing card just like the big leaguers, and a trip to McDonalds afterward. At the high school level it is the belief that an athlete's worth is tied only to his or her ability to earn a college scholarship. At the college level, it is the shot at the pros that is most important. And for the pros, it is the big contract, complete with the fancy sports car and high-priced agent. And at all levels, it is the belief that it just isn't that important unless it is worthy of an ESPN highlight. We have become blinded by the hype.

As a product of the system and as one who still believes in the value and essence of the games themselves, coming to the realization that, on balance, organized sport is no longer about "higher purposes" has been painful. But sport has changed too dramatically over the past twenty-five years for us to even pretend that such a connection continues to exist. Whether it was Latrell Sprewell's vicious choking of his coach, athlete salaries exceeding $100 million, one too many eight-year-olds never getting off the bench because the coach's ego needed to win a pee-wee league game, or the seemingly never-ending parade of universities being placed on

NCAA probation, somewhere, the institution of organized sport in America crossed over a line to where it has become devoid of meaning. Somewhere along the line the scales have tipped to where its overall influence on our culture has become more negative than positive.

Can It Change?

Will America's mammoth sports enterprise ever change? Will its influence in our culture ever wane? Is it possible? Games have been played by civilized man for thousands of years. Could something as wildly popular as organized sport collapse from its own weight?

Obviously, our current system of sport will not collapse, or even change significantly, tomorrow. That, however, is no reason to dismiss the possibility. With science, technology, and globalization of all aspects of American society advancing at rates that only twenty years ago were unimaginable, who knows what the world will look like in fifty or one hundred years? Anything is possible. It is not unrealistic to expect the role that organized sport plays in our society to be significantly different in twenty-five, fifty, or one hundred years.

What if, for example, our cultural consensus regarding the relative importance of the development of the mind versus the body began to shift? There are some indications that this shift may, in fact, be occurring already. Over the past two decades, America's economy has been changing from one based upon industrial might to technological and information-based services. Clearly, the skills necessary to succeed in the workplace of the future will have far more to do with brain than brawn. The great "industrialists" driving the economic engine of the future will likely be those who, in high school, were in the computer club and marching band, the same "geeks" and "nerds" who were ridiculed by the "jocks." The wave of the future is technology, information management, innovation, and the Internet.

Succeeding in such an economy will require intellectual and creative skills of the mind nurtured in the classroom rather than muscles built in the weight room and on the playing field.

As with any monumental shift in societal attitudes, it begins with those who will comprise our future generations. As our children discover the limitless possibilities available to anyone who can master such skills, is it unreasonable to expect that a generation's definition of desirable personal talents, characteristics, and interests could change? Perhaps in thirty years, it will be the jocks who are looked upon as being "nowhere" and "uncool." Perhaps in fifty years, it may be far more exciting, glamorous, and lucrative in the eyes of these children of the Internet age to master the marketplace of technology and information rather than a jump shot or a slam dunk.

And is it too far-fetched to think that high school athletes may not even have the opportunity to attend college on an athletic scholarship? Aside from the many questions regarding the ways in which highly competitive, mega-commercialized athletic programs undermine the academic and institutional integrity of our colleges and universities, there are serious questions about what higher education will look like in fifty years. Currently, almost every American institution is developing on-line offerings of its courses, each one chipping away at the notion that a university must have bricks and mortar and a physically present student body to exist. If all that will be required to access a college education is a computer, if we can earn a college degree from the comfort of our living rooms, will it be necessary for universities to sponsor athletic programs?

If intercollegiate athletics were expelled from higher education, what impact would it have on high school sports? Would the trend filter down to the high school level? Will high schools be forced to pare away all but the most essential educational functions as a result of financial pressures that will only become more contentious in the future? And what influence would such developments have on the long-held notion that participation in organized sports is an effective supplement to the educational process? Would such a shift signal or, in fact, be the result of, a shrinking of the perceived role and influence of organized athletics in our culture? Is it possible that we might find that highly competitive, elite athletics was not so essential after all? In such an environment, is it inconceivable that the role of our educational institutions in this area would be to sponsor programs that demand broad-based participation designed to develop lifelong fitness habits as opposed to the current programs for the athletic elite?

As this changing cultural consensus relating to our nation's educational priorities begins to take hold, its influence will undoubtedly carry over into the home. Against this backdrop, what if even more convincing research surfaced indicating that participation in highly competitive athletics does not, in fact, build all of those positive character traits that we have long assumed? Continued rampant cheating, overzealous coaches, and abusive training regiments could contribute to a general sense that organized sports has gotten so out of control that it negatively affects children. In such an environment, would it be unreasonable to envision parents becoming less inclined to encourage their children to participate in organized athletics? Perhaps parents would no longer go to such great lengths to organize or drive their children to and from such highly competitive, pressure-packed activities. Parents may come to believe that it is better for their children to develop interests in activities in which they can participate for their entire lives such as jogging, aerobics, swimming, and recreational basketball and volleyball. Given that the key to future economic prosperity will be dependent upon one's intellectual skills, perhaps parents will begin to look upon sports as simply an activity to keep physically fit rather than as an end-all, be-all, have-to-make-it-to-the-pros obsession. They may even decide that it is not only easier, but also more beneficial, to let their kids surf the Internet or take piano lessons rather than participate in a traveling all-star team.

There are some indications that such a change in attitudes may already be occurring. For example, in May 2000, voters in Mobile County, Alabama, voted to approve a property tax increase that saved high school sports and other extracurricular activities in the state's largest school system. Most of the pre-vote attention focused on the need to pass the referendum to continue to allow county high schools to sponsor sports, particularly football. The referendum passed by a margin of 56 percent to 44 percent—hardly an overwhelming endorsement of high school sports. And this, in the football-crazed state of Alabama.

Losing a Connection to Sports

One of the reasons organized sport is so wildly popular is that most Americans, particularly men, have had a very direct connection to the athletic experience. At some point in their lives, most men, and now an increasing number of women, were involved in athletics on a very meaningful experiential level. Whether it be pick-up games in the streets or as a member of the high school football team, most Americans have played one or more sports. That participation in organized sports for most did not last past high school does not matter. The fact is, most sports consumers have participated in organized sports at some point in their lives. It is hard to imagine that such involvement does not have a direct impact on their continued interest in, and consumption of, sports. Further, most children dreamed of attending a big-league game. And because it was affordable to do so, usually, they did. I remember vividly, the first time I laid eyes on Yankee Stadium's lush, emerald-green baseball diamond. I was awestruck. A large part of our interest in sports derives from our ability to relate in a very direct way to what we are watching. Having played and attended big-league games as a youth provides us with a vivid link back to our pasts, bringing back memories of simpler times.

Today, kids have many more diversions: television, computers, the Internet, and an infinitely larger and increasingly segmented entertainment market. Youth sports have become too organized, complete with uniforms and with parents organizing, scheduling, and driving their children to and from games and practices. And it is a lot more work simply to get together with a bunch of kids to play a game than it used to be. In many cases, it is easier to stay home and watch television or play on the computer. As a result, I do not get the sense that there are playgrounds and ballfields crowded with children playing stickball, touch football, and basketball as in the past. Further, professional games are prohibitively expensive, pricing many families out of the market. The only opportunity many children have to watch a pro game is on television; that is, of course, if it doesn't start too late as is the case with the World Series. Even so, the television sports experience is a very shallow one.

Could all of these diversions, coupled with how expensive attending live events has become, result in a future generation of consumers, parents, and business leaders whose experience with sports as children was limited and superficial? When that generation matures, what will be its attitude toward organized athletics? Is it possible that the role and influence of athletics will take on less significance and, as a result, the cultural consensus of valued personal characteristics and abilities might be different from that which exists today?

Is it unreasonable to imagine a day when our society values and glorifies intellectualism more than athleticism? Rather than glorifying their every move, will we ever tire of athletes' boorish and obnoxious ways? Is it possible that some day athletes will be considered a poor example of the dominant values and characteristics of our culture, looked upon not as heroes, but rather as sad caricatures, mired in a state of perpetual adolescence, clinging to memories of their youthful glory days, unable to assimilate into a mature adult world, with no great societal value other than being able to provide a few fleeting moments of mindless entertainment? Is it conceivable that we could outgrow our obsession with sports? Is a real-life "Revenge of the Nerds" possible?

If our societal consensus changes in this way, there will be no shortage of those who will line up to boot the culture of elite athletics out the door. In so many ways, and at so many levels, athletes and those in the athletic establishment have behaved as if they are entitled, that they are better than everyone else simply because they can run fast and jump high and their names appear in the newspaper. Could we, as a culture, tire of such behavior or, more serious, come to resent it? Perhaps such resentment is already boiling under the surface of our collective conscientiousness.

Daniel F. Chambliss is Sidney J. Wertimer Professor of Sociology at Hamilton College. In a write-up of a book he was asked to review for *Society*, he considered the evolution of athletics from a historical perspective:

> It may be that the sports behemoth of our time may begin soon to crumble under the weight of so many bodies, with such varied agendas. The Olympics could disintegrate into so many peripheral, semi-visible or "extreme" sports, each appealing to some different cultural group (surfers, shooters, roller derby aficionados). If the cultural consensus as to what is heroic fades; if cynicism about cheating, and money, and drugs in sport grows; if the attention-to-focusing power of network television fragments in the submarkets of hundreds of cable channels (not to mention internet sites) for all kinds of entertainment; if parents no longer provide the transportation, the money, and the moral support for long-term training for children whom they increasingly do not know—if all of this happens, which is not that far-fetched an idea, perhaps high-performance sport, resting on years and years of committed training that begins in childhood, will fade away altogether. And high performance sport will have been just a blip, a single-century Western cultural oddity, lost in the long stretch of world history. (Chambliss 2000, 90)

Achieving Balance

Sport in America has never been pure. Puritan leaders in colonial America, for example, considered leisure activities, particularly sports, "raucous pastimes, all that they deemed sensual or self-indulgent, all activities that opened the floodgates to violence and passion, all that distracted men and women from diligent work and pious worship" (Gorn and Goldstein 1993, 9). And its relationship with the educational community has always been uneasy. But while never perfect, we were always certain that, on balance, the values and benefits of organized sports outweighed its negatives. Today, I am no longer certain of that. Organized sport has changed dramatically since I was a boy playing pick-up basketball, football, and baseball in the streets and fields of northern New Jersey. It has become too everything—too large, too important, too much money involved, too much pressure to win, and all too soon. It has assumed a place in our culture of far too much importance.

Balance is important. If a basketball player spends all of her time developing her right hand, eventually, defenses will adjust by over-playing her to the right. Without a well-developed left hand, she is far less effective. If a football team runs the ball 95 percent of the time, it is far easier to defend than if it had a more-balanced offensive attack. Balance is the key to athletic effectiveness and life itself. Sports' role and standing in our country has become out of balance.

The answer, however, is not to eliminate organized sports in America, but rather to rethink, as both individuals and as a society, the role that athletics should play in our lives and culture. Just because there are significant problems in the way we conduct and the emphasis we place on youth sports programs, does not mean that we should eliminate them. Rather, they must be altered dramatically. Specifically, they must be deorganized. Adults must loosen their stranglehold grip on the organization and conduct of youth sports activities so that children can get more out of them, particularly so they can have more fun. We must give youth sports back to the kids.

Nor should elite sports programs be eliminated. But serious consideration should be given to whether they should be removed from our educational institutions. Perhaps the responsibility for the development of elite programs and athletes should be borne by independent clubs and organizations that are not associated with educational institutions. It is perfectly reasonable, however, to expect that our educational institutions provide athletic opportunities and programs that are educationally grounded, designed for broad-based participation and the development of lifelong health and athletic participation habits.

Nor is it my intent to deny a city or region a professional football or basketball franchise. Rather, it is to call for a more responsible prioritization of civic resources relating to sports. Professional sports franchises are perfectly capable of funding the construction of their own stadiums. Until the last fifteen years, that was the norm. In these times of declining public resources for increasingly difficult civic challenges, spending tax dollars on professional sports franchises is publicly irresponsible.

For example, rather than using public tax dollars to build a new football stadium for wealthy owners and millionaire players, wouldn't it be better to spend that money on the development of educational initiatives to inform people of the importance of life-long exercise and athletic participation as well as the development of programs and opportunities to enable them to act on it? Clearly, such a shift in community spending patterns is a much better use of public resources and a more productive use of sport as a cultural and societal resource.

And I am not advocating that you stop watching or attending sporting events. It is fun to watch sports. But do we need to watch as much as we do? Absolutely not! There are far too many other things to do.

The issue is balance and perspective. We must regain perspective regarding the role, purpose, and importance of sport in our culture.

Getting Back in the Game

Part of sports' great appeal is that it allows us to escape from the ordinary routine of our daily lives. Sport allows us to soar with great champions. We can share in amazing accomplishments of human endurance, courage, and will. Why, then, am I taking all of the fun out of sports? Why can't I simply sit back and enjoy the games? Who wants to listen to all of this negativity when all you really want to do is relax in front of the television for a while?

As much as I would like to forget about sports' problems and simply enjoy the games, I cannot. Sports' influence on our lives and culture is simply too great for such concerns to be swept under the rug. Everywhere we turn, sports-related images, attitudes, and behaviors are pervasive—from the workplace, to the schools we attend, to what we see on television, to the taxes we pay. Sport has an impact on and influences, in one form or another, virtually every aspect of our lives. It is simply too important to stand by as it continues to evolve into something that we are no longer comfortable with and no longer feel good about.

There is no greater benefit of sport than that of experiencing the euphoria of being in the game. There is no better feeling and no more educational and personal growth experience than being right there in the middle of the action testing your strength, skills, savvy, determination, and intelligence against others, putting it all on the line in the heat of battle. Win or lose, the point is to be in the game, to be in the middle of the action, to participate.

Sport has also taught us that it is acceptable to sit on the sidelines and watch those games. We have become comfortable with passively sitting on the sidelines and bearing witness to what the games have come to represent. Just like we are lulled to sleep while watching a game while lying prone on the sofa in front of the television on a lazy Sunday afternoon, we have been lulled into accepting what organized sport in America has become. But our sports-induced coma must end. It is time to get up, dust ourselves off, stretch a little, and get back in the game!

It is time to reclaim sport in America. We can no longer sit passively on the sidelines and continue to watch while it is overtaken by the values of the entertainment culture. Sports were never meant to be passive. We must reclaim responsibility for shaping organized sports' proper role in our society. Parents, coaches, educational and civic leaders—we all bear responsibility. We have been sitting on the sidelines and watching as sport has evolved into something we are no longer comfortable with and no longer feel good about.

Sport also teaches us to never quit, that the game is not over until the last second ticks off the clock or the last out is registered. While I do not believe that we have quit, we have, however, been in denial about organized sport in America. Simply put, we must face reality about what organized sport has become in our society and the consequences of that evolution. I hope that the arguments, research, and stories offered in the previous pages have helped to shed light upon not only the ways in which sport has evolved, but also the ways in which we can, as individuals and as a culture, reclaim it for more worthy purposes. Ultimately, it is the responsibility of the individual to break an addiction. And in the case of a societal addiction, we all have a role to play. We must assume responsibility for getting back into the game—all of us.

It pains me when, after critically analyzing something that has been an integral part of my life—something that I love and value—I find that it has changed so dramatically that I no longer recognize it. Perhaps that is my problem alone. But I doubt that it is. And as much as I would like to trivialize its impact, to just write off the current state of sport in America as something that will never change, I know that it will because it has before.

We must get back into the game because organized sport in America must change. Our society can no longer afford for sport's violent, win-at-all-cost mentality to erode the ideals of a democratic and civil society. With our population becoming more obese, we can no longer accept the notion that athletic participation should be relegated to a minority of elite athletes. As we struggle to meet the rapidly changing educational, economic, and social demands of the twenty-first century, we must get back into the game because we can no longer continue to support an athletic culture that promotes anti-intellectualism, undermines educational values and institutions, and systematically creates "dumb jocks." And we simply cannot afford the continued use of tax dollars to build stadiums for wealthy owners and millionaire players and to supplement the budgets of college athletic programs when our bridges, inner cities, and schools are crumbling.

Something must change. But can it? Will it? Absolutely. Sports' influence and standing in our culture will change. Nothing can grow unabated forever. Even a star burns brightest just before it explodes. The institution of sport in America is like a house of cards, ever in danger of collapsing from its own weight. It is like a runaway freight train that will surely derail at the next great bend in the tracks. It has become grossly distorted from what it was meant to be and indeed from what we want and need it to be. How much more of organized sports' negative influence can we continue to absorb as a culture before we rise up and scream, "Enough!"?

A heroin addict in denial of his addiction will continue to inject the drug into his veins, despite being fully aware of the tremendous damage it is inflicting on his body. Similarly, we, as individuals and as a society, are in denial. We continue to embrace a sports culture, injecting it into our homes, schools, minds, and relationships, despite the fact that, deep in our hearts, we know that it has come to be harmful to us. Thus, the question is, can we kick the habit?

REFERENCES

Adler, Patricia A., and Peter Adler. 1991. *Backboards and Blackboards: College Athletes and Role Engulfment*. New York: Columbia University Press.

Athletic Footwear Association. 1990. *American Youth and Sports Participation*. North Palm Beach, Florida.

Barry, N. H. 1992. *Project ARISE: Meeting the Needs of Disadvantaged Students through the Arts*. Auburn, Ala.: Auburn University.

Benedict, Jeff, and Don Yeager. 1998. *Pros and Cons: The Criminals Who Play in the NFL*. New York: Warner Books.

Bilberry, Darren. 2000. In *Sports in Schools: The Future of an Institution*, ed. John Gerdy. New York, Teachers College Press.

Bissinger, H. G. 1990. *Friday Night Lights: A Town, a Team, and a Dream*. New York: Addison Wesley.

Brand, M. 2001. "Academics First: Rejuvenating Athletics Reform." *Trusteeship* 9:2 (March/April): 19–22.

Brown, J. S. 1995. As appeared in *Imagine*, written and compiled by Andrew Bailey for Synectics. London: White Dove Press.

Bunce, Donald, and Dennis Wilson. 1996. "Spring Practice Can Be a Safer Activity." *NCAA News* (April 29): 4.

Carter, Stephen L. 1996. *Integrity*. New York: Basic Books.

Chambliss, Daniel F. 2000. "Books in Review." *Society* 37:3 (March/April): 89–90.

Chu, Donald. 1989. *The Character of American Higher Education and Intercollegiate Sport*. Albany, N.Y.: State University of New York Press.

Clisura, Paul. 1995. In *Quotations with an Attitude: A Wickedly Funny Source Book*, ed. Roy L. Stewart. New York: Sterling Publishing Co.

Coakley, J. 1986. *Sport in Society: Issues and Controversies.* St. Louis, Mo.: Times Mirror/Mosby College Publishing.

Covey, Stephen R. 1989. Quote from Einstein, p. 42, in *The Seven Habits of Highly Effective People.* New York: Simon and Schuster.

Crosset, Todd. 2000. In *Sports in Schools: The Future of an Institution,* ed. John Gerdy. New York: Teachers College Press.

Crosset, Todd W., Jeffrey R. Benedict, and Mark A. McDonald. 1995. "Male Student-Athletes Reported for Sexual Assualt: A Survey of Campus Police Departments and Judicial Affairs." *Journal of Sport and Social Issues* 19:2 (May): 126–40.

The Dali Lama. 2000. "Infinite Compassion: Real Happiness Lies at the End of Suffering." *Forbes ASAP* (October 2): 237.

Danielson, Michael N. 1997. *Home Team: Professional Sports and the American Metropolis.* Princeton, N.J.: Princeton University Press.

Dawidoff, Nicholas. 2000. "The International Pastime?" *New York Times* (March 23).

Denlinger, Ken. 1994. *For the Glory.* New York: St. Martin's Press.

DiBiaggio, John. 2000. "Knight Compass Steers NCAA's Reform Path." *NCAA News* (September 11): 4–5.

Dowling, William C. 2000. "Sports, Race, and Ressentiment." *Society* 37:3 (March/April): 29–34.

Duderstadt, James J. 2000. *Intercollegiate Athletics and the American University: A University President's Perspective.* Ann Arbor: University of Michigan Press.

Duderstadt, James J. 2000. "Some Observations on the Current State and the Future of Intercollegiate Athletics." Presented to the Knight Commission on Intercollegiate Athletics (October 18). Washington, D.C.

Dudley, William, ed. 1994. *Sports in America: Opposing Viewpoints.* San Diego, Calif.: Greenhaven Press.

Eastman and Beaudine. 1996. "Broad Range of Talents Needed for Today's Athletic Directors." *NCAA News* (November 4): 13.

Edwards, Harry. 1984. "The Black 'Dumb Jock': An American Sports Tragedy." *College Board Review* 131 (Spring): 8–13.

Engh, Fred. 1999. *Why Johnny Hates Sports: Why Organized Youth Sports Are Failing Our Children and What We Can Do about It.* Garden City, N.Y.: Avery Publishing Group.

Entine, Jon. 2000. *Taboo: Why Black Athletes Dominate Sports and Why We Are Afraid to Talk about It.* New York: Public Affaris.

Euchner, Charles. 1993. *Playing the Field: Why Sports Teams Move and Cities Fight to Keep Them.* Baltimore, Md.: Johns Hopkins University Press.

Flynt, W. 1994. *Alabama: The History of a Deep South State.* Tuscaloosa: University of Alabama Press.

Flynt, W. 1990. Speech delivered at Young Men's Business Club's Man of the Year Banquet (April 25). Birmingham, Alabama.

Fulks, Daniel L. 2000. *Revenues and Expenses of Intercollegiate Athletic Programs: Financial Trends and Relationships.* Indianapolis, Ind.: NCAA.

Galbraith, John Kenneth. 1996. *The Good Society: The Humane Agenda.* New York: Houghton Mifflin.

Gardiner, M., A. Fox, and F. Knowles as reported in *Nature* 232 (May 1996).

Goldberg, Isaac. 1949. P. 82 in *The Dictionary of Humorous Quotations*, ed. Evan Esar. New York: Dorset Press.

Gorn, Elliott J., and Warren Goldstein. 1993. *A Brief History of American Sports*. New York: Hill and Wang.

Gragg, Derrick. 2000. In *Sports in Schools: The Future of an Institution*, ed. John Gerdy. New York: Teachers College Press.

Gross, Mike. 1999. *Lancaster Intelligencer-Journal* (February 14), C-6.

Gup, Ted. 1998. *Chronicle of Higher Education* (December 18), A-52.

Hamann, D. L., and L. M. Walker. 1993. "Music Teachers as Role Models for African-American Students." *Journal of Research in Music Education* 41:303–19.

Harrison, C. Keith. 2000. "Black Athletes at the Millennium." *Society* 37:3 (March/April): 35–39.

Hatab, Lawrence J. 1991. In *Rethinking College Athletics*, ed. Judith Andre and David N. James. Philadelphia, Pa.: Temple University Press.

Hoberman, John. 1997. *Darwins's Athletes: How Sport Has Damaged Black America and Preserved the Myth of Race*. New York: Houghton Mifflin.

Hoberman, John. 2000. "The Price of "Black Dominance." *Society* 37:3 (March/April): 49–56.

Hugo, Victor. 1995. As appeared in *Imagine*, ed. Andrew Bailey for Synectics. London: White Dove Press.

Institute for International Sport. 1999–2000. *Men's College Basketball Sportsmanship Research*. Kingston: University of Rhode Island.

Isaacs, Neil. 1978. *Jock Culture, U.S.A.* New York: W. W. Norton.

Jones, Canada Bill. 1995. P. 122 in *Quotations with an Attitude: A Wickedly Funny Source Book*, ed. Roy L. Stewart. New York: Sterling Publishing Co.

Journal of American College Health. 1998, May. As reported in "Study Shows Athletes Top College Drinkers," *Dayton Daily News*, May 7, 1998, 7-C.

Knight Foundation Commission on Intercollegiate Athletics. 1991. *Keeping Faith with the Student-Athlete*. Charlotte, N.C.: Knight Foundation.

Kyle, Donald G. 1993. *Athletics in Ancient Athens*. Leiden, The Netherlands: E. F. Brill.

Lancaster Intelligencer Journal. 1999. (January 14), C-2.

Lapchick, Richard. 1996. *Sport in Society: Equal Opportunity or Business as Usual?* Thousand Oaks, Calif.: Sage Publications.

Lapchick, Richard. 1991. *Five Minutes to Midnight: Race and Sport in the 1990's*. Lanham, Md.: Madison Books.

Lefkowitz, Bernard. 1997. *Our Guys: The Glen Ridge Rape and the Secret Life of the Perfect Suburb*. Berkeley: University of California Press.

Lester, Robin. 1995. *Stagg's University: The Rise, Decline, and Fall of Big-Time College Football at Chicago*. Urbana: University of Illinois Press.

Lipsyte, Robert. 1992. *New York Times Magazine* (April 2), 55.

Lomax, Michael E. 2000. "Athletics vs. Education: Dilemmas of Black Youth." *Society* 37:3 (March/April): 21–23.

Longman, Jere. 2001. "Despite His Critics, Carter Was Right." *New York Times* (May 21), D-3.

McCabe, Robert. 2000. In *Sports and Schools: The Future of an Institution*, ed. John Gerdy. New York: Teachers College Press.

McCall, Nathan. 1994. *Makes Me Wanna Hollar: A Young Black Man in America*. New York: Random House.

Meggysey, Dave. 1971. As appeared in Jack Scott, *The Athletic Revolution*. New York: Free Press.

Michener, James. 1976. *Sports in America*. New York: Random House.

Miracle, Andrew W., and C. Roger Rees. 1994. *Lessons of the Locker Room: The Myth of School Sports*. Amherst, N.Y.: Prometheus Books.

Mohl, Bruce. 1998. "Cable Rates Could Take a Big Jump." *Boston Globe* (June 22), 1.

"Money." 1973. Written by Roger Waters, recorded by Pink Floyd.

Morbidity and Mortality Weekly Report. 1997, March 7. U.S. Department of Health and Human Services/Center for Disease Control and Prevention.

Murphy, Cait. 1998. "The Folly of Taxpayer-Funded Stadiums." *Fortune Magazine* (December 21).

Nack, William. 2001. "The Wrecking Yard." *Sports Illustrated* 94:19 (May 7): 60–75.

National Association of College and University Business Officers. 1993. *The Financial Management of Intercollegiate Athletics Programs*. Washington, D.C.

National Center for Educational Statistics. 1990. *National Education Longitudinal Study, 1988. First Follow-up.* Washington, D.C.

National Coalition for Music Education. 1997. *Music Makes the Difference (Fact Sheet)*. Reston, Va.

National Collegiate Athletic Association. 2000. *NCAA Division I Graduation-Rates Report*. Overland Park, Kans.: National Collegiate Athletic Association.

National Collegiate Athletic Association. 1999–2000. *NCAA Minority Opportunities and Interests Committee's Two-Year Study of Race Demographics of Member Institutions*. Overland Park, Kans.: National Collegiate Athletic Association.

National Collegiate Athletic Association. 1991. *The Public and the Media's Understanding and Assessment of the NCAA*. Pole conducted by Louis Harris and Associates, New York. Indianapolis, Ind.: National Collegiate Athletic Association.

Putnam, Douglas T. 1999. *Controversies of the Sports World*. Westport, Conn.: Greenwood Press.

Putnam, R. D. 1995. "Bowling Alone: America's Declining Social Capital." *Journal of Democracy* 6:65–78.

Rauscher, F., G. Shaw, L. Levine, K. Ky, and E. Wright. 1994. *Music and Spatial Task Performance: A Causal Relationship*. Irvine: University of California.

Reid, Elwood. 1998. In *The Best American Sports Writing*, ed. Bill Littlefield. New York: Houghton Mifflin.

Rosentraub, Mark S. 1997. *Major League Losers: The Real Cost of Sports and Who's Paying for It*. New York: Basic Books.

Rothstein, Richard. 2000. "Do New Standards in the Three R's Crowd out P.E.?" *New York Times* (November 29), A-29.

Russell, Bill. 1979. *Second Wind: The Memoirs of an Opinionated Man*. New York: Random House.

Ryan, Joan. 1995. *Little Girls in Pretty Boxes: The Making and Breaking of Elite Gymnasts and Figure Skaters*. New York: Warner Books.

Sack, Alan, and Ellen J. Staurowsky. 1998. *College Athletes for Hire: The Evolution and Legacy of the NCAA's Amateur Myth.* Westport, Conn.: Praeger Publishers.

Schultz, Richard D. 1991. "NCAA State of the Association Address." Nashville, Tennessee (January 7).

Scott, Jack. 1971. *The Athletic Revolution.* New York: Free Press.

"Secret Agent Man." Recorded by Johnny Rivers. Written by Sloane and Barry.

Shields, David Lyle, and Brenda Jo Bredemeier. 1995. *Character Development and Physical Development.* Champaign, Ill.: Human Kinetics.

Shulman, James L., and William G. Bowen. 2001. *The Game of Life: College Sports and Educational Values.* Princeton, N.J.: Princeton University Press.

Shulman, James J., and William G. Bowen. 2001. "Playing Their Way In." *New York Times* (February 22), A-29.

Smith, Ronald A. 1988. *Sports and Freedom: The Rise of Big-Time College Athletics.* New York: Oxford University Press.

Sporting Goods Manufacturing Association. 1997. *State of the Industry Report.* Delivered at the Sporting Goods Manufacturing Association's Super Show (February 13). Atlanta, Georgia.

Staurowsky, Ellen J. 2000. "Lessons from IU Case May Be Unexpected." *NCAA News* (June 5): 4–5.

Stoll, Sharon. 1996. Correspondence to John Gerdy (July 19).

Thelin, John R., and Lawrence L. Wiseman. 1989. *The Old College Try: Balancing Athletics and Academics in Higher Education.* Report No. 4. Washington, D.C.: George Washington University.

Torpor, Bob. 1995. "Athletics and Marketing." *Marketing Higher Education* 9:3 (March): 6.

Twain, Mark. 1949. As appeared in *The Dictionary of Humorous Quotations,* ed. Evan Esar. New York: Dorset Press.

Underwood, John. 1984. *Spoiled Sport: A Fan's Notes on the Troubles of Spectator Sports.* Boston: Little, Brown, and Co.

U.S. Department of Health and Human Services. 1997. *Morbidity and Mortality Weekly Report* (March 7). U.S. Department of Health and Human Services/Center for Disease Control and Prevention.

Venerable, Grant. 1989. "The Paradox of the Silicon Savior." As reported in *The Case for Sequential Music Education in the Core Curriculum of the Public Schools.* New York: Center for the Arts in the Basic Curriculum.

Vescey, George. 1999. "Don't Worry: Sportsmanship Won't Be Catching." *New York Times* (February 21), sec. 8, p. 9.

Vinella, Susan. 1998. "Select Teams' Goals Bench Some Kids." *Youth Sport Coach* (August): 1, 6.

Voltaire. 1949. In *The Dictionary of Humorous Quotations,* ed. Evan Esar. New York: Dorset Press.

Washington Post. 1999. (January 12), A-10.

Watterson, John Sayle. 2000. *College Football: History, Spectacle, Controversy.* Baltimore, Md.: The Johns Hopkins University Press.

Wetzel, Dan, and Don Yeager. 2000. *Sole Influence: Basketball, Corporate Greed, and the Corruption of America's Youth.* New York: Warner Books.

Wolff, Alexander. 1995. "Broken Beyond Repair." *Sports Illustrated* 82:23 (June 12): 20– 26.

Women's Sports Foundation. 2000. *Introduction to Fitness.* East Meadow, N.Y.

Wong, Edward. 2001. "New Rules for Soccer Parents: 1) No yelling. 2) No hitting refs." *New York Times* (May 6), 1, 30.

Zimbalist, Andrew. 1999. *Unpaid Professionals: Commercialism and Conflict in Big-Time College Sports.* Princeton, N.J.: Princeton University Press.

Zimbalist, Andrew, and Roger G. Noll. 1997. *Sports, Jobs, and Taxes: The Economic Impact of Sports Teams and Stadiums.* Washington, D.C.: Brookings Institution Press.

INDEX